RENEWALS 458-4574

Hinduism and Secularism

Also by Arvind Sharma

THE CONCEPT OF UNIVERSAL RELIGION IN MODERN HINDU THOUGHT

A DOME OF MANY COLOURS (*co-editor*)

FEMINISM AND WORLD RELIGIONS (*co-editor*)

HINDUISM FOR OUR TIMES

OUR RELIGIONS (*editor*)

PHILOSOPHY OF RELIGION: A Buddhist Perspective

RELIGION AND WOMEN (*editor*)

THE ROPE AND THE SNAKE: A Metaphorical Exploration of Advaita Vedānta

TODAY'S WOMAN IN WORLD RELIGIONS (*editor*)

THE PHILOSOPHY OF RELIGION AND ADVAITA VEDĀNTA

Hinduism and Secularism

After Ayodhya

Edited by

Arvind Sharma
Birks Professor of Comparative Religion
McGill University

palgrave

First published 2001 by
PALGRAVE
Houndmills, Basingstoke, Hampshire RG21 6XS and
175 Fifth Avenue, New York, N. Y. 10010
Companies and representatives throughout the world

PALGRAVE is the new global academic imprint of
St. Martin's Press LLC Scholarly and Reference Division and
Palgrave Publishers Ltd (formerly Macmillan Press Ltd).

ISBN 0–333–79406–0

This book is printed on paper suitable for recycling and
made from fully managed and sustained forest sources.

A catalogue record for this book is available
from the British Library.

Library of Congress Cataloging-in-Publication Data
Sharma, Arvind.
    Hinduism and secularism : after Ayodhya /
    Arvind Sharma.
        p. cm.
    Includes bibliographical references and index.
    ISBN 0–333–79406–0 (cloth)
        1. Religion and politics—India. 2. Secularism—India.
    3. Barbari Masjid (Faizabad, India)—History. 4. Ayodhya
    (Faizabad, India)—History. I. Title.
    BL2015.P57+
    322'.1'0954—dc21
                                                    00–040450

10   9   8   7   6   5   4   3   2   1
10   09   08   07   06   05   04   03   02   01

Printed and bound in Great Britain by
Antony Rowe Ltd, Chippenham, Wiltshire

Contents

Contributors

John J. Carroll, is Chancellor Professor of Political Science at the University of Massachusetts, Dartmouth. He is currently working on a comparative study of strategies for guaranteeing religious rights in pluralist societies. His recent publications include an analysis of constitutional traditions in the American states, and the theory of religious freedom in American constitutional law.

Matthew A. Cook, was educated at the University of California at Santa Cruz (anthropology/south Asian studies) and the University of Texas at Austin (Asian studies). His early work focuses on the role of party factionalism in shaping the politics of Hindu nationalism at large. He is now working on a Ph.D in anthropology at Columbia University. His publications and research examine the politics and histories of India, as well as anthropology. Currently, he is writing on the role culture and capitalism play in the advent of – and local resistance to – nineteenth-century British colonialism in Sindh.

Koenraad Elst, grew up in a Catholic family in the Dutch-speaking part of Belgium. After a brief juvenile flirtation with Marxism he was drawn to exploring the spiritual domain, especially through Asian philosophies and disciplines like Aikido, Taijiquan and Yoga. He then went on to earn an MA degree in Chinese Studies, Indo-Iranian Studies and Philosophy. He earned his doctorate in 1998 at Catholic University, Leuven, with a dissertation on the ideological development of Hindu nationalism (publication forthcoming). While doing research in Indian philosophy at Benares Hindu University, he started taking an interest in the ongoing Rushdie and Ayodhya controversies and the larger debate on secularism. He has published several books on the historical Ayodhya file, sharply dissenting from the regnant Islamic-cum-secularist consensus and its amplifiers in the Western universities and media. He has also written on ethnic and caste conflict in India, the doctrinal and psychological basis of Christianity and Islam, the existing threats to freedom of expression, language policy issues, Buddhism and Ambedkarite neo-Buddhism, and on more abstruse topics of Chinese and Indian philosophy.

Steven A. Hoffmann, is a Professor of Political Science at Skidmore College. He is the author of *India and the China Crisis* (1990). His current research interests include India–US relations and "atmospherics," on which he will be working at the Woodrow Wilson Center in Washington, DC. His most recent publications have appeared in *Economic and Political Weekly*, and in Jasjit Singh, ed., *Asian Security in the 21st Century* (1999).

Subhash C. Kashyap, is a well-known political scientist and expert in constitutional law and parliamentary affairs and author of many prestigious works. He served as Secretary-General of Lok Sabha, the Parliament of India, during 1984–90. Earlier he had been Head of the International Centre for Parliamentary Studies. Recipient of many distinctions and honors within and outside India, he has been US Congressional Fellow of the APSA (Washington, DC), UN (UNDP) Fellow, Fellow of the Academy of American and International Law, SMU (Dallas), etc. He has received the Motilal Nehru Award twice and several State Prizes for his works in law and political science. He is currently member-secretary of the Committee recently appointed by the government of India to review the Indian Constitution.

Vasudha Narayanan, is Professor of Comparative Religion at the University of Florida. Her books include *The Way and the Goal* (1987) and *The Vernacular Veda* (1994). She is the co-author of *The Tamil Veda* (1989) and a co-editor of *Monastic Life in Christian and Hindu Traditions* (1990). Her forthcoming books include: *The Hindu Tradition: An Introduction* and *The Hindu Tradition in the United States*. She was awarded a John S. Guggenheim Fellowship in 1991 and an NEH Fellowship in 1998–9. She is currently vice-president of the American Academy of Religion.

Arvind Sharma, is the Birks Professor of Comparative Religion in the Faculty of Religious Studies at McGill University, Montreal, Canada.

Shrinivas Tilak, obtained his Ph.D from McGill University and has since taught at several Canadian universities: at the University of British Columbia in Vancouver and the University of Manitoba in Winnipeg, as well as at McGill and Concordia Universities in Montreal. Hermeneutics is one of his many interests, which finds an expression in his *Religion and Aging in the Indian Tradition* (1989).

Dhirendra K. Vajpeyi, is a professor in the Dapartment of Political Science, University of Northern Iowa, Cedar Falls. He has authored, co-authored, and edited 14 books, including *Environmental Policies in the Third World*, co-edited with O.P. Dwivedi (Greenwood, 1995); *Technology and Development; Local Government and Politics in the Third World; Indira Gandhi's India; Water Resource Management; A Comparative Perspective*, (Praeger, 1998); *Ethnic and Religious Minority Politics in South Asia*, (co-ed.); and *Modernizing China*; and many articles in academic journals. At present, he is Secretary of the International Political Science Association's Research Committee on Technology and Development, and Vice-Chair of the Research Committee on Local Politics and Government. Presently he is working on *Deforestation, Environment, and Sustainable Economic Development.*

Theodore P. Wright, Jr., is Professor Emeritus of Political Science at the State University of New York at Albany. He has conducted research in both India and Pakistan and his most recent publication is "The Indian State and its Muslim Minority; from Dependence to Self-Reliance?" in Yoginder Malik and Ashor Kapur, eds., *India: Fifty Years of Democracy and Development* (1998).

Introduction

Arvind Sharma

The demolition of the Babri Masjid on December 6, 1992 not only razed a landmark; it also constituted a landmark in the history of India. Now, eight years later, this fact is no longer in dispute; what could be and is disputed is the exact nature of its significance.

This volume has been assembled to help us think more deeply about that significance. The mosque may be gone but the issue the controversy around it signified is still with us. If anything, its posthumous significance bids to rival, if not exceed, its significance while it stood.

The first essay, by Theodore P. Wright, Jr., locates the issue in the context of the Muslim community in India and assesses its significance in terms of the past history of the community and its present divisions. After all, the Babri Masjid was a mosque, and it seems appropriate to begin a discussion of the controversy surrounding it with that of the community the mosque represented. The Babri Masjid, however, possessed a symbolic significance for secularism in India as well, and the essay by John J. Carroll explores this dimension. India has kept the name of secularism but has given it a peculiar habitation, which must not be lost sight of.

If the Babri Masjid possessed a unique significance for Islam and for secularism, it acquired over the seven years preceding its demolition (if it had not possessed it earlier) enormous significance for Hinduism as well. Its symbolic potency, however, was not intrinsic but parasitic on its association with Rama, and the concept of Ramarajya – the Hindu symbolic shorthand for the ideal state. Matthew A. Cook, in his excursion on this topic, demonstrates how the divergent understandings of the same concept, in the liberal press and by Hindu nationalists, leave dangerous room for a profound misunderstanding.

The next chapter, by Dhirendra K. Vajpeyi, makes us land with a thud from the theoretical stratosphere into the rough and tumble of Indian politics, while the next chapter, by Subhash C. Kashyap, makes us privy to the Machiavellian maneuvers which are carried out under the bright lights of idealistic rhetoric on the Indian political scene. These two essays serve to illustrate how electoral politics influence outcomes conventionally couched in doctrinaire terms. Like a sudden twister, such politics can, in a moment, wreck an otherwise ideologically placid landscape.

News, it has been said, is the first draft of history. In India, however, even the rough draft of historical writings is capable of making news, so deeply is the present in the grip of the past. A whole school of historiography has tried, since independence, to divorce religion and politics in the writing of Indian history. Steven A. Hoffmann reviews this effort, which assumes a special relevance in the long run.

The next two chapters, as if to redress the balance, shift the focus onto Hindu perceptions of politics and history, which had a bearing on the events of Ayodhya, even as they are being shaped by it now. Nagging, it is said, is the repetition of unpleasant truths; how, then, are we to describe its first presentation?

These two chapters present two unvarnished Hindu perspectives on the present and the past, and might offend the liberal scruples of some, or even many, readers. This is as good a reason as any for including them, for the "truth" that grates us is as true for someone else as the truth which pleases us. Shrinivas Tilak analyzes the pathologized discourse about *Hindutva* from a Hindu nationalist perspective, while the chapter by Koenraad Elst on current so-called "communalist" Hindu thought is the first opportunity many readers will have of familiarizing themselves, even in resistance, with a mode of thought which those who actually brought down the Mosque could or would not articulate as such, but once articulated, will have little difficulty in accepting.

The long last chapter by Vasudha Narayanan restores the liberal perspective, or perhaps even the liberal vision. But it is no longer an innocent vision, for we know by now that there is competition. The relations between the two communities have unfortunately deteriorated in Tamil Nadu since this piece was written.

What is still wanting is a spiritual vision of the event. I regret that our desire in this respect must remain unfulfilled for now. It is not easy to do. The day it *is* fulfilled, the time would be ripe for a very different kind of volume on this very topic!

1
The Muslim Minority Before and After Ayodhya

Theodore P. Wright, Jr.

The early literature on development, race, ethnicity and minorities tended to assume that "majority" groups are bound to become dominant once the residues of colonialism are liquidated by independence.[1] Either assimilation into a new nation would take place voluntarily on the model of the American "melting pot" or political democracy, civil rights and the secular state would assure that the weight of numbers would make the distribution of political, economic and social values coincide eventually with the ethnic proportions in a country's population. The newly preponderant majority would then feel secure enough to be generous and allow all minorities which did not want to assimilate, even those which were colonial or pre-colonial "former ruling elites", to preserve their cultural identities.[2] If there were a clash of goals between a newly dominant majority seeking to impose assimilation and such a now "subordinate" but once dominant minority striving to retain its separate identity, then the latter would "get what's coming to it": subordination, expulsion or extermination, for its longtime "oppression" of its erstwhile "mass subjects", to use R.A. Schermerhorn's terminology.[3] Who in academia worries, for instance, about the fate of long-settled white colonists in Algeria, Kenya, Zimbabwe or South Africa after the black African majority comes to power or about Turks in Bulgaria, Manchus in China or the Anglo-Irish in Ireland?[4]

Before Ayodhya

In India, the Nehruvian constitution and its dispensation defined secularism in a quite different way from that current in the West and especially the United States. It was taken to mean not a "wall of separation between religion and state," but rather equal, not proportional, treatment of all faiths.[5] The document itself provided for considerable governmental intervention in the tradition and practices of the Hindu majority in order to promote an alien agenda of reform, e.g., the abolition of untouchability and the various provisions such as widow remarriage and divorce through the Hindu code bill of 1955.[6] Regarding the religious practices of the largest minority group, Muslims, the constitution mandated a uniform civil code, superseding the *shariat*, but this has remained a dead letter under Muslim pressure in a democracy in which blocks of votes are important.[7]

Although some Muslim politicians have made "communal," that is, specifically Muslim, demands upon the Indian polity since shortly after independence,[8] the long period (1947–67) of "one-party dominance" by the Indian National Congress with its ideology of secular socialism obscured conflict between Hindus and Muslims. Muslim members of the Constituent Assembly gave up the British-accorded separate electorates and reserved legislative seats. But there was always a section of Hindu politicians, chiefly to be found after 1951 in the Bharatiya Jan Sangh party, who wanted to define Indian nationality in terms of a common denominator kind of Hinduism to which Muslims must conform in certain symbolic ways.[9]

Unfortunately for the domestic peace and stability of many ex-colonial polities and even a few in the so-called First World, the benign expectations of "nation-building" outlined above have been increasingly negated in recent years by the phenomenon of "majority backlash": a violent reaction to what a significant number of majority members perceive as excessive or unfair privileges retained by some minorities, like Indian Muslims, because of their former period of rule, or awarded to others at the bottom of the Hindu caste hierarchy after independence as compensation for past disadvantages due to discrimination.[10] The latter provision referred initially to supposedly temporary quotas set up as "reservations" of legislative seats, university admissions and civil service positions for the Scheduled Castes or Untouchables (now called Dalits) and the Scheduled Tribes. Not only have these ineluctably become permanent,[11] but in 1989 the Mandal Commission Report was adopted by the Government of India which extended some preferences to the "Other Backward Castes" just above the Untouchables.[12] This could increase the ascriptive allocation of government jobs to over half of the population. The upper-caste Hindus, especially Brahmins, who had adapted their traditional religio-literary intellectual skills to Western notions of modernity and had accepted open competition with merit allocation of rewards to individuals, found their hard-won competitive advantage whittled away by arbitrary, anti-modern group benefits. It is in this context of well-meant "compensatory discrimination"[13] that one may better understand the rise of "Hindutva" in India in the late 1980s with its polarizing effect, not so much on "Backward" versus "Forward" caste relations, but between all Hindus and the more vulnerable Muslim minority.[14] It also explains the passionate denunciations by the Bharatiya Janata Party, successor to the Jan Sangh, of "pseudo-secularism" on the part of Congress Party governments and their supporting intellectuals.

The politically mobilizing "backlash" perception outlined above, whether objectively valid or not, is exacerbated by what I have called the "ethnic numbers game":[15] the fear that the Hindu majority's somewhat artificial census preponderance of 80 percent, the basis for the legitimacy of the "Rashtravadis" or sons of the soil claims to political hegemony, is being reversed by dynamic trends such as differential birth and migration rates, religious and linguistic conversion or changes in state boundaries. The fates of Lebanon and Kosovo warn us that such group status reversals can happen. In these circumstances, we may find an ostensible majority group acting very defensively like an actual minority. The example of Sri Lanka springs to mind.[16] As a result, the potential for "zero-sum game" (your gain is our loss) group conflict rises sharply. The policies adopted in reaction to this by a threatened majority (sons of the soil hiring preferences in Maharashtra, "English Only" in the USA, "Malayanization")[17] are likely then to become self-fulfilling prophecies and produce even more polarization and counter-mobilization, a vicious spiral of conflict. I do not mean to imply the inevitability of escalating group conflict however; the Quebec case shows the possibility of a more benign outcome.[18]

After Nehru's death in 1964, the apparent consensus on the secular and pluralistic nature of the Indian state and people began to erode. As an index of that, the toll of communal, mostly Hindu–Muslim, riots rose again sharply.[19] The 1970s also saw the sudden oil-financed revival of Islamic fundamentalism in the Middle East and Iran with its spillover effects in South Asia:[20] Arab Gulf jobs and remittances, disproportionately enjoyed by Muslims among Indians, Arab aid to decaying Islamic buildings and languishing institutions in India (the "hidden hand" of the Indian press when not referring to the CIA), and the program of Islamization in neighboring Pakistan.[21] All of these developments gave to a broader spectrum of the Indian intelligentsia than the RSS[22] an almost paranoid feeling of beleaguerment. Even so distinguished and modern an Indian intellectual as T.N. Madan shocked the American

Association for Asian Studies in 1987 by asserting that "at present secularism in South Asia as a generally shared credo of life is impossible, as a basis for state action impracticable, and as a blue-print for the foreseeable future impotent. . . . The principal question . . . is not whether Indian society will eventually become secularised as Nehru believed it would, but rather whether it is desirable that it should."[23]

By the early 1980s, this attitude came to be called in the press the "Hindu backlash," a sense that the dwindling caste Hindu majority was a victim of what in the United States was being called "reverse discrimination" against the likewise declining white majority.[24] While the Indian phrase targeted especially the system of reserved seats in higher education, legislatures and civil service for the Scheduled Castes and Tribes, violent reaction, as in the Ahmedabad riots of 1983, quickly spread to attacks on the more feared but more vulnerable Muslim minority.[25]

This new, broader Hindu militancy took organizational form during the 1981 crisis over the conversion to Islam of several villages of Untouchables in the South Indian state of Tamilnadu. This hemorrhaging aroused the specter of eventual (2057 AD) group proportion reversal for caste Hindus in the whole country.[26] Yuvraj Karan Singh of Jammu and Kashmir, notably the only sizable state in India in which the Hindus are a minority, revived the Vishwa Hindu Parishad, which took upon itself the reconversion (*shuddhi*) of the defecting ex-Untouchables.[27]

The next step in Hindu–Muslim communal polarization was the Muslim agitation in 1985 to override an Indian Supreme Court decision which awarded alimony to Shahbano Begum, an elderly Muslim divorcee, in apparent contravention of Muslim Personal Law.[28] The new Prime Minister who accepted this demand, Rajiv Gandhi, was seen by many Hindus, both communal and secular, to have surrendered to an insistent coalition of orthodox *ulema* for the sake of expediency, in order to win the Muslim "block vote."[29] The stage was set for Hindu militants to demand some balancing concession by government to the majority community.

Thus it was that a long-dormant legal dispute over ownership of an obscure mosque, built by the Mughal emperor Baber in 1528 at Ayodhya in Uttar Pradesh, at the alleged site of the birth of the Hindu hero-divinity Rama (hence Ramajanmabhoomi), suddenly flared into national prominence. A century earlier, a British court had denied permission to the *mahant* of a commemorative *chabutra* outside the mosque to build a temple over it.[30] In late 1949, however, in the heated aftermath of Partition, some local Hindus broke into the mosque one night and set up idols of Rama and Sita inside it, thereby desecrating the edifice from the Muslim point of view. A local magistrate, probably in collusion with the intruders, ordered the mosque to be locked, thus excluding both Muslims and Hindus, ostensibly to prevent further communal strife.[31] Various individuals and organizations filed suits and countersuits which were never finally disposed of by the courts, probably on the principle of "letting sleeping dogs lie."[32]

In June 1984 a former Congress Party State Minister of UP, Dai Dayal Khanna, had had a vision of restoring Rama's birthplace and founded the "Shri Rama Janmabhoomi Mukti Yagna Samiti" to do this, at the instance, apparently, of the Vishwa Hindu Parishad.[33] It seems clear that the initiative in this communal conflict was from the side of militant members of the Hindu majority, bent upon a symbolic victory over descendants of their onetime Muslim rulers. Their mouthpiece, the weekly journal *Organiser*, had been publishing a long series of articles listing Hindu temples which it asserted had been forcibly converted into, or demolished to make way for, mosques during the seven centuries of Muslim invasion and rule.[34] Muslims quite naturally feared that the Ayodhya dispute was only the opening salvo of a planned campaign to deprive them of some of their principal places of worship and historic monuments of their former dominance. Major mosques at Varanasi and Mathura were specifically targeted.[35] In any case, after a year's delay in the plan owing to Indira Gandhi's assassination in the Fall of 1984 and the temporary diversion of Hindu wrath to the Sikh minority, the drive to restore Rama Janmabhoomi was resumed in 1985. Well-planned *rath yatras* (chariot processions) converged upon Ayodhya from far parts of UP. It culminated in a court order on February 1, 1986 to unlock the mosque and admit Hindu devotees to worship the idols. The city was again becoming a major pilgrimage center for Hindus.

Muslim "communal" organizations like the Majlis-i-Mushawarat (Muslim Consultative Council)[36] and the Muslim Personal Law Board were not slow to respond, and within two weeks created the Babri Masjid Protection Committee. There were rumors that Arun Nehru, Prime Minister Rajiv Gandhi's cousin and erstwhile henchman, instigated the court order in order to placate Hindu voters angered by the government's aforementioned concession to Muslim orthodoxy on overriding the Shahbano Begum decision.[37] A yet more Machiavellian motive could have been to continue to divert majority attention from the even more dangerous Hindu–Sikh confrontation in the Punjab.[38]

Waves of riots rippled out from Ayodhya to violence-prone cities of UP like Meerut and even to the old city of the national capital itself.[39]

Leading roles on the Muslim side were played by two incongruously paired figures: Syed Shahabuddin,[40] retired Indian foreign service officer, opposition MP and, in his student days, Marxist youth leader, and on the orthodox side, Syed Abdullah Bukhari, Shahi Imam of the Jama Masjid in Delhi and fiery opponent of the Gandhis, mother and son, since 1976.[41] Thus the coalition of what I shall presently be calling orthodox, revivalist and modernist Muslims which had played such an important role in turning the Congress Party out of office nationally for the first time in 1977 appeared to be reforming. As with the contemporaneous Shahbano agitation, few Muslim intellectuals of secular persuasion were willing publicly to advocate compromise on this emotionally charged issue.[42]

Desperate to regain the initiative from the Hindu militants (collectively called the Sangh Parivar) and to impress the Congress Party with the seriousness of Muslim alienation, the Protection Committee decided in December 1986 to urge their fellow Muslims to boycott Republic Day celebrations on January 26 and to stage a massive demonstration in New Delhi the next March 30 as preparation for a march on Ayodhya and the offering of *namaz* (prayers) at Babri Masjid in violation of court injunction.[43] The UP government hastily prohibited all such religious processions.[44] Under intense pressure, Shahabuddin withdrew the call for *bandh* (strike) at the last minute.[45] This caused a split in the Babri Masjid Protection Committee and the establishment of yet another committee.[46]

In the Fall of 1990, Hindu *karsevaks* (volunteers) attempted to take the mosque by storm but were fired upon by the police and several were killed, which cost the Congress state government the next election.[47] The worst rash of Hindu–Muslim riots since Partition swept over the state and beyond. The Babri Masjid Protection Committee persuaded Congress and the Left parties to support a proposal to freeze ownership of all religious edifices as of Independence Day in 1947.[48] The stage was set for the most communally polarized general election since the one in 1946 just before independence.[49]

In analyzing Indian elections, there is a tendency by both non-Muslim Indian and foreign journalists to treat the Muslim minority stereotypically as an undifferentiated "fundamentalist" whole[50] with perhaps a few modernists on the periphery. It would be more fruitful to employ a more complex taxonomy[51] and to categorize Indian Muslims according to their various goals, methods and orientations.

With regard to minority goals, American sociologists of what were then called "minority" or "race relations" used to assume from the narrow experience of the United States that all ethnic, religious and racial minorities wanted assimilation, or at least integration, into the dominant majority culture.[52] In the past thirty years, however, the neo-ethnicity movement has propagated the opposite belief that our and their aim is, or should be, "pluralism,"[53] a multicultural society akin to the secularist vision of the "composite national culture" of the Indian National Congress in the Nehru era.[54] Contrary to both of these successive assumptions, Richard Schermerhorn[55] elaborated in 1970 a more inclusive schema not only of what he called "subordinate" groups' goals, but also of "dominant" groups' intentions for the subordinates, plus recognition that the aims of both sides could change over time. He further postulated that conflict between them arises from an incongruency of goals, a situation in which one side, be it majority or minority, desires assimilation while the other wants separation, whereas if both want the same goal, whether it be the former or the latter, harmony will prevail.

In this construct, one can view the goal of the Hindutva forces for the Muslim minority, as far from being the expulsion or extermination suggested by analysts on the Left who liken them to fascism, but rather as enforced assimilation. This goal is rejected by most Muslims who wish to preserve their separate cultural, if not political, identity. It can be argued that the modal goal of the Hindu majority in India for all minorities, because of the threats of secessionist movements (Sikh, Kashmiri, Tamil, Naga, Assamese) has been shifting from voluntary pluralism to compulsory integration. Toleration of difference is declining as in Europe, just at the time that it has been increasing in America as the goal of "diversity." This is the meaning of the attack on "pseudo-secularism" with its double standards for majority and minorities.

Finally, for a more complex typology of Indian Muslims, Hamilton A.R. Gibb long ago classified them, according to their reactions to the challenge of Western modernity, into four types: orthodox, revivalist, modernist and secularist.[56] As noted above, these have proven useful in analyzing shifting coalitions of Muslim organizations in Indian elections of the 1970s.[57]

Historically first among Gibb's types are the orthodox, those who accept the entire Muslim tradition, including Sufism, as it has come down to the present. It is represented by the Jamiat-ul-Ulema-i-Hind, a segment of the Deobandi ulema[58] which has a longstanding alliance with the Congress Party, going back to Mahatma Gandhi's adoption of their goal of preservation of the Turkish Khilafat in 1919.[59] Maulana Abul Kalam Azad, Nehru's longtime Minister of Education, was the chief representative of the Muslim *ulema* in the Indian leadership of the 1950s.[60] He seems at times to have harbored the illusion that independent India would constitute a sort of *millet* (autonomous peoples) system in which the ulema would control their fellow Muslims by administering the *shariat* in their own *qazi* courts. In part, this has been operative through the unconstitutional persistence of a separate Muslim personal law, though administered by the regular court system. The Shahbano decision showed the orthodox that secular-trained judges could not be relied upon to uphold Islam. In 1993, some of them actually demanded the creation of independent *shariat* courts.[61] India to them would be *Dar-ul-Aman*, a place of tolerant pluralism midway between *Dar-ul-Harb* (the land of war) and *Dar-ul-Islam* (the land where Islam dominates).[62] Such an arrangement, while compatible with the practice of traditional Hindu rule, is clearly contradictory to both the modern vision of one law for all citizens, and Hindutva or Hindu nationalism which also demands a single nationality and court system for all Indians, but defined in terms of a common denominator Hinduism.

By the 1991 election, the orthodox were rather sparsely represented by candidates like Z.R. Ansari who had been instrumental in getting the parliament to revoke the Supreme Court's decision in the Shahbano case,[63] Maulana Hashmi and Mufti Mohammed Sayed among Congress candidates, and the late Maulana Muzaffar Hussain Kachocchivi of the Samajwadi Party, former Prime Minister Chandrasekhar's fragment of the Janata Dal party. But the *ulema* were heavily involved in both of the Babri Masjid Protection Committees,[64] as is Syed Abdullah Bukhari, who has taken a rather hyperbolic and adamant position toward compromise on Babri Masjid.[65]

A deviant *alim*, however, is Maulana Wahiduddin Khan, a member of the pietistic and apolitical *Tabligh-i-Jama'at*.[66] In his journal, *al-Risala*, and in interviews with *Organiser*, the RSS weekly,[67] he took the position that Muslims should surrender the Babri Masjid as a token of goodwill to Hindus on the Quranic ground that a mosque should never be built on an illegally obtained site.[68]

Gibb's second rubric is the revivalists or fundamentalists, to employ a much abused and by now pejorative term which is incorrectly applied by the Western press to practically all but the most secular Muslims.[69] Their aim is to purify Islam of all the interpretations and syncretistic practices such as saint veneration which have been added since the golden age of the Khulaf-ur-Rashidun (the rightly-guided first four Caliphs).[70] The principal organization embodying this perspective is the Jama'at-i-Islami, founded by Maulana Abul-ala Maudoodi, a lawyer, in 1941. Unlike its counterpart in Pakistan where the Jama'at is a legal party and runs candidates, in India it does not take part in elections except to endorse sympathetic candidates. It did join the Muslim Majlis-i-Mushawarat (Muslim Consultative Council) in 1964 to act as a pressure group. The Jama'at pursued a somewhat more realistic and conciliatory policy on the Babri Masjid issue than the ulema during the direct negotiations with Hindu leaders in which both participated,[71] More broadly, it has attempted to initiate a dialogue with Hindu militants like K.R. Malkani, the former editor of *Organiser*,[72] over the whole range of sore points between the two communities. In the long run, however, it is ideologically committed to the utopian goal of the conversion of India to a Muslim majority, though it has been increasingly pragmatic in practice. In the 1991 election it urged upon Muslim voters the strategy of choosing whichever candidate of any religion or party had the best chance of defeating the BJP.

The third type are "modernists" bent upon adapting Islam through interpretation (*ijtihad*) of the holy scriptures to what they regard as the imperatives of survival in the modern age, perhaps comparable to Reform Judaism.[73] They are more concerned with the fate of Muslims as a people than with Islamic theology and observance. The Muslim League and its Quaid-i-Azam, Mohammed Ali Jinnah, represented the goal of most Muslims before independence, the establishment of a separate state of Pakistan. But those remaining in India, especially in South India where they have repeatedly elected two MPs in Muslim majority districts of Kerala, agitate issues of benefit mostly to the North Indian Muslim elite: official status for the Urdu language, proportional representation in the civil service, the survival of Aligarh Muslim University as a minority institution, preservation of Muslim Personal Law and, an issue of vital interest to all Muslims, suppression of communal riots.[74] Sultan Salahuddin Owaisi, the perennial MP from Hyderabad on the ticket of the Majlis Ittihad-ul-Muslimin, who won again in 1991 and is a member of both the Majlis-i-Mushawarat and the Babri Masjid committee, falls also into this category.[75]

In North India, most Leaguers joined the Congress after Partition. In 1991 the modernists suffered almost total defeat in the Congress debacle in UP and Bihar: Tariq Anwar, Salim Sherwani, Akbar "Dumpy" Ahmed, A.R. and Mohsina Kidwai, and M.J. Akbar. The exception was Salman Khursheed, grandson of the late President of India, Zakir Husain, who thereby won a seat in the union cabinet and is now the Congress chairman for UP.[76] This group of modernists tend to be strident proponents of what the BJP calls "pseudo-secularism," is against Hindutva, and in favor of whatever position the Congress Party takes on Babri Masjid, such as leaving the decision to the courts.[77]

A maverick modernist is Syed Shahabuddin who won reelection in 1991 by belatedly abandoning his personal party, the *Insaan* (humanity), for the Janata Dal in his home state of Bihar. It can be surmised that his personal beliefs are more modernist than the positions he has had to espouse on Shahbano Begum, Salman Rushdie's blasphemous novel, *The Satanic Verses*, which he got banned in India,[78] and on the Babri Masjid, in order to win a following among the ulema and the majority of pious Muslims.[79]

Fourth, there is the category of what the orthodox call "Muslim by name only" which I have designated "secularist" because they value Muslim culture but do not believe in or practice the religion.[80] In this they are comparable to many of the Zionist Socialists who founded the modern state of Israel. Ironically, they are to be found at opposite ends of the political spectrum in India: the various branches of the Communist Party in Kerala and West Bengal (where they won six seats in the Lok Sabha on CPM and CPI tickets in the 1991 poll) and on the right wing in the BJP. Of the latter, examples are the party's exogamous Secretary General and Union cabinet minister, Sikandar Bakht, Arif Beg, an unsuccessful candidate in Madhya Pradesh in 1991, and Aizaz Rizvi, the sole Muslim in the BMP's post-1991 provincial cabinet in UP[81] It is, of course, difficult to ascertain whether these Alfred Lilienthals of Islam[82] genuinely believe that Hindutva is broad enough to encompass Indians of all religions, as the BJP asserts, or are following the path of expediency and thereby provide the party with a token façade of Muslim names in return for the benefits of office. As mentioned earlier, it cannot be automatically assumed that all people externally identifiable with an ethnicity reject assimilation as a goal. Both Communist and BJP Muslims had to toe their parties' line on Babri Masjid, such as the proposal for its physical removal from the Ramjanmabhoomi site, or, on the Left, for declaring it a national historical monument.[83] The Marxists among them, of course, reject Hindutva out of hand as "reactionary" and "obscurantist."[84] Congress has had its share of secularists, like the late Mohammedali Currimbhoy Chagla of Bombay, and Arif Mohammed Khan of UP who lost out on the Shahbano Begum dispute as well as in the 1991 election. Perhaps Rafiq Zakaria who lost in Aurangabad (Maharashtra) on the Janata ticket and the cricketer Nawab of Pataudi (husband of Rabindrinath Tagore's granddaughter, Sharmila), who lost in Madhya Pradesh, should be included in the secularist group.

In conclusion of this part of the analysis, Muslim leaders and spokesmen are not unanimous even about Hindutva, let alone on the specific issue of the Babri Masjid. Accordingly, far from being the Congress "vote bank" beloved of journalists, they were badly split in the 1991 election as they were in the previous general election, principally between the Janata Dal, its offshoot, the Janata Dal Samajwadi, and the Congress, except in West Bengal (CPM) and Kerala (Muslim League). The electoral strategy suggested by some leaders to vote for whichever candidate had the best chance of defeating the BJP turned out to be too sophisticated for the voters and signally failed in many constituencies in 1991, when the various centrist parties were unable to make electoral adjustments among themselves.[85] This allowed the party of militant Hinduism to greatly increase its share in parliament and to win control of the state government in crucial UP, the historic Muslim citadel which contains the disputed religious site at Ayodhya.

Foes of the BJP, both Muslim and Hindu, have been quick to cry "fascist,"[86] but at least publicly that party took in 1991, as it has in subsequent elections, a nationalist rather than a specifically anti-Muslim position in its manifestoes[87] : (l) relocate rather than demolish Babri Masjid in order to rebuild Ramajanmabhoomi; (2) amend Article 30 of the Constitution to give equal access to all applicants to all Muslim educational institutions; (3) turn the Minorities Commission into a general Human Rights Commission; and (4) delete the special constitutional status of Jammu and Kashmir in Article 370 from the constitution. Although the escalation of communal riots and killings may seem to belie this noncommunal stance, the party is far from the openly discriminatory and implicitly genocidal policies of Nazi Germany. It was at least conceivable in 1991 that the ascent to power in New Delhi of the BJP would not spell the unmitigated disaster for Muslims which its opponents predicted.[88] The question remains open and pressing for India as for Europe and the United States whether nation-building is ultimately compatible with ethnic pluralism.

After Ayodhya

Then, on December 6, 1992, the whole framework for the discourse over secularism in India changed fundamentally when a carefully prepared assembly of Hindu volunteers (*karsevaks*, including *sanyasin* or holy men) again attacked the Babri Masjid and this time succeeded in demolishing it. They then laid the foundations for a temple to Ram in its place. The difference in outcome from 1990 was that in 1992 a BJP state government was in office and the police stood aside.

Some observers as well as participants in the action thought in the immediate aftermath of the horrendous Hindu–Muslim communal riots which followed that they portended the death knell of the secular state in India. It was anticipated that the BJP would win the next general elections and alter the nature of the Indian state in keeping with its ideology of Hindutva.[89] However, in retrospect, nothing so drastic has yet happened. Institutionally, the Congress Party remained in power, if shakily, in New Delhi until the 1996 elections. A Congress-proposed constitutional amendment to "delink" religion from politics[90] failed to come to a vote in parliament because even the other secular opposition parties suspected the intentions of the ruling party. But in the 1993 byelections necessitated by the Centre's dismissal, immediately after the demolition, of the BJP state governments in Uttar Pradesh, Rajasthan, Himachal Pradesh, and Madhya Pradesh, the BJP lost to a Janata Dal Samajwadi-led coalition in UP and to Congress in MP, retaining only Rajasthan and the Delhi State[91] and in 1995 winning Maharashtra in harness with the local Shiv Sena.

The English-language press by August had reduced coverage of the Ayodhya incident to the usual futile judicial inquiry, ostensibly to fix blame for the worst of the post-Ayodhya riots, those in Bombay in both December 1992 and January 1993.[92] Like a Saturday afternoon movie serial of the 1930s, India seems to stagger on from crisis to crisis without any decisive change for better or worse. Opponents of Hindutva often cite the parallel with Germany in 1932.[93] But when the BJP won electoral pluralities nationally in 1996 and 1998 it had to form coalitions with regional parties on condition of excluding the communal parts of its manifesto from the government's common program. Only in the unlikely event of it winning an absolute majority on its own in 1999 might the dire prognostications of December 1992 become pertinent again. Will the experience of leading a diverse coalition cause the "domestication" or "deradicalization" of the BJP to ordinary parliamentary politics as happened to some of the European Communist parties in the 1960s?

Specifically, however, what has been the fate of the Muslim minority which suffered most grievously in the riots, to the tune of up to a couple of thousand dead?[94] So far, the author's principal impression is of the utter inadequacy of the response by the Muslim political, religious, and intellectual elite. Because of the nature of the event which precipitated the crisis, the press quite naturally interviewed Muslim members of the All-India Babri Masjid Action Committee (BMAC) and its splinter, the Babri Masjid Movement Coordinating Committee (BMMCC): Salahuddin Owaisi, MP, Sulaiman Sait and G.M. Banatwalla (Muslim League MPs), Azam Khan (ex-Minister in Madhya Pradesh), Maulana Jafaryab Jilani, Javid Habib (journalist, once President of the Student Union at Aligarh Muslim University),[95] Syed Shahabuddin, UP and editor of *Muslim India*, and last but not least, the rambunctious Syed Abdullah Bukhari.[96]

Besides their individual electoral constituencies and committees, who do they represent in a crisis so vitally concerning the whole Muslim community?[97] As noted earlier, the Indian political system no longer provides the Muslim minority with reserved seats chosen by separate electorates and the extraparliamentary minority organizations (NGOs) do not generally have leaders elected by the memberships. So Sulaiman Sait and Banatwalla, for instance, though hailing from Bangalore and Bombay respectively, have to get elected from Muslim majority constituencies in Kerala although they do not speak Malayalam, the language of their constituents. The Congress and Janata Dal Muslim parliamentarians elected in 1991[98] by largely Hindu voters were understandably silent, at least in public, in the aftermath, given the failure of their parties, especially the ruling Congress, to protect either the symbolic mosque or Muslim lives, homes, and businesses from planned destruction. Salman Khursheed, MP, and Ghulam Nabi Azad, MP from Madhya Pradesh but from Kashmir originally, were apparently designated the spokesmen for the Muslim minority within the central cabinet. Sikandar Bakht, MP, former member of the Janata Party cabinet (1977–9) and subsequently again in the BJP cabinet in 1998–9, had the thankless task of explaining his party's role in the demolition and riots to audiences both domestic and foreign.[99] *Organiser*, the mouthpiece of the RSS, even has its own Muslim columnist, Muzaffar Hussain.[100]

The English-language press, to its credit, also sought out the opinions of an unusual number of ordinary Muslims, often survivors of the killings and burnings, and thereby tapped a huge wave of disillusionment with both the Congress and Opposition political leadership, Hindu as well as Muslim.[101] This disaffection with democratic politics was undoubtedly the origin of the series of retaliatory bomb explosions, chiefly in Mumbai, during 1993.[102]

A few Muslim notables and celebrities had the courage to stand against the counterproductive postures and demands of the community's mainstream spokesmen. Asgher Ali Engineer of Bombay/Mumbai, a perennial rebel of the Daudi Bohra sect of Ismailis,[103] had written already in 1990 that "every human life is much more precious than a hundred masjids and temples . . . We should, therefore do everything possible to resolve this issue through constructive dialogue in the spirit of reconciliation."[104] Now he warned Muslims against attempting retaliation for the demolition.

At the level of the modern-educated Muslims, Professor Imtiaz Ahmed of Jawaharlal University[105] convened on January 25, 1993 a 500-strong meeting of academics and cinema celebrities[106] at which the few politicians present were shouldered aside: "You have talked enough, and now listen to us."[107] The convenor tried, apparently in vain, to reorient his co-religionists to "real" (that is, material and secular) issues like jobs and education. The conference finally voted four resolutions. (1) It called on the government to reassert its secular character and to stop patronizing unrepresentative members of both majority and minority communities. (2) It condemned irresponsible statements by "Muslims with vested interests," including the Urdu press. Specifically, it condemned the renewed call to boycott Republic Day, only urging government to downplay that celebration in view of the recent riots. (3) It urged the government to settle speedily the issue of whether, where, and how to replace the demolished mosque. (4) It urged progressive Muslim intellectuals to organize as a lobby to press for reform from within the community.[108]

The pacifist Maulana Waheeduddin Khan continued to plead, as before the demolition, for the surrender of the mosque's site to Hindus without recompense as a token of goodwill.[109]

What is striking, however, about the reactions of most of the Muslim leadership, if not the rank and file, is the provocative and unrealistic character of their demands in view of their dangerously isolated position. They, except for Bukhari,[110] were sane enough to realize that it was suicidal to call upon foreign Muslim countries like Pakistan or Saudi Arabia to intervene in India's domestic turmoil, especially in the context of the Kashmir uprising, although the Council of Muslim Organizations did protest the demolition and riots.[111] Yet, the best that the BMAC could think to do was once again to attempt to stage a march on Ayodhya to offer *namaz* at the site of the destroyed mosque.[112] Later, like Shahabuddin in 1991, it urged Muslims not to celebrate Republic Day on January 26, a gesture sure to infuriate most Hindus. The Muslim Personal Law Board, a conclave of *ulema* who assumed leadership when the BMAC lost its *raison d'être* after the destruction of the mosque, unreasonably rejected the government's compromise plan to rebuild the mosque next to the Ram Mandir which had been begun by the *karsevaks* on its site.[113] The only small token of accommodation to majority opinion was the ruling of Ahl-e-Hadees in 1993 that the "triple *talaq*," the divorce of a Muslim wife by her husband in one sitting, was un-Islamic.[114] The Muslim Personal Law Board refused to accept even this. The Muslim Intellectual Group founded by Imtiaz Ahmed cautiously took up the issue during a conference in August 1993 and appointed a committee to urge upon the Muslim Personal Law Board a reconsideration of its position in the light both of the Quran and of current conditions.[115]

In the meantime, the Vishwa Hindu Parishad (VHP) and the BJP had raised the stakes of conflict by hinting that they might press in due time demands for further mosque demolitions beginning with the Mughal Aurangzeb's in Varanasi and Mathura.[116] Some *sadhus* who had urged on the *karsevaks* at Ayodhya even demanded the return to Hindus of the Taj Mahal and the Jama Masjid of Delhi, both of which they claimed were constructed by the Mughals on the sites of Hindu temples or palaces.[117]

Had the BMAC been willing to yield and relocate the Babri Masjid, as Javid Habib apparently urged during the crucial negotiations in 1990–1, it might have bargained with its Hindu counterparts for an end to such demands, that is for their adherence to the Protection of Religious Edifices law which Congress got passed in 1991 after the election. At least then Muslims would have had an acid test of their opponents' sincerity or perfidy if the latter revived the demand on some future occasion.

It is perhaps symptomatic of what I have called above the "former ruling elite" mentality that the North Indian Muslim leadership and their "urduizing" cohorts from the south have been unable to see their situation strategically, but have continued fruitlessly to press various demands in moralistic and legalistic terms.[118] To do so may momentarily attract the favorable attention of Amnesty International, Asia Watch, and the more Wilsonian interventionist members of the Clinton Administration in the USA,[119] but in India itself it simply fires the resentment even of moderate Hindus.[120]

Among political parties, there has been convincing evidence that the Congress Party has been "playing the Hindu card" at least since 1980.[121] After all, it was Indira Gandhi's son, Rajiv, who reopened the Babri Masjid in 1986 to Hindu worshippers.[122] So the party which most Muslims had regarded as their chief protector is now unwilling to risk defeat by majority backlash with any truly effective measures such as ordering police to fire on the attacking Hindu *karsevaks*, the act which in 1990 had cost the Janata Dal dearly in the next election in UP. In the 1992 crisis, that Party's Chief Minister in Bihar did manage to contain riots,[123] but his is a badly fragmented party, a weak reed for Muslims to depend on. Yet in the Fall 1994 byelections, Muslim voters did turn to an alliance with the Other Backward Castes to stave off a BJP victory.[124]

The Marxist parties and the National Front, which are arguably the most credible defenders of secularism in the political spectrum, were not able because of overconfidence to prevent Calcutta's first major communal riots since 1964 in West Bengal, the one major state they ruled.[125]

What have all these political maneuverings to do with the larger issue of secularism versus fundamentalism in India with which we began? Constitutionally, India has never had an American-style separation of the state from religion. Ideologically, secularism, incorporated into the constitution as a term belatedly by Indira Gandhi's Emergency amendments in 1976, is understood more in the sense of equal treatment of all religions. But does equal treatment mean proportionate and how does one reconcile it with the kind of equality of individuals implied by liberal constitutionalism?

For the more revolutionary of the Marxists, "secularism" would mean the extirpation of what they call "obscurantism" by forceful state action as in the former Soviet Union, although this has not been the pragmatic policy of Marxist state governments in India when in power in Kerala and West Bengal.

Muslim, like Hindu, liberal modernists are closest to the recent American, if not European, conception of secularism as a "wall of separation" in which all religion is to be consigned to the sphere of private belief and practice.[126] This goal, so ascendant a generation ago among modern Indians as among most Westerners, is now on the defensive in South Asia, perhaps worldwide, due to the manifest failures of secular states in a postmodern era to provide their citizenry with its material let alone spiritual needs.

In these grim circumstances, the best that Muslims may be able to obtain in India is some *modus vivendi* with the political representatives of the Hindu majority under which they can live as "Hindu Muslims" symbolically without demanding special treatment. This is what Ismailis and Parsis have successfully done for centuries, and, one might add, as Jews have had to do in the United States until about 1967. To demand more, however "right" or "just" it may be in the abstract, has proven again in the Babri Masjid episode to be severely dysfunctional for the Muslim poor who get killed and burned out in the communal riots. Now even the Muslim middle class, whose lives were threatened in the Bombay riots in January 1993,[127] have a stake in compromise. The BJP still insists that its aim for minorities is one of integration, not expulsion or genocide. Let this be tested by negotiation and practice.[128]

Notes

1   Myron Weiner, "Political Integration and Political Development," *The Annals*, 358 (March 1965), pp. 52–64.

2   For this category, see Theodore P. Wright, Jr., "Identity Problems of Former Elite Minorities," *Journal of Asian Affairs*, I, 2 (Fall 1976), pp. 58–64.

3   R.A. Schermerhorn, *Comparative Ethnic Relations*, New York: Random House, 1970, p. 13. See quotation in Anthony Lewis column, *New York Times*, Feb. 6, 1983.

4   Typical of this attitude is Donald Rothchild's *Racial Bargaining in Independent Kenya: a Study of Minorities and Decolonization*, London: Oxford University Press, 1973.

5   Donald E. Smith, *India as a Secular State*, Princeton: Princeton University Press, 1963, ch. 5.

6   J.D.M. Derrett, *The Death of a Marriage Law*, New Delhi: Vikas, 1977.

7   Tahir Mahmood, *An Indian Civil Code and Islamic Law*, Bombay: Tripathi, 1976, p. 17.

8   Theodore P. Wright, Jr., "The Effectiveness of Muslim Representation in India," in *South Asian Politics and Religion*, ed. Donald E. Smith, Princeton: Princeton University Press, 1966, pp. 105–8.

9   N.C. Chatterjee of the Hindu Mahasabha listed these in 1951 as: acceptance of the Ramayana and Mahabharata epics, discarding of Arabic names and Muslim Personal Law. Donald E. Smith, *India as a Secular State*, p. 375.

10 Theodore P. Wright, Jr. and Omar Khalidi, "Majority Hindu Images, Stereotypes and Demands of the Muslim Minority in India: the Backlash," *Journal of the Institute of Muslim Minority Affairs*, XII, 2 (July 1991), pp. 321–34.

11 Myron Weiner and Mary F. Katzenstein, *India's Preferential Policies*, Chicago: University of Chicago Press, 1981.

12 Marc Galanter, *Competing Equalities: Law and the Backward Classes in India*, Delhi: Oxford University Press, 1984.

13 Ramesh Thakur, "Ayodhya and the Politics of India's Secularism: a Double-standards Discourse," *Asian Survey*, XXXIII, 7 (July 1993), pp. 645–64. See Laura Dudley Jenkins, "Caste, Class, and Islam: Debating the Boundaries of 'Backwardness' in India," paper delivered at the Association for Asian Studies, Annual Meeting, March 1999.

14 Edward Desmond, "Fatal Fires of Protest," *Time*, Oct. 15, 1989, p. 63.

15 Theodore P. Wright, Jr., "The Ethnic Numbers Game in South Asia: Hindu–Muslim Conflicts over Family Planning, Conversion, Migration and Census," in *Culture, Ethnicity and Identity*, ed. William C. McCready, New York: The Academic Press, 1983, pp. 405–27.

16 On the Sinhalese minority complex see C.R. de Silva, "The Sinhalese–Tamil Rift in Sri Lanka," in *The States of South Asia: Problems of National*

     Integration, eds. A. Jeyaratnam Wilson and Dennis Dalton, Honolulu: University Press of Hawaii, 1982, pp. 155–74.

17   Mary Fainsod Katzenstein, *Ethnicity and Equality: The Shiv Sena Party and Preferential Policies in Bombay*, Ithaca: Cornell University Press, 1979.

18   "Quebecers Seem Interested in Success not Secession," *New York Times*, 27 Jan. 1985.

19   Theodore P. Wright, Jr., "The Failure of the Indian Minorities Commission, 1977–1981," *Indian Journal of Politics*, XX, 1 and 2 (March–June 1986), pp. 152–76; Steven I. Wilkinson, "What Large Datasets Can Tell us About the General Explanations for Communal Riots," *Towards Secular India*, I, 4 (Oct.–Dec. 1995).

20   Theodore P. Wright, Jr., "Indian Muslims and the Middle East," *Journal of South Asian and Middle Eastern Studies*, VI, 1 (Fall 1987), pp. 48–56.

21   Anita Weiss, ed., *Islamic Reassertion in Pakistan*, Syracuse: Syracuse University Press, 1986.

22   Walter K. Andersen and Shridhar D. Damle, *The Brotherhood in Saffron: The Rashtriya Swayamsevak Sangh and Hindu Revivalism*, Boulder: Westview, 1987.

23   T.N. Madan, "Secularism in its Place," *Journal of Asian Studies*, 46, 4 (Nov. 1987), pp. 43–51.

24   Nathan Glazer, *Affirmative Discrimination*, New York: Basic Books, 1975. Wright and Khalidi, "Majority Hindu Images," op. cit.

25   Bachi J. Karkaria, "Sabarmati on Fire," *Statesman* (April 13, 1985), p. 12; "Unintended Victims of the Gujarat Agitation," ibid. (Jan. 22, 1985), p. 13.

26   Abdul Malik Mujahid, *Conversion to Islam: Untouchables' Strategy for Protest in India*, Chambersburg, Penn.: Anima Books, 1989. Frank Fanselow, "The Genesis of Communalism in Tamil Nadu: The Minakshipuram Mass Conversion of Harijans to Islam," paper delivered at the Association for Asian Studies annual meeting, Boston, March 13, 1999; forthcoming in *Eastern Anthropologist*.

27   Dev Dutt, "Conversions," *Seminar*, 269 (Jan. 1982), pp. 41–5.

28   Theodore P. Wright, Jr., "The Shahbano Begum Case: Women's Rights vs. Muslim Personal Law in India," *Developing Countries*, Special Studies, no. 155, Council on International Studies and Programs, SUNY Buffalo, ed. Claude Welch, 1989, pp. 119–44.

29   Violette Graff, "The Muslims of India," in *Islam and the State in the World Today*, ed. Olivier Carre, New Delhi: Manohar, 1987, pp. 195–232, for Muslim voting patterns in the 1984 election.

30   Ashwini Bhatnagar, "Opening the Floodgates," *Illustrated Weekly of India* (April 6, 1986), pp. 23–34.

31   "Old Wound Reopened by Rusty Lock," *Link* (March 2, 1986), pp. 4–5 reports that the deputy commissioner of the time, K.K.K. Nayer, later admitted his role in this conspiracy and had to resign. He then became an MP on the Jan Sangh ticket. See also Aslam Abdullah, "The Threat to India's Mosques," *Arabia* (April 1986), pp. 34–6.

32   M. Mahmud, "Babri Masjid; Fact versus Fiction," *Radiance*, (Feb. 22–8, 1987), pp. 6–8 for the legal details.

33   Inderjit Badhwar with Prabhu Chawla and Farzand Ahmed, "Hindu Militant Revivalism," *India Today* (May 31, 1986), pp. 30–8.

34 Ganeshilal Varma, "Conversion of Hindu Temples in Karnataka," tenth of a series dating from Oct. 21, 1984, *Organiser* (May 10, 1987), pp. 8–12.

35 Badhwar, op. cit., mentions a list of 25 other Muslim shrines which the VHP claims were Hindu temples. See also Walter K. Andersen's paper, "The Rashtriya Swayamsevak Sangh; Hindu Revivalism in Action," delivered at the Midatlantic Regional meeting of the Association for Asian Studies, Lehigh University (Oct. 30, 1987), p. 21.

36 Z. Masood Quraishi, "Electoral Strategy of a Minority Pressure Group: the Muslim Majlis-i-Mushawarat," *Asian Survey*, 8, no. 12 (Dec. 1968), pp. 976–87.

37 Neerja Chowdhury, "The Communal Divide," *Secular Democracy* (May 1986), p. 28, repeating a charge made by Chowdhury in *Statesman*, April 30, 1986.

38 The opposite strategy, one of Sikh–Muslim alliance for minority human rights against the Government of India, was proposed by Jagjit Singh Chauhan, the self-styled Khalistan leader in London. *Statesman Weekly*, April 5, 1986, p. 6.

39 These were reported in *India Today*: "The Barabanki Bomb" (June 15, 1986), "Fires of Hate" (July 15, 1986), "A Communal Flashpoint" (May 15, 1987), "A Deadly Confrontation" (June 15, 1987), "The Agony of Meerut" (June 15, 1987).

40 See the vitriolic exchange between Shahabuddin and M.J. Akbar, a secularist Muslim editor in Calcutta, in the pages of *Illustrated Weekly of India*, Aug. 10, 1986.

41 For Bukhari's entry into politics, see Theodore P. Wright, Jr., "Muslims and the 1977 Indian Elections: A Watershed?", *Asian Survey*, XVII, 12 (Dec. 1977), pp. 1207–20.

42 For instance, the defense of Shahabuddin's role in the Ayodhya dispute, "Muslim Voice Ignored," by retired Indian Ambassador and Vice Chancellor of Aligarh Muslim University, Badr-ud-din Tyabji, of the famous Nationalist Muslim clan of Bombay, in *Statesman Weekly* (March 21, 1987). Also A.G. Noorani, the noted civil libertarian's defense of the Muslim position in "The Babari Masjid Case," *Economic and Political Weekly of India* (Jan. 17, 1987), pp. 71–2.

43 "Declaration of Delhi on Babari Masjid Adopted by the All-India Babari Masjid Conference, 22 December, 1986," *Newsletter* of the Consultative Committee of Indian Muslims of the USA and Canada, January 1987. For a critical report, "A Contentious Call," *India Today* (Jan. 11, 1987), pp. 10–13.

44 *Statesman Weekly* (May 23, 1987), p. 1.

45 "Babri Masjid Hawks to Go Ahead with Agitation," *The Hindu Weekly* (Feb. 14, 1987), p. 3.

46 Koenraad Elst, *Ram Janmabhoomi vs. Babri Masjid*, New Delhi: Voice of India, 1990, p. 153.

47 Asgher Ali Engineer, "Ram Janmabhoomi Karseva and Communal Violence," in his *Politics of Confrontation*, Bombay: Ajanta, 1992, pp. 113–26.

48 The Places of Worship (Special Provisions) Bill was introduced in August 1991 and passed in September. *The Hindu* (Aug. 31, 1991), p. 1 (Sept. 21, 1991), p. 4.

49 *Communalisation of Politics and 10th Lok Sabha Elections*, ed. Asgher Ali Engineer, Delhi: Ajanta, 1993.

50 For instance, *India Today*'s characterization of the 1991 contest between M.J. Akbar and Syed Shahabuddin as "Secularism vs. Fundamentalism" (May 15, 1991).

51 Theodore P. Wright, Jr., "Typology of South Asian Muslims: a Taxonomic Exercise," in *Islam in Southern Asia*, ed. Dietmar Rothermund, Wiesbaden: Franz Steiner Verlag, 1975, pp. 49–53.

52 Milton Gordon, *Assimilation in American Life*, New York: Oxford University Press, 1964.

53 For instance, *The Mobilization of Collective Identity: Comparative Perspectives*, eds. Jeffrey Ross and Ann Baker Cottrell, Lanham, Md.: The University Press of America, 1980.

54 For a critique of the "counterfeit secularism" into which this has degenerated, see Arun Shourie, *Religion in Politics*, New Delhi: Roli, 1987, ch. XI.

55 R.A. Schermerhorn, op. cit., p. 83.

56 H.A.R. Gibb, *Mohammedanism*, Oxford: Oxford University Press, 1949.

57 Theodore P. Wright, Jr., "Muslims and the 1977 Indian Elections: a Watershed?", op. cit.

58 Barbara D. Metcalf, *Islamic Revival in British India: Deoband, 1860–1900*, Princeton: Princeton University Press, 1982.

59 Ziya-ul-Hasan Faruqi, *The Deoband School and the Demand for Pakistan*, Bombay: Asia, 1963.

60 Ian M. Douglas, *Abul Kalam Azad*, Delhi: Oxford University Press, 1988.

61 Rafiq Zakaria, "Islamic Courts in India," *India Today* (Nov. 15, 1993), p. 106, and Muzaffar Hussain, "Proposed Islamic Courts Signify Conspiracy to Deny Muslim Women's Rights," *Organiser* (Jan. 9, 1994), p. 7.

62 Syed Shahabuddin and Theodore P. Wright, Jr., "Indian Muslim Minority Politics and Society," in *Islam in Asia*, ed. John Esposito, New York: Oxford University Press, 1987.

63 See note 28 above.

64 "Two Faces of Shahabuddin," *Organiser* (Jan. 8, 1989), p. 2.

65 A letter to the editor in *Organiser* (July 14, 1991) claimed that the Shahi Imam was quoted in *Kerala Koumudhi*, on May 6, 1991, to have threatened "that, in case of Hindu Rashtra [being enacted], he will order the twenty-five crores of Muslims in India, to unleash a 'bloody revolution' and cut this country into pieces," and to have threatened in 1990 during the communal riots "that he was capable of bringing [a] foreign army into India to protect Indian Muslims." He eventually endorsed the Janata Dal for Muslims voters. *The Hindu* (May 11, 1991).

66 Maulana Waheeduddin Khan, *Tabligh Movement*, New Delhi: Islamic Centre, 1986.

67 Waheeduddin Khan interview in *Organiser* (Aug. 5, 1990) and *Hindustan Times* (June 27, 1993) as reported in *Muslim India* 130 (Oct. 1993), 449.

68 Editorial, *Al Risala*, no. 27 (April 1986), p. 2; Maulana Waheeduddin Khan, "Not by Grievances Alone; Indian Muslims' Failure," *Times of India*, Sept. 15, 1987; personal interview, Jan. 24, 1991.

69 Abdul Rehman Momin, "On 'Islamic Fundamentalism,' the Genealogy of a Stereotype," *Hamdard Islamicus*, X, 4 (Winter 1987), pp. 35–46.

70 Leonard Binder, *Religion and Politics in Pakistan*, Los Angeles: University of California Press, 1961, ch. 3.

71 "Jamaat Advisory Council Resolutions," *Radiance* (Nov. 2, 1991), p. 8; for the breakdown of the negotiations between the Babri Masjid Action Committee and the Vishwa Hindu Parishad, see Bhasker Roy, "AIBMAC: Divided House; Rift among Muslim Leaders," *India Today* (March 15, 1991), p. 38.

72 See Abdul Moghni's reply in *Radiance* (Nov. 13, 1988), p. 3, to Malkani's "Resolving Religio-Cultural Differences in the Service of the Indian People," *Manthan* (June 1988).

73 Binder, op. cit., ch. 2, "Ijma Modernism."

74 Ibid.

75 Theodore P. Wright, Jr., "The Revival of the Majlis Ittihad-ul-Muslimin of Hyderabad," *Muslim World*, LIII, 3 (July 1963), pp. 234–43.

76 Notably, Khursheed took a position in 1992 at Jamia Millia Islamia against removal of the ban on Salman Rushdie's novel *The Satanic Verses* when it was urged by a more secularist historian. For a detailed history of Muslim voting in a key UP constituency see Violette Graff, "Religious Identities and Indian Politics: Elections in Aligarh, 1971–1985," in *Islam, Politics and Society in South Asia*, ed. AndreWink, Delhi: Manohar, 1991, pp. 133–77. For the kinship ties of some of these elite UP Muslims, see Theodore P. Wright, Jr., *Muslim Politics in South Asia: Who You Are and Who You Marry*, the Aziz Ahmad Lecture, 1991, Toronto: Centre for South Asian Studies, pp. 5–16.

77 The Congress manifesto waffled on Babri Masjid by opting for either a negotiated settlement or abiding by the court's verdict, but without demolishing the mosque and guaranteeing the status quo as of August 15, 1947 for all other religious structures. *Radiance* (May 19, 1991). The account of the manifesto in *The Hindu* (April 27, 1991), p. 2, did not mention the first part.

78 Theodore P. Wright, Jr., "The Rushdie Affair: the Spread of Communalism from South Asia to the West," *Plural Societies*, XX, 3 (Dec. 1990), pp. 31–40.

79 For a typical misrepresentation of his position, see "Kishanganj Secularism vs. Fundamentalism," *India Today* (May 15, 1991).

80 Violette Graff, "Islam et Laicité," in *Islam and the State in the World Today*, ed. Olivier Carre, op. cit., pp. 43–57. Theodore P. Wright, Jr., "Indian Muslim Politics and the Challenge of Communism," *Asian Thought and Society*, VIII, 4 (Nov. 1983), pp. 218–24.

81 "Four Muslims on BJP List," *The Hindu* (May 11, 1991), p. 3.

82 Reference to the most conspicuous of anti-Zionist American Jews, author of the book, *What Price Israel?*, New York: Devin Adair, 1953.

83 "Are We Abusing History?", report on a document prepared by historians at Jawaharlal Nehru University, *Illustrated Weekly of India* (Feb. 25, 1990).

84 Typically, see Sumanta Banerjee, "'Hindutva Ideology and Social Psychology," *Economic and Political Weekly* (Jan. 19, 1991), pp. 97–101.

85 "Muslim Tactics Boomerang," *Organiser* (July 21, 1991), p. 16. Both Muzaffar Hussain, writing for *Organiser* (July 28, 1991), p. 5, and Syed Shahabuddin, in his journal *Muslim India*, 105 (Sept. 1991), p. 386, agree

that Muslim representation in Parliament at 27 has declined to the lowest
level since 1962 when it was 23.

86   For example, Harbans Mukhiya of Delhi University speaking at Rensselaer
Polytechnic Institute, Troy, NY, March 15, 1993.

87   "Party Manifestoes," *Organiser* (May 19, 1991).

88   Three columns in *The Statesman* by Sunanda K. Datta Ray "The BJP's
Dilemma: Posturing for the Faithful," (Aug. 24, 1991) and Amulya
Ganguli, "The BJP's Dilemma: Law and Order vs. Ram Temple" (Aug. 10,
1991) and "BJP in the Dock: Hindu Rashtra vs. Akhand Bharat" (Aug. 31,
1991), argue that the desire for power at the Centre will modify the party's
militancy. For a subsequent example, see "BJP Woos Muslims in UP," *Hindu*
(Feb. 1991), p. 4. A more negative view of the compatability of BJP success
with Muslim survival is implicit in Asgher Ali Engineer's "Communal
Riots, Before, During and After Lok Sabha Elections," *Economic and Political Weekly of India* (Sept. 14, 1991), pp. 2135–8.

89   For instance, Edward Gargan, "Peril to the Indian State: a Defiant Hindu
Fervor Threatening India's Secular Character," *New York Times* (Dec. 9,
1992).

90   "Religion Bill Goes to Select Committee," *Times of India* (Aug. 7, 1993), pp.
5, 12. This included both the Constitution (80th Amendment) Bill, 1993,
and the Representation of the People (Amendment) Bill, 1993, They would
have the effect of disqualifying at the stage of filing nomination any candidate suspected misusing religion for political purposes.

91   "Sharing the Spoils," *India Today* (Nov. 30, 1993), pp. 16–30.

92   *India Today* (Aug. 15, 1993), p. 16.

93   For example, Rashid Talib, "Hindutva: Flattery by Imitation," *Seminar*, 402
(Feb. 1993), pp. 37–42.

94   Derek Brown, "India Counts Cost Following Week of Sectarian Violence,"
Guardian (Dec. 14, 1992), p. 9, estimated 1,150 killed and 5,000 wounded
from the first-round of riots. Deaths in the second round in Bombay in
January would probably raise the total deaths to over 2,000, small compared to the slaughter in the Punjab in 1947, estimated to have reached
half a million.

95   Violette Graff, "Religious Identities," note 20.

96   For his decline in influence, Hardiner Baweja, "A Fall from Grace: the
Imam's Expanding Businesses and Ostentatious Lifestyle are Eroding his
Following," *India Today* (July 31, 1993), pp. 90–2.

97   Omar Khalidi, "Muslims in Indian Political Process; Group Goals and Alternative Strategies," *Economic and Political Weekly* (Jan. 2, 1993), pp. 43–54.

98   Theodore P. Wright, Jr., "The Reaction of Muslims to Hindutva in the 1991
Indian Elections: the Crisis of Secularism," delivered at the 12th European
Conference on Modern South Asian Studies, Berlin, Sept. 26, 1992. Sha-
habuddin, in a rather partisan gesture, called upon Muslim ministers to
resign in protest against the failure of the Centre to protect the Babri
Masjid. *Times of India* (Jan. 16, 1993), p. 13.

99   "Bakht in US to Refurbish Image," *Times of India* (Jan. 16, 1993).

100 For example, Mozaffar Hussain, "Islamic Fundamentalism Overtaking
India," *Organiser*, May 2, 1993, p. 7.

101 "A Nation Divided," *India Today* (Jan. 15, 1993), pp. 14–19, shows Hindus

47.7% and Muslims 86.1% disapproved of the mosque demolition; Hindus divided 32.1% vs. Muslims 59.9% on whether using military force would have stopped it; but a majority of Muslims opted for rebuilding both temple and mosque, contrary to their leaders' position. See also "Strangers in their Own Land," ibid., p. 44. Charu Gupta and MKS found in "The Muslims and the News," *Mainstream* (Feb. 13, 1993), pp. 15–19, much more negative and stereotyped reporting in the vernacular press.

102 "Bombs in Bombay; Twelve Explosions Tear through the City, Killing More than 300," *Time* (March 22, 1993), p. 22. Subsequent investigation blamed Ibrahim Memon, a Muslim crime boss, and the Government of India attempted to implicate Pakistan Intelligence.

103 Asgher Ali Engineer, *The Bohras*, New Delhi: Vikas, 1980.

104 Asgher Ali Engineer, *Babri Masjid*, p. 14.

105 Editor of the pathbreaking series of four volumes on the empirical reality of Muslim life in India beginning with *Caste and Social Stratification among the Muslims*, Delhi: Manohar, 1973.

106 Theodore P. Wright, Jr., "Muslim Mobility in India through Peripheral Occupations: Sports, Music, Cinema, and Smuggling," in *Asie du Sud: Traditions et Changements*, eds. Marc Gaborieau and Alice Thorner, Paris: Editions du Centre National de la Recherche Scientifique, Collection des Colloques Internationaux, 1979, pp. 271–8. Film actress Shabana Azmi played a prominent role both in Bombay and abroad in attempting to restore communal amity in a secular context. *India Today* (June 30, 1993), p. 563.

107 Syed Zubair Ali, "Muslim Intellectuals Strive for Change," *Times of India* (Jan. 26, 1993), p. 4.

108 Rashmee Z. Ahmed, "A Revolution Begun?", *Sunday Times of India Review* (Feb. 7, 1993), p. 1. In August, the Muslim Intelligentsia Meeting inveighed against triple *talaq* (divorce at one sitting), which the Ahl-e-Hadees had declared un-Quranic but the Ulema had supported. Imtiaz Ahmad, *The Triple Divorce Issue: a Muslim Perspective*, New Delhi, n.d.

109 "Wahiduddin Khan on Leaving Babari Masjid to the Conscience of the Hindus," *Muslim India*, 130 (Oct., 1993), p. 449, reprinted from *Hindustan Times* (June 27, 1993).

110 For example, Musaffar Hussain, "Islamic Fundmentalism Overtaking India" (May 2, 1993), p. 7

111 Reactions by Muslims abroad included "Muslims on the Rampage in Pakistan and Bangladesh: Mobs attack Hindu Temple and Indian Property after Mosque Destroyed," *Guardian* (Dec. 8, 1992), p. 11.

112 "BMAC Bid to March on Ayodhya Foiled," *The Hindu* (Jan. 8, 1993), p. 5.

113 See Umashanker Phadnis, "Indian Muslims' New Leadership Plans Mass-contact Drive," *Dawn* (April 28, 1993), p. 15 for the Muslim Personal Law Board's rejection of Prime Minister Rao's compromise package proposal.

114 "Talaq in One Sitting Violates Quran," *Economic Times* (Aug. 9, 1993).

115 The Muslim Intelligentsia Meeting joined the debate to inveigh against triple *talaq*. The convention then was addressed by Maulana Wahiduddin Khan and such lay luminaries as Yunus Salim (former MP), Syed Hamid (former Vice Chancellor of Aligarh Muslim University), Professor Tahir

Mahmood (legal expert on Muslim Personal Law), and the cinema star Dilip Kumar (Yusuf Khan). "Muslim Intelligentsia Meet; Resolutions," for which I am indebted to Imtiaz Ahmad. In defence of the Ulema, see Iqbal Masud, "Anti-Ulema Fever," *Economic and Political Weekly* (Oct. 30, 1993), pp. 2387–8. Later the Muslim Personal Law Board proposed an independent set of Shariat courts. "Divisive Justice; Shariat Courts Provoke a Barrage of Criticism," *India Today* (Nov. 30, 1993), p. 33.

116   "Ominous Signs: Krishnajanmabhoomi," *India Today* (Nov. 30, 1993), p. 4.

117   "Sadhus Now Claim Jama Masjid Also," *Hindu* (Jan. 9, 1993). The latter claim goes back to P.N. Oak, *The Taj Mahal is a Hindu Palace*, Bombay: Pearl, 1968.

118   Barrister A.G. Noorani of Bombay is the chief exemplar of the legalistic approach to Muslim grievances; e.g., "Talaq Talk: Bad in Law and Theology," *Statesman* (July 31, 1993), p. 10.

119   For example, "India Struggles Toward Calm after Savagery: Asia Watch Seeks Probe of Police Conduct," *New York Times* (Dec. 13, 1992). For the debate over American foreign policy towards rights in the Clinton Administration, see Stephen Stedman, "The New Interventionists," *Foreign Affairs*, 72, no. 1 (1992), pp. 1–16.

120   Theodore P. Wright, Jr., "Limitations on the Human Rights Approach to Problems of the Muslim Minority in India," *Indo-American Journal of Human Rights* (March 1989), reprinted in *Muslim India*, 86 (Feb. 1990), p. 88.

121   Violette Graff, "The Muslim Vote," in *Electoral Politics in India: a Changing Landscape*, eds. Subrata K. Mitra and James Chiriyankandath, New Delhi: Segment Books, 1992.

122   A.G. Noorani, "The Babri Masjid–Ram Janmabhoomi Question," in *Babri Masjid Ramjanmabhoomi Controversy*, ed. Asgher Ali Engineer, Delhi: Ajanta, 1990, pp. 56–78.

123   "Bloody Aftermath," *India Today* (Dec. 15, 1992), pp. 42–3, mentions Chief Minister Laloo Prasad Yadav's nurturing of Muslim–Yadav unity in Bihar as the cause of the state's relatively low incidence of post-Ayodhya riots.

124   See Inderjit Badhwar, Zafar Agha, Javed Ansari, "Saffron Setback" on the Muslim voters' role, *India Today* (Dec. 15, 1993), pp. 26–33.

125   "Violence Grips Calcutta," *Statesman* (Dec. 12, 1992), p. 6.

126   This seems to be the view of Dr. Rasheeduddin Khan's journal *Secular Democracy*, which is not surprising in view of his Ahmadiyya origins. This sect has been persecuted in Pakistan during periods of Islamization.

127   One of the noticeable differences of the 1992–3 communal riots from previous ones, especially in Bombay, was the systematic attacks on middle-class Muslims. Edward Gargan, "Police Complicity Found in Bombay Riots," *New York Times* (Feb. 4, 1993), pp. 1, 8.

128   "The BJP," said its president, Murli M. Joshi, "would not recognise the minorities as permanent minorities. Our party is not for treating anybody as a minority . . . all those belonging to India should be one." *Indian Express* (Jan. 25, 1993), p. 1. This was the position of American liberals before the introduction of "affirmative action" in 1965.

2
In the Shadow of Ayodhya: Secularism in India

John J. Carroll

Introduction

The destruction of the Babri Masjid mosque in Ayodhya has sent powerful and disturbing shockwaves through Indian society. Fifty years after independence, the country remains deeply troubled by communal divisions, the seriousness of which were graphically illustrated by Ayodhya and the fury which followed. Each side in the dispute over the sacred site has blamed the other for the rioting and problems which ensued. The Bharatiya Janata Party (BJP) has accused the Congress Party of following a policy of "pseudo-secularism" that has heightened religious divisions by pandering to minorities at the expense of the Hindu majority. Congress for its part has held the BJP directly responsible for the destruction in Ayodhya and the violence which followed, and rapidly replaced BJP governments with Central rule in four of India's largest states. India's numerous left parties have accused the BJP of following policies of religious intolerance designed to exploit communal tensions in the cause of a purified Hindu state, and the Congress Government of dithering while the crisis gathered.

In the aftermath of Ayodhya, as Indians have tried to puzzle out what went so terribly wrong, they have turned to debating the meaning of secularism and its application to Indian society. This has been a natural and constructive response to events which have raised questions about the workability of the regime rules under which the nation's religious divisions are managed. Not only is the relationship of the religious majority toward minorities under debate, but also the posture which the government should take toward the country's numerous religious groups.[1]

The debate has been passionate and wide reaching. The idea of a secular state, enshrined in the Preamble of the Indian Constitution as a fundamental aspiration, has come under extraordinary attack as a failed experiment, while others have risen to its defense. Some have attacked secularism as a Western concept inappropriately applied to the Indian state without respect for the profound religiosity of the Indian people.[2] Others have argued that the concept has not been conscientiously applied, but sacrificed instead for political convenience and electoral advantage.[3] Still others believe that the concept of secularism should be abandoned and India redefined as a Hindu state.

This analysis will examine the practice of Indian secularism to better understand why the system is so troubled. The emphasis will be on contemporary theories of secularism, and how India has actually operationalized the theory. In respect to the latter, we shall look closely at how the Indian government positions itself in respect to the official sponsorship of religious rituals, public prayer, and other devout displays. This is a question of great symbolic importance because it sets the tone for relationships between religions and the state, and the government's posture on this question may be seen to imply an answer to a further and more serious inquiry: does the state prefer one group rather than another, and if so, with which group (or groups) does it stand? We shall also look at the implications for individual conscience of India's brand of secularism.

This is an analysis with modest goals. Tensions between India's various communities – language, ethnic, religious, and regional – have a long and turbulent history. The application of social theory, whether it be federalist, parliamentary, or secularist, will bring no easy solution to such problems, and to think otherwise is a delusion. Nonetheless, the thoughtful application of theory may help ameliorate tensions under certain circumstances. The argument here is a simple one, and one which I believe a majority of Indian intellectuals still endorse: that secularism offers the best hope for managing India's religious difficulties, despite powerful opposing forces which might still render those strategies ineffective.

Theory of secularism

Religion has long been recognized as a potential competitor with the state for the allegiance of humankind. The demands of God may be made as loudly as those of Caesar; however, religion holds the trump with its promise of salvation and the threat of eternal damnation. A state which actively competes with religion for the allegiance of citizens is likely to be at considerable risk, for while it may win in the short run through force of arms, it may suffer the permanent disaffection of those it has suppressed.

A major goal of secularism is to protect the state from instabilities associated with religious controversy.[4] For this reason, secularism has been an inviting theory around which to organize religion–state relationships because it claims to minimize the divisiveness inherent in the pluralism of contemporary society. Theorists of secularism have argued that religious groups will use government as an arena for struggle, in which each seeks official endorsement for its own brand of religious orthodoxy.[5] Citizen is set against citizen and efforts are made to the draw in the government as a partisan of each side. The results may be destabilizing if losing groups believe the state is allied with the winners, and hence, is operating without legitimacy beyond the sanction of faith. Losers may react by seeking to overthrow the state as a means of recapturing official orthodoxy. To avoid such dangers, the secular state stands aloof from religious controversy: it does not enter disputes over religious dogma, avoids intrusion in the internal affairs of religious groups, and avoids the appearance of partiality toward one sectarian group or another.

Another major goal of secularism is to secure religious freedom for persons of faith and official tolerance for those without, positions which are now counted among the basic human rights. Religious belief and practice lend meaning to some peoples' lives and, thus, have value as forms of self-expression and modes for the exploration of existence. As a matter of public policy, the secular state does not dictate the terms of individual belief, which belongs in the private sphere. Individuals should be free to adopt whatever faith they choose, to preach their religion in public, and to practice openly within the limits of public morality and order. In addition, secularists sometimes argue that religious pluralism strengthens the state by providing alternative life models from which citizens can choose, and by enriching the public policy debate by bringing to bear diverse perspectives on morality and justice. In this way, the secular state may draw substantial benefits by fostering a rich cultural and public life marked by diversity within a system of managed conflict.

Even though the secular state allows religious groups to manage their own affairs, proclaim their doctrines, and practice their faiths with a minimum of interference, on occasion the demands of religion and the state conflict, as in the case of religiously-based conscientious objection to military service. Under such circumstances, secularism requires that the state enforce "neutral" rules which are adopted and applied through procedures which are themselves as even-handed as possible. These rules should be stated as broad constitutional, statutory, or judicial principles which are applied evenly to all groups. They establish the conditions under which religious exceptions to general-purpose rules may be made, if at all, and when they may not. In this way, conflict between religion and the state is managed so that it does not appear that the state is aligned with one religious group in opposition to others. All are subject to the same rules and the same processes, operating within a broader framework of religious freedom.

Finally, secularism seeks to protect religion from debasement by the state. This goal distinguishes the contemporary theory of secularism in both India and the United States from its old associations with theory hostile to religion.[6] It is a secular state that is the goal, rather than a secular society. Religion is not relegated to the private sphere in order to marginalize it, but to protect it. Clearly, the temptation of politicians to wrap themselves in their national flag is exceeded only by the temptation to wrap themselves in holy scripture. Religion lends the appearance of legitimacy to government and its actions, and as such religious associations are often sought by political leaders to improve their standing or that of their party. In so doing, politicians adapt religion to their own needs and may distort and misuse it, offending those who believe their sacred doctrine or ritual has been profaned. This is a particularly difficult area for secularism, in part because breaches tend to occur in the grey area between what is religious and what is cultural.[7]

Secularism as a theory for the organization of the state offers potential incentives which are extraordinarily attractive, both to government and to individual citizens. In the first place, secularism shows the state how to remove itself from the hazardous terrain of religious dispute, thus reducing the likelihood of political instability. In the second place, secularism puts strong emphasis on human rights by requiring the state to respect individual and sectarian autonomy in the religious sphere. However, secularism is not easy to apply, requiring as it does considerable discipline from government officials. They should resist the temptation to overtly exploit religious doctrinal divisions for partisan gain. They should be sensitive to the symbolic content of the messages they send, and to the distinction between their private and public behaviors. They should understand the difference between the religious and secular spheres, and the limited demands which public policy can make on citizens of faith. In sum, they should have an understanding of secularism and how it is expected to operate, and have some willingness to conform themselves to its requirements.

Characteristics of Indian secularism

While the western theory of secularism is associated with the arguments above, there are some ideas which are characteristic of the Indian conception. One such idea is that secularism means governmental tolerance for all religions rather than separation of church and state in the Jeffersonian sense.[8] The Indian view is that government need not stand aloof from religion, but may encourage and accommodate religious practices. This idea has been implemented in a number of ways: the nation has created national holidays to commemorate religious festivals or to recognize leaders of the many faiths; the President and Prime Minister pay countless official visits to religious sites, including Hindu temples, mosques, and Christian churches; public places, including government offices, are often decorated with religious icons.

In its official embrace of religious values, government may not exclude any of the major groups. Government must accommodate Christian, Parsi, and Islamic practices as well as Hindu; it should be inclusive and show no favoritism, but otherwise need not distance itself from sponsorship. Although some Indian intellectuals, particularly those on the left, understand secularism as requiring a rational public life separated from religion, and perhaps even government hostility to religion as a conservative and undemocratic force, Indian secularism is generally not of this type. In the Indian context, secularism denotes a regime which stands as a neutral outside religious divisions – there is no established church – although it may cooperate with religious groups and accommodate the religious feelings of its people.

Another Indian theme is that all religions are aspects of the same phenomenon and that Christian, Hindu, Islamic, and other faiths are manifestations of a basic unity. It makes little difference how one worships: form and content are secondary to the underlying oneness. From this perspective, religious tolerance requires a willingness to view – even actively embrace – alternative beliefs and forms of worship as equivalent. The person who thinks one religion is superior to another, the believer who thinks his truth excludes other truths, is intolerant. Variations on this theme are the subject of government campaigns to reduce communal feeling. In railroad stations and government offices throughout India, the sayings of Mahatma Gandhi and the Nehrus are prominently displayed. The official message is that the various religions are but "leaves" on a "single tree"; and that the God of the Christian, Hindu, Parsi, and Muslim is the "same."

Indian secularism also differs from the Western view in its concern that the state be able to reform religious institutions. The Indian Constitution allows the state to regulate religion for "social welfare and reform" and to throw open "Hindu religious institutions of a public character to all classes and sections of Hindus."[9] Under this provision, the state has prohibited both bigamous marriages and sati, and has opened temples, under most circumstances,[10] to untouchables. In so doing, government sought reform of the caste system, which many still view as the major obstacle to economic and social modernization. At the same time, provisions such as this are not entirely consistent with secularism because they invite government to regulate the management of religious life.[11]

In sum, Indian secularism is set within a constitutional and social framework which is profoundly ambiguous. The word "secularism" itself is a late addition to the Constitution, having been formally incorporated into the Preamble by amendment in 1976. While the Amendment codifies the general understanding of the nature of the Indian state, the original document contains a variety of provisions which taken together lack "conceptual clarity," as one commentator put it.[12] Freedom of conscience and religious practice are specifically safeguarded by the Constitution, but the same provision allows the State to regulate for the purposes of "social welfare and reform," and to restrict the "economic, financial, political or other secular" activities of religious groups.[13] The line between the secular and religious activities *of religious groups* is extraordinarily difficult to locate, which in turn means that government regulations may intrude on decisions central to religious observance, e.g., expenditures by temples for religious celebrations,[14] the level of which denote the importance of the occasion and the intensity of religious feeling. Elsewhere the Constitution provides for autonomy of religious schools, but limits this autonomy where governmental assistance has been provided.

Among the directive principles of state, ideas which are to guide government but are not enforceable at law, are the creation of a common civil code and the protection of cattle. Both of these principles speak to sensitive and continuing issues which have split citizens along religious lines: the continuation of the Muslim civil code excepting that community from the ban on polygamy, and continuing their divorce and other practices;[15] and the prohibition of cow slaughter in response to Hindu sentiments.[16] The politics of these directive principles continue to symbolize what some perceive to be the special treatment of politically powerful religious groups, and are a continuing source of communal resentments.

Accommodation and the neutrality of the state

The idea of accommodation allows government to provide public opportunities for citizens and officials to recognize the sacred. This has led to a number of practices in which government sponsors, or appears to sponsor, religious displays, rituals, and public prayer. In contrast, secularism requires the state to avoid such entanglements so that it is insulated from the disputes which may result. Practices which on their surface may appear benign are not always so, and may carry undercurrents of doctrinal and sectarian dispute.

Perhaps the most widespread of these accommodations is the placement of religious displays on government property. Wherever one goes, be it the Bank of India, a police station, the revenue office, a train station, or on a city bus, one is likely to see a religious icon, often in the form of a small shrine. Such displays, which have been erected by government officials and employees, may be of substantial size, and are usually attached to a wall in full public view, rather than sitting on the bureaucrat's desk, as the family portrait is semi-privately placed.

The significance of such displays is, of course, subject to interpretation: are they private expressions of religiosity, officially sanctioned expressions of religious belief, or both? Some Indians see them as purely private displays and inoffensive as such, others object to (a) the religious encroachment on government, that is to say, neutral space, (b) the official tolerance or sponsorship of the display, and (c) the predominance, as might be expected, of majority group displays.

In addition to displays of this sort, there are encroachments of a more permanent nature. Wherever temples or other religious edifices are erected, and that could be anywhere, authorities are exceedingly reluctant to disturb them, even where structures encroach on public land and inconvenience others. In the center of Hyderabad, for example, a temple has been erected in the middle of a major thoroughfare, and has grown steadily and incrementally to substantial size. It now sits as a permanent building on its own traffic island. Elsewhere, in this city as in others, one can find religious buildings, small or large, within government compounds, well-established and flourishing under the direct gaze and care of officialdom.

Religious observances are regularly injected into other aspects of government life. State or city buses may stop enroute to allow the driver and conductor to do pooja, or even to board a temple priest who accepts offerings from the passengers and bestows blessings. High government officials of both the center and the states frequently visit temples and other religious sites as part of their official schedules. While any one of these events may be trivial in itself, cumulated they are fraught with difficulty. When government is transformed into an arena for religious expression it ceases to be a neutral space.

The problem is not alleviated by the Indian understanding that all religions must be accommodated, because there is disagreement over what that idea means. If government wishes to be perceived as secular, it must rule with an "even hand" or be accused of sectarianism. But this is a riddle without solution. In India, as elsewhere, religious groups are of unequal size: India has a dominant majority (86 percent Hindu), a sizable minority (Muslims 12 percent), and numerous smaller but influential communities (Christian, Sikh, Parsi, Jain, and Buddhist, each under 3 percent). From the majority perspective, government rules with an "even hand" when its accommodations reflect majority numbers. Consequently, multiple state visits to Hindu temples and ubiquitous displays of Lakshmi or Ganesh confirm the majority and are symbolic to it of fairness. For many in the minority, equality is interpreted as equal treatment – one for one or nearly so – despite disparities in size. With anything less, they are constantly reminded of their vulnerability, their minority status and lack of power. Public officials sensitive to sectarian differences are faced with an ongoing dilemma: they constantly seek to avoid offense but cannot help giving it. Compensations toward minorities slight majority sentiment; recognition of majority status reinforces awareness of minority vulnerability. It is a calculation which government cannot help but lose, even when it acts with the best of intentions. In the end, each group is acutely aware of how others seek advantage – to demonstrate power, spread the faith, enrich sectarian coffers – and is resentful of success.

Having established a policy of accommodation, government inevitably becomes a battleground for sectarian advantage. The implications are endless and all too real: displays are transformed into symbolic statements about relative power; some encroachments may be purposefully provocative and government will be expected to tolerate, if not protect them; the administrative arms of government, such as the police, may be politicized along religious lines; and so on. The end result is that government, willingly or not, becomes an arena for sectarian competition. In consequence, government is perceived by all sides as playing favorites, although the perception of who is favored differs depending on the perspective of the observer.

Coercion and public ritual

The Indian idea that the various forms of religious expression are different aspects of an underlying unity also causes problems for secularism. At root, this belief denies a central reality of religious life: that every aspect of the sacred is contested between sects. There is no agreement on the existence or nature of God, the manifestations through which the sacred may be known, if or how the sacred should be worshipped, requirements for a moral life, the possibility of salvation and how to achieve it. Consequently, when toleration requires affirmations of any sort, problems for individual conscience are encountered. This can be illustrated by a recent incident in Kerala.

The Hindu reported on March 5, 1993, that the Kerala state industry minister, Mr. P.K. Kunhalikutty, a member of the Muslim League, refused to light a lamp at ceremonies honoring the inauguration of a new company, apparently claiming the practice was un-Islamic. The newspaper reported:

> Mr. Kunhalikutty was to originally preside over the function which the chief minister, Mr. K. Karunakaran, was to inaugurate. Since Mr. Karunakaran did not turn up, the minister was asked to inaugurate the function, which was presided over by Jesudas.
>
> After delivering the inaugural address, Mr. Kunhalikutty headed straight for his seat when Jesudas requested him to light the lamp. The minister returned but asked Jesudas instead to light the lamp. Jesudas lighted a few wicks and repeated his request which was turned down.
>
> Jesudas then raised his voice to ask the minister whether lamps were not lit at night in his area (Malappuram district). The minister shot back that they used only electricity.
>
> Jesudas wondered how secularism could be ushered in at this rate, said the eyewitness. In his presidential address he dwelt at length on religion and argued that religions do not preach divisiveness.

This incident raises the problem of tolerance in the Indian concept of secularism, and what behaviors can reasonably be expected of people who hold religious views. Jesudas believed that persons who have religious objections to a practice associated with another faith should put their objections aside and participate in a spirit of ecumenism. His view is associated with the idea that the various religions are but manifestations of a single phenomenon, that the God of the Christian and the Muslim, to paraphrase the government slogan, is the God of the Hindu.

Secularist theory argues that tolerance requires each person to indulge the other in their own practices, but individuals who do not believe should be excused. This is the position adopted by the US Supreme Court when it released Jehovah's Witnesses from their obligation to salute the flag,[17] a position subsequently adopted by the Indian courts in a similar controversy.[18] Nonetheless, the common belief and practice is that the social obligation to avoid "divisiveness," as Jesudas put it, requires believers to conform.

In India, this problem is commonly raised by majoritarian practices, such as here, the lighting of a lamp to begin a ceremony or the breaking of a coconut. It is frequently argued that these are cultural rather than religious practices; it is not uncommon, for example, to find offerings of broken coconuts and flowers placed before Christian images, such as statues or the crèche. Given such evidence, many Indians find it difficult to understand how anyone can raise religious objections to participation. As one Hindu friend put it, "I cannot open a building by cutting a ribbon. It's just not Indian." Nonetheless, there is a widespread understanding that these practices carry religious connotations. In a recent case decided by the Andhra Pradesh High Court challenging the breaking of coconuts and the chanting of mantras at state functions, the court upheld these practices even while observing that the ceremonies were "meant to invoke the blessings of the Almighty"; further, the Court also held that display of pictures of gods in public places was permitted because they "only symbolize the devotion of the persons concerned toward the Almighty."[19]

The problem for secularism is that these practices are coercive. For some, participation in the religious rituals of another faith may be more than their conception of right action allows. When participation is expected in a public setting, such as the incident in Kerala, there are powerful social pressures at work toward conformity. Consequently, when government officials sponsor prayer or ritual at official ceremonies they are in effect coercing some to affirm what they do not believe. The usual result is to lend majoritarian practices the stamp of official approval, and to brand the person who objects as outside the consensus. This brings the state a long way from the neutrality between sects that secularism requires.

Regulating religion

The neutrality of government is also compromised by the tradition of regulating religious affairs. The Constitution allows government to legislate for social reform, as well as exercise the traditional police powers over religion to secure public order, morality, and health. This has meant a comparatively wide sweep to government power, and a tendency to look there for solutions of religious disputes.

The Ayodhya affair illustrates the problems associated with this approach. The mosque at Ayodhya was demolished by militant Hindus who believe this to be the site of a prior temple commemorating the birthplace of Lord Ram. This promised to be the opening round of a series of confrontations at other ancient places, where temples were said to have been destroyed and mosques built in their place. The dispute over the site had been simmering for decades, but was brought to crisis by a group who occupied Ayodhya, began worship of their own idols, and proceeded to take down the mosque. The dispute pitted Hindu fundamentalists against Hindu moderates, and Hindus against Muslims. The result was weeks of rioting across India and countless dead.

Faced with a communal crisis as intense as any since partition, the government moved quickly to restore order. Among the steps taken were arrest of leaders of the demolition movement and the communal groups which had urged them on, a ban on communal organizations of every persuasion, removal of BJP governments in four states with installation of emergency rule from Delhi, and various efforts to restore peace in riot-torn areas. In addition, the government decided to intervene in the specifically religious aspect of the dispute.

Immediately after the mosque's destruction Prime Minister P.V. Narasimha Rao announced that his government would rebuild the mosque and assure erection of a Hindu temple as well. Having made these commitments, he placed the government in an extraordinarily delicate position, assuring that they would remain at the center of the dispute. To carry out their decision, they would have to decide the exact placement of both temple and mosque, both matters of great dispute, the relative size of each structure, and assure access to both. These are precisely the sorts of considerations that the theory of secularism would have government avoid, i.e., judgments about essentially religious questions that are the subject of sectarian rivalry. Interestingly, the Indian public had a different idea of how the government should proceed: almost half (46 percent) preferred a secular structure such as a school or museum, while smaller numbers preferred a temple or mosque be built.[20] Reporting on their own poll, *India Today* surveyed the complexities into which the government had plunged:

> The Government's decision to rebuild the mosque – which came even as Muslims in both India and abroad began clamoring for it – finds no favor with the electorate. The decision does, however, have pockets of support – the Muslim and the southern voter.
>
> About location, the most acceptable option – to 37 percent of voters – was that the temple and the mosque be built side by side. For the only-temple and mosque away [from the site] options taken together, the support is as high as 44 percent. The Government's option of only a masjid [mosque] at the site finds practically no takers. The only-temple option finds great support in the north and among BJP backers, while Congress(I) backers, Muslims and the south prefer the "unity" option.[21]

The Ayodhya affair is indicative of the extent to which India's governments are involved with the supervision and regulation of religion and religious disputes. In Tamil Nadu, to take another example, the Chief Minister directs a Temple Administration Board which is seeking to rejuvenate Hindu ritual by sponsoring refresher classes for temple priests, who are themselves on the state payroll. In Karnataka, the former chief minister published advertisements in the national papers boasting of his efforts to rejuvenate the temples and rituals. All of these actions, and myriad others, have eroded the expectation that the state is sensitive to secular principles and committed to them.

Discussion

It is difficult to conclude with Donald Eugene Smith, who looked at this issue almost 30 years ago, that India is a secular state. The label remains, the Preamble to the Constitution is in place, but policy decisions keep government continuously entangled in religious controversies: the more serious and divisive the issue, the more likely it seems that government will intervene.

Despite the secularist label, India is an *accommodationist* state, intent on finding room for religious expression at official levels, regulating and manipulating religious groups for political and social ends. In partial consequence, the Indian political system has not dealt successfully with its religious divisions. The integrity of the state is threatened by separatist movements which are drawn along religious lines; communal hostilities have intensified as militants have sought to rally Hindus behind the saffron flag; Muslims, for their part, are shaken by recent events, and are divided over tactics and uncertain of their future.[22]

Secularism requires behaviors that are extraordinarily difficult for Indians to adopt. The whole fabric of Indian life is steeped in public religiosity, and government plays a major role. Nonetheless, India has no established religion, the courts have remained as true to the conception of a neutral state as the Constitution would allow, and the majority of Indians demonstrate their continued goodwill and good sense. It is not surprising to find that the Indian public would have preferred a secular rather than religious disposition of the Ayodhya site. On a related matter, the same poll shows that majorities of every community, including Muslims, support adoption of a common civil code,[23] which would complete the unfinished and messy business of that directive principle.

India's religious divisions are among its most serious, and better ways are needed to cope with them. It would be wise, despite the contrary record, for government to start disengaging from its religious entanglements and in so doing, to release some of the pressures on the Indian state. The process could begin gradually, by withdrawing from activities which are largely symbolic rather than substantive. There is no constituency for withdrawal of aid to religious schools nor an end to regulation of the temples, but senior officials could reduce the number of their visits to religious sites, and the disposition of Ayodhya could be treated as a civil matter and left to the judgments of the land courts. In addition, some controls could be placed over religious exhibits on government property. All of these steps would be painful at first, both personally and politically, but they would begin to create new expectations about government behavior, and new perspectives on its neutrality.

While some movement in the direction of secularism would be helpful, it will not end religious divisiveness. All nations have scarce resources, and groups are inevitably divided among themselves for their share of the pie. Development will not occur evenly, and religious, geographic, caste, and class tensions will result. In addition, there are those in India who have a different vision of its future and who believe that the creation, or recreation, of a Hindu state is its destiny. This is an essentially romantic movement whose vision has proved attractive in a time of considerable social and economic dislocation. Ayodhya was meant to be a challenge to the status quo and a confrontation with the "pseudo-secularism" of recent decades. It is a challenge that requires an equally decisive response. What better way, perhaps, than through a renewed concern with secularism which tempers the divisive policies of accommodation that seem to have reinforced communal tensions?

Notes

1   This discussion is part of a larger debate that is questioning the very fundamentals of the Indian state, its social, political and economic organization.

2   Pramod Menon and Gautam Sen, "What Is Wrong with Secularism," *The Radical Humanist*, 57, no. 1 (April 1993), pp. 25–9. M.N. Karna, "Meaning of Ayodhya," *Seminar*, 402 (Feb. 1993), pp. 31–4.

3   H.A. Gani, "Failure of Indian Secularism," *The Radical Humanist*, 57, no. 1 (April 1993), pp. 31–6.

4   Justice William Brennan of the US Supreme Court has developed a sophisticated and powerful theory of secularism (although he does not call it that) on which much of this analysis draws. See, especially, his dissenting opinion in *Marsh* v. *Chambers*, 463 US 803 (1983), for a statement of the public-policy goals of secularism.

5   See arguments of Justice Hugo Black in *Everson* v. *Board of Education*, 330 US 1 (1947).

6   Nonetheless, there are secularists who view religion as a backward and irrational force, the influence of which should be actively limited by government. See S.L. Verna, "Reformulation of Indian Secularism," *Indian Journal of Political Science*, 46, no. 1 (Jan.–March, 1985), pp. 32–48.

7   This question is sometimes litigated in societies operating under secular constitutions. Courts are inclined to validate such practices on grounds that the state seeks merely to recognize popular customs. See the Jain challenge, as a debasement of their faith, to official celebrations of a Jain prophet, *Suresh Chandra* v. *Union of India*, AIR 1975 Delhi 168. On a similar theme, the US Supreme Court reduced Christmas to a "national folk festival" while upholding an officially sponsored display of the Christian crèche, *Lynch* v. *Donnelly*, 465 US 668 (1984).

8   It has been argued that there can be no secularism without, at a minimum, separation of church from state, with each confined to its own sphere of responsibilities (Ved Prakash Luthera, *The Concept of the Secular State and India* (London: Oxford University Press, 1964)). Abraham Vazhayil Thomas discusses these questions in his *Christians in Secular India* (Cranbury, NJ: Associated University Presses, 1974), pp. 15–20. The term "secularism" is used here because it is how Indians commonly describe their own system, and it is the official term as well. While the Indian system contains some elements of separation, it can best be characterized as a system in which government accommodation of religious values is the norm.

9   Article 25.

10   Public access to temples may be limited when ritual requires it. *Venkataramana Devaru* v. *State of Mysore*, AIR 1958 SC 255.

11   This problem is discussed by Donald Eugene Smith in *India as a Secular State* (Princeton: Princeton University Press, 1963).

12 G.R.S. Rao, "Secularism in the Indian Republic: Emerging Issues and Implications," Professor V.R. Bhonde Memorial Lecture, Nagpur University, Feb. 21–2, 1991.

13 Article 25.

14 *The Commissioner, Hindu Religious Endowments, Madras* v. *Sri Lakshmindra*, 1954 SCR 1005.

15 See particularly the Muslim Women Act of 1986, reversing a decision by the Supreme Court (*Mohammed Ahmed Khan* v. *Shah Bano Begum*, AIR 1985 SC 945) upholding a right to maintenance of a Muslim divorcee.

16 *M.H. Quareshi* v. *State of Bihar*, AIR 1958 SC 731, unsuccessful challenge to prohibition on cow slaughter as a denial of the occupation of butcher. See also Mohammed Mutaza Khan, "Politics of Secularism: a Case Study of Cow Slaughter in India," *Indian Journal of Politics*, 17, no. 2 (June, 1983), pp. 85–102.

17 *West Virginia* v. *Barnette*, 319 US 624 (1943).

18 *Bijoe Emmanuel* v. *State of Kerala*, (1986) 3 SCC 615; AIR 1987 SC 748. The Indian case involved expulsion from school for refusing to sing the national anthem.

19 Reported in *The Hindu*, Aug. 12, 1992, p. 4. The quotation is from *The Hindu* report, not a direct quotation from the Court's judgment.

20 "*The Hindu*–CPSS Opinion Poll: Ayodhya, Mandal Low in List of Priorities," *The Hindu*, Jan. 25, 1993, p. 7.

21 "Ayodhya: After the Demolition," *India Today*, Jan. 15, 1993, p. 20.

22 Christians also have reason to worry, as the BJP entered a controversy in Goa about the path of a new railroad connection to Bombay by casting the controversy as a Christian–Hindu dispute.

23 *The Hindu*, Jan. 25, 1993, p. 7. For all India, 81 percent approved; 88 percent of Hindus; 87 percent of Christians; and 52 percent of Muslims.

3
Reconstructing "Ram Rajya": Tradition, Politics, and the Bharatiya Janata Party

Matthew A. Cook

India is full of divisions. It is divided linguistically: 13 officially recognized languages and hundreds of dialects. India is divided ethnically: Aryan, Dravidian, and Asian ethnic groups are all found within its borders. India is divided politically: separatist movements have popularity in the states of Kashmir, Punjab, and Assam. India is divided socially: problems of caste exist throughout the country and caste warfare occurs in the state of Bihar. India is divided religiously: it is home to Hindus, Muslims, Jains, Christians, and Buddhists.

As a political party the Bharatiya Janata Party (BJP) wishes to overcome these divisions by stressing the concept of unity. In this way it hopes to succeed in taking control of the government from the Congress Party, which has ruled India – except for a short period – since independence. Dr. Murli Manohar Joshi, former President of the BJP, states:

> Our [the BJP] approach [to politics] is to emphasize the bonds of unity in India.
>
> (Tierney, 1991: 36)

In addition, the BJP stressed the importance of unity in the naming of the 1992 *Ekta Yatra*: *Ekta* in Hindi means unity, or literally "oneness," and *Yatra* translates as pilgrimage. Once again, Dr. Joshi repeatedly stated, during the period in which he traveled through most of the states in India, that the purpose of the Ekta Yatra was to promote Indian unity (*India Today*, 1992: 42).

What devices does the BJP use in order to promote unity in India among such a diverse population? Historian Brian Stock, in *Listening for the Text*, states that traditions give a sense of unity (Stock, 1990: 161).

Similarly, the BJP attempts to to use this idea of tradition to promote unity through the regular use of ancient Indian symbols: for example, the BJP's election symbol, the lotus (an ancient Hindu and Buddhist symbol), and the BJP flag, colored both saffron and green (the holy colors associated with the Hindu religion and Islam respectively). Perhaps the most important use of symbols by the party involves the concept of Ram Rajya. The desire to establish Ram Rajya in India remains one of the most important examples of the BJP's use of traditional Indian concepts to gain popular and political support.

The use of Ram Rajya in BJP speeches coincides with the rise in popularity of the BJP. The term Ram Rajya derives from the traditional Hindu folk text, *The Ramayana:*[1] *Ram*, which refers to Rama, the *The Ramayana's* mythical warrior/king protagonist, and *Rajya*, which refers to his kingdom or state, is considered a "Golden Age" marked by prosperity and unity in the Hindu tradition. The BJP desires to *establish* Ram Rajya, which implies that India is not currently in this state. The way to achieve Ram Rajya is to vote the BJP into power. In this sense, Ram Rajya becomes symbolic of an India ruled by the BJP.

Press critical of the BJP represents the party, its desire to establish Ram Rajya, and the policies with which it would rule, as "regressive." These representations rest on the use of language that connotes backward movement:

> It [the BJP] . . . aspires *to restore* [emphasis mine] Rama Rajya, a mythical golden age of Hindu civilization when the Hindu god Rama ruled.
>
> (Desmond, 1991: 35)

> His party, he [L.K. Advani] says, would make India a Hindu state . . . The result, Advani tells his fast-growing band of supporters, *would be a return* [emphasis mine] to Rama Rajya, which the Hindus believe to be a golden age when their warrior god Lord Ram ruled the world.
>
> (Bhandare and Fernandes, 1993: 30)

> Far from ushering in a golden mythical age of Ram Rajya, the BJP's policies seek *to take us back* [emphasis mine] to the medieval age . . .
>
> (Bhandare and Fernandes, 1993: 30)

By connoting backward movement, the texts represent the BJP, its policies, and Ram Rajya, as regressive.

After living in India and conducting fieldwork on the BJP, I have difficulties accepting this representation. Many of the BJP supporters

I spoke with considered the BJP, its vision of India (Ram Rajya), and its policies to be "progressive" (Dasgupta, 1993: 9). Furthermore, the meaning of Ram Rajya has a great impact on a wide range of Indians – from well-educated Brahmans to poor laborers.

Why do press representations of Ram Rajya (and party policies on which it would be based) contradict those of BJP members/supporters? Is this discrepancy simply *prima facie*, or does this difference cut more deeply, revealing underlying assumptions about Indian society? This paper takes the latter point of view. The first section examines the accounts by which the press represents Ram Rajya as "regressive." It argues that the press constructs this representation with a "post-Englightenment" understanding of the concept of tradition, and therefore fails to recognize that the BJP's talk of Ram Rajya has little to do with returning to the past, but everything to do with gaining political power in the present. The second section considers what the term Ram Rajya reveals about the complex structure of the BJP.

Interpreting Ram Rajya: tradition and "post-Enlightenment" discourse

The concept of tradition has a well-documented meaning in "post-Englightenment" discourse. Historian Brian Stock, in *Listening to the Text*, states that tradition usually occurs in opposition to the concept of change (Stock, 1990: 159). Stock maintains that because popular culture associates change with modernity, "tradition automatically came to mean the culturally changeless and historically immobile" (Stock, 1990: 159).

People also associate tradition with the past (Hobsbaum and Ranger, 1983: 1; Pelikan, 1984: 9–10; Shils, 1981: 54–5). Stock states, "In classical sociological theory, tradition is most easily defined as the stage of society from which we all emerged" (Stock, 1990: 159). The tendency of "post-Enlightenment" discourse (from which all social sciences developed) to describe tradition as a past stage from which we evolved is documented in Folkloristics/Anthropology. Scholars consider folklore both "traditional," as well as a "survival" (Dundes, 1969: 2–3; Shils, 1981: 18). A "survival" refers to phenomena left over from earlier stages of history which have lost their original meanings and functions. The use of "tradition" and "survival" concurrently to describe folklore results in phenomena intrinsically connected to the past. Folklorist/anthropologist Allen Dundes, in *The Devolutionary Premise in Folklore Theory*, notes the tendency to associate traditional phenomena, specifically folklore, with the past:

Even a cursory examination of the intellectual history of folklore scholarship reveals a definite unquestioned basic premise that the golden age of folklore occurred in the past, in most cases specifically the far distant past.

(Dundes, 1969: 5)

Dundes's comments, and Stock's observation of classical sociological theory with the concept of "survival," both underline that "post-Englightenment" discourse assumes traditional materials (in this case, folklore) come from the past (Pelikan, 1984: 651; Shils, 1981: 12). Furthermore, by stating that there is a belief in a particular "golden age," Dundes highlights the assumption that traditional phenomena have set and definable boundaries in the past; these boundaries render them objectifiable. This ability to objectify (i.e. to make concrete, static) occurs because traditional phenomena in "post-Enlightenment" discourse *are not* associated with change (Stock, 1990: 159).

The fact that "post-Enlightenment" discourse treats tradition as "objective" phenomena of the past, has had a profound effect on the way Western-trained thinkers have set about representing the world. For example, Western academics try to discover, by tracing back through time, the "original," "objective" versions of traditions. Folklorist/ Anthropologist Alan Dundes notes:

Just as ethnographers carefully sifted through unavoidable details obviously only recently added through acculturative contact in an attempt to discover the pure unadulterated original native culture, so practitioners [folklorists] of the Finnish historical-geographic method sought to work backwards through the unfortunate changes (or . . . mistakes and errors) in order to find the pure unadulterated [read changeless] original Ur-form.

(Dundes, 1969: 9)

Anthropologist/Ethnographer Michelle Rosaldo echoes Dundes by noting: "[there has been] a persistent tendency to appropriate ethnographic data in the form of a search for origins" (Rosaldo in Clifford and Marcus, 1986: 110). James Clifford, in *Writing Culture: the Politics and Poetics of Ethnography*, adds even greater legitimacy to Rosaldo's and Dundes's observations. He states that in anthropological literature there has been a descriptive "pattern of *retrospection* [emphasis mine] that laments the loss of a 'good' country, a place where authentic social and natural contacts were once possible" (Clifford, 1986: 113). Dundes, Rosaldo, and Clifford exemplify the tendency to treat traditions as phenomena that can be "discovered" by tracing them back (or retro-spection) through time to an "original" version: the "Ur-form," a "golden age," or even the "good" country. Clifford notes that the per-ception of these constructions (and by association, tradition) as pure and unadulterated are derived from a "western" source: The Bible's Garden of Eden (Clifford, 1986: 113).

Press critical of the BJP represent its desire to establish Ram Rajya and the policies which constitute it as "regressive." This "regressive" repre-sentation is based on language that connotes backward movement. Many question the accuracy of this representation: For example BJP supporters consider the party's vision of India to be "progressive" (Dasgupta, 1993: 9). The BJP's version of Ram Rajya conflicts with journalists' representation beause the two occupy different "positions" in Indian society.

What we say is always "positioned": we write and speak from specific places, times, and cultures. As a result of our "position," statements must always be understood as being "in context" (Hall, 1990: 222). The BJP, and its critical press, occupy different "positions" in contemporary India: one is a political party, and the other a communication business. The two positions conceptualize Ram Rajya from quite different con-texts, therefore they represent it differently.

To understand the "context" from which the critical press labels Ram Rajya as "regressive" one must examine the definition of "tradition" in "post-Enlightenment" discourse: traditional phenomena are associated with changelessness and thereby objectifiable; traditional phenomena are associated with the past, not modernity or the future. Because the term Ram Rajya derives from *The Ramayana*, a *traditional* Hindu text, the critical press represents it (like Dundes's and Rosaldo's traditional phenomena) as an objective point in the past to which the BJP wishes to return.[2] The influence of this particular understanding of "tradition" remains particularly important because it results in the press misun-derstanding that BJP references to the establishment of Ram Rajya have little to do with returning to the past, but everything to do with gaining political power in the present at the expense of the BJP's main rival: The Congress Party.

The politics of traditions: Ram Rajya and Congress culture

India has a "dominant party political system" – a multiparty system in which one party has continuously been dominant (Manor, 1988: 63). This party has been the Congress Party.[3] The Congress Party's influence occurs throughout all India: streets and parks have the names of Congress Party leaders, statues all across India commemorate Congress Party politicians, the Congress Party controls the Indian economy in a state-dominated economy. Public museums tell of the Congress Party's fight against colonialism and its creation of the modern Indian state (Thompson, 1993). The Congress Party's influence has been so great that historian Ainslie Embree, in *India's Search for National Identity*, states, "it's [The Congress Party's] voice was the voice of India" (Embree, 1980: 19) It surprises no one that the party has had an enormous role in the construction of India's history. Historian/Anthropologist Nicholas Dirks, in *Colonialism and Culture*, states that history,

> is a system of organizing the past that depends upon certain narratives, assumptions, and voices and that continues to have important stakes throughout the social and political order.
>
> (Dirks, 1992: 14)

Dirks portrays history not as neutral dates and facts, but as something created or deliberately "organized." Whoever "organizes" the past then engages in a political act. Historian Gyan Prakash supports this interpretation:

> History's power to constitute what exists and has existed makes the writing of histories a profoundly "worldly" activity . . . historical writing as a political practice.
>
> (Prakash, 1992: 382)

If one takes the position that "In India . . . the politics of the academy can never be separated from the politics outside its own institutional confines" (Dirks, 1992: 14), what does an examination of the influence of non-academic institutions on the portrayal of Indian history reveal? Despite Indian historiography being very complex, a survey of Indian history books and museums reflects the politics of India's dominant party: postcolonial Indian history roughly coincides with the exploits of the Congress Party (Thompson, 1993).

Within the Congress Party the Nehru family has been particularly prominent. It has produced three Prime Ministers who have governed India through 35 of its 44 years of independence. The Nehru family's role in postcolonial India has been so all-pervasive that commentators portray the family as both a "dynastic heritage" and a "national icon" (Ludden, 1992: 273). Journalist and BJP National Executive member Jay Dubashi states of the Nehru family's relationship with India:

This is the world Nehru created and we have to live in it. Everything is being named after one Nehru or the other [i.e. Indira Gandhi, or Rajiv Gandhi] as if the family had taken over the country. In Bombay, the other day, they named the new port as Nhava Seheva, Jawahar Port, to go with the existing Indira dock not far away. It is only a matter of time before whole cites will be named after Jawaharlal or Indira, and, in due course, this country, which is supposed to be India that is Bharat will be known as Nehrustan.

(Dubashi, 1992: 108)

Due to this dominance, the Nehru family has had a great influence on the construction of India's recent history. This influence, which is reflected in the "Nehruvian" policies of Jawaharlal Nehru, his daughter Indira Gandhi, and her son Rajiv, were aimed at creating a modern centralized state and economy (Ludden, 1992: 257–79). As a result of this influence, postcolonial history constructed an India of "big hydroelectric projects and steel mills" with rhetoric based on a "modern sensibility founded on scientific thinking" (Prakash, 1992: 362).

References to the establishment of Ram Rajya help the BJP challenge the dominant position of both the Congress Party and the Nehru family. BJP opponents argue that this challenge uses traditional Indian concepts, like Ram Rajya, to "remold the people of India to become one monolith called Indians" (G. Cook, 1993: 24). This "vote bank," for the BJP, "homogenizes" the Hindu community, which make up 80 percent of India, into one "ostensible" unit. While this argument provides insights into Indian politics, especially when examining the work groups allied with the BJP (i.e. the Vishwa Hindu Parishad (VHP), the Rashtriya Swayamsevak Sangh (RSS), and the Bharatiya Mazdoor Sangh (BMS)), ultimately it does not clarify the reasons why the BJP refers to establishing Ram Rajya.

The BJP doesn't actively need to promote a Hindu "vote bank"; its allies promote such a "bank." In fact, it behoves the BJP *not* to get involved in creating this "bank."[4] Those involved in creating a Hindu "vote bank" cannot agree on who constitutes a "Hindu"; therefore if the BJP were to actively enter this debate it would be in the "no win" political position of having to side with one set of supporters against another set.[5] While the BJP greatly benefits at the expense of the Congress Party from the promotion of a Hindu "vote bank," BJP references to Ram Rajya remain primarily part of another political strategy. This strategy challenges the political dominance of the Congress Party and Nehru family; it undermines the latter's influence on the construction of postcolonial Indian history.

Dennis Austin and Peter Lyon, in "The Bharatiya Janata Party," quote L.K. Advani, the BJP president, who states that the party's prime resolve was "to break the mold of Nehruvian politics" (Austin and Lyon, 1992: 40). As part of this resolve, the BJP uses rhetoric that conflicts with that of the "Nehruvian" construct of India. For example, the BJP capitalizes on issues concerning religious shrines and pilgrimage sites, as opposed to hydroelectric projects and steel mills. It employs the rhetoric of theatrics, religious myth, and dreams rather than Nehru's modern "sensibility" founded on scientific thinking (Austin and Lyon, 1992: 36–50).

BJP references to the establishment of Ram Rajya challenge the dominance of "Nehruvian" politics; rhetorically constructing an alternative India, one ruled by the BJP, the party destabilizes the historically dominant "Nehruvian" construction of India. The term Ram Rajya employs multiple layers of meaning: on one level it is an India ruled by the BJP, on others it simultaneously refers to a mythical "Golden Age" from the Hindu tradition. This level of meaning emphasizes a "glorious" far past, and thus brings into question the "glory" of the near past. Considering that India's near past has been oriented toward the exploits of the Congress Party, led by the Nehru family, this subtle suggestion represents an attempt by the BJP to subvert the latter's power by questioning its construction of India. In this way the BJP questions the glory of "Nehru's India" and justifies a change in leadership. The BJP reasons: You've experienced Nehru's vision of India for 40 years now and it wasn't the "best." Our vision is better; it will be like a "Golden Age," so please vote for us.[6]

This technique of justifying one's political will to govern by using the past to undermine your opponent's power, develops out of the colonial experience. Historian/anthropologist Nicholas Dirks, in *Colonialism and Power*, states:

> Orientalism also refers to a much more sophisticated body of scholarship, embodied in such practices as philosophy, archeology, history, and anthropology, all glorifying the classical civilizations of the East (at the same time they glorify even more the scholarly endeavors of the West that make possible their recuperation) but suggesting that all history since the classical age was characterized by decline, degradation, and decadence. Orientalism . . . shared fundamental premises about the East, serving to denigrate the present, deny history, and repress any sensibility regarding contemporary political, social, or cultural autonomy and potential in the colonized world.

(Dirks, 1992: 9)

Gyan Prakash notes that the British used orientalist textual and institutional practices to question "the will to govern of your opponents" by glorifying the past, in order to justify their colonial rule in India (Prakash, 1992: 355). The BJP uses this same technique in making references to Ram Rajya; however they change the players, and thus attempt to denigrate "Nehru's India."

Ram Rajya as political tradition: many versions; one umbrella

Thus far, I have examined representations of Ram Rajya conflict, and why press representations fail to help one understand the BJP as a political party. I also have shown how the BJP's talk of establishing Ram Rajya in India fulfills multiple functions that are aimed largely at undermining the Congress Party, and more specifically how the BJP uses the Ram Rajya metaphor to undermine the Nehru family's dominant position in Indian politics, while at the same time promoting the party's vision of India. Difficulties arise in understanding the concept because BJP references to Ram Rajya serve multiple functions simultaneously. Furthermore, the BJP's demographics complicate analysis of the term. In this sense an analysis of the term Ram Rajya reveals much about the rather complicated structure of the BJP.

Austin and Lyon state:

> [The saffron brotherhood – a metaphor for the BJP and its allies] is broad and not always of one mind or purpose. There are not only extremists and moderates, but economic nationalists alongside free market enthusiasts, and the BJP has to contend ideologically within its own saffron brotherhood.
>
> (Austin and Lyon, 1993: 45)

The party's supporters make it difficult to understand what the BJP means when it states it will establish Ram Rajya. One just can't ask the "real" BJP to please stand up and define its vision of India because many, and sometimes conflicting, ideologues want to be heard.

Understanding that the BJP's support comes from a rather eclectic group remains extremely important. Only after identifying such ambiguities can one abandon the impossible task of finding an "objective meaning" for Ram Rajya and to focus on how the concept brings a variety of ideologies under one big BJP "tent." Perhaps the most important feature of the slogan is how the BJP uses Ram Rajya to make this "big tent." Understanding this shifting perception of "tradition" helps explain the complexity of the meaning of Ram Rajya and sheds light on the political complexity of the BJP.

The meanings of tradition

Despite the position of post-Enlightenment philosophy that forms "part of the past," it shouldn't be assumed that this philosophy denies the ties of phenomena with the present. Western social science has always maintained that continuity exists between traditions of the past and the present. For example, traditions have been considered markers of identity for whole societies and cultures (Handler and Linnekin, 1984: 27; Shils, 1981: 19). Such a conceptualization of tradition treats it as an unchanging core of traits that are handed down from one generation to the next (Kroeber, 1948: 411; Hobsbaum and Ranger, 1983: 1; Pelikan, 1984: 19–20; Shils, 1981: 34–5). Anthropologists Richard Handler and Jocelyn Linnekin, in *Tradition, Genuine or Spurious*, have critiqued this understanding of tradition by pointing out how it has been constructed on a "nature" metaphor:

> Tradition is likened to a natural object, occupying space, enduring in time, and having a molecular structure ... [it is] modeled after a natural object – bounded, discrete, and objectively knowable.
>
> (Handler and Linnekin, 1984: 286)

Likening tradition to a natural object reinforces the perception of traditional phenomena as something unchanging. But traditions are not unchanging. Like all aspects of social life they remain "changing and contestable" (Clifford and Marcus, 1986: 6). Therefore, traditions *should not* be conceptualized as phenomena handed down from the past, but rather, as Handler and Linnekin argue, as phenomena "symbolically reinvented in an ongoing present" (Handler and Linnekin, 1984: 280). While this understanding of tradition does not imply a total lack of continuity with the past, it does imply that, despite having histories, traditions don't necessarily depend on "objective" relationships to the past for their meaning. Traditions become redefined according to context (Cohen, 1987: 660; Hobsbawn and Ranger, 1983: 2–5; Pelikan, 1983: 12–15; Shils, 1981: 258–61). The use of Ram Rajya in Indian politics illustrates this argument.

Ram Rajya derives from the traditional Hindu text, *The Ramayana*, and refers to a "golden age" that coincides with the BJP establishing a government in Delhi. Its use in Indian politics is not new. In addition to the BJP, both Mahatma Gandhi and Jaya Prakash Narayan spoke about Ram Rajya.

Mahatma Gandhi embeds Ram Rajya in the Hindu cosmology. This cyclic cosmology identifies four stages or *yugas*: *Satya* (the "Golden Age" – a period of truth, justice, and prosperity), *Treta* (a "good" period, but not the best), *Dvapar* (a "corrupt" period, but with time to make things good again), and *Kali* (a totally "corrupt" period). The Kali yuga ends with *Pralaya* (a time of total destruction), *Srsti* (a time of creation) follows Pralaya. Srsti then returns the cosmology back to Satya to form a complete circle. Hindus conceive the present as the Kali Yuga. Mahatma Gandhi associated Kali Yuga with the rule of the British Raj, and believed, once the British were gone, India would come "out of the *Kal[i] Yug[a]*, into a a new era of freedom and plenty – *Ram Rajya*" (Naipaul, 1976: 15). In this sense, Ram Rajya represents a "golden age" that is defined by the "removal" of the British from India and self-rule.

During periods following independence, political figures gave Ram Rajya a new political interpretation. For example, just prior to the "emergency" of the 1970s, a different definition of Ram Rajya emerged. The "emergency" was a period of political unrest when political infighting "broke-out" within the Congress Party. Many Congress Party politicians and sympathizers were upset by the "iron hand" with which Indira Gandhi ruled the party, and with the direction in which she was taking India. In reaction to these factors, a group of former Congress Party politicians decided to "get rid of her": They charged Indira Gandhi with electoral corruption. In reaction to these charges, Mrs. Gandhi suspended the Indian Constitution and declared a state of "emergency." This act enabled her to censor newspapers critical of her and arrest political foes.

Political figure Jaya Prakash Narayan, a leading Indira Gandhi critic, defined Ram Rajya during the "Emergency" in the following manner:

> *Swaraj* means *Ramraj*. Swaraj means that every village will have its own rule. Every village, every *mohalla* and town will manage its own affairs.
>
> (Narayan in Naipaul, 1976: 155)

In this context, Ram Rajya does not symbolize self-rule on a national level, but a village level. Narayan's "golden age" is when every village can rule itself without interference from Indira Gandhi or the Center (the Indian federal government).

Mahatma Gandhi's and Jaya Prakash Narayan's two differing definitions of Ram Rajya clearly illustrate Handler and Linnekin's argument that traditional phenomena are "reinvented [or redefined] in an ongoing present" (Handler and Linnekin, 1984: 280). The unstable meanings produced by this process of reinvention may appear at odds with the BJP's emphasis on "unity": Gandhi's and Narayan's versions of Ram Rajya could be viewed as competitive visions of India. I disagree. The BJP, by using the term Ram Rajya, is attempting to develop its own vision of India as well as incorporate the political support that accompanies Gandhi's and Narayan's visions. In this sense, Ram Rajya functions as an allegory. James Clifford, in reference to Northrop Frye's *Anatomy of Criticism*, states that an allegory is a type of metaphor that "implies the existence of at least two meanings of the same words" (Clifford, 1986: 98). Clifford concludes, after noting that all words have allegorical features, that this makes it particularly difficult to view any one layer of meaning as "privileged, [and] accounting for the rest" (Clifford, 1986: 98).

The BJP's use of Ram Rajya as an allegory has been central to the party's blossoming power: multiple layers of meaning enable the party to appeal not only to "neo-Gandhians" (Manor, 1988: 79) and remnants of Narayan's Janata Party, but also to Hindu extremists from the Vishwa Hindu Parishad (VHP) and Bajrang Dal, as well as these groups' mother organization, the nationalist Rashtriya Swayamsevak Sangh (RSS), and free market enthusiasts (Singh and Ghimire, 1993: 38–9).[7]

By making the establishment of Ram Rajya an election goal the BJP has been able to build previously unthinkable political alliances. They have brought neo-Gandhian groups under the same tent as the Rashtriya Swayamsevak Sangh: a group indicted in the assassination of Mahatma Gandhi. The key to understanding how the BJP has worked these political alliances lies in conceptualizing "traditions" not in the conventional way as unchanging, but as contemporary ongoing phenomena. The shifting meaning of the traditional Hindu concept of Ram Rajya in Indian politics clearly illustrates Handler and Linnekin's argument that "traditions" are reinvented in the ongoing present. Ram Rajya's shifting meaning allows the BJP to reap great political benefits: By using the concept they gain support from groups historically associated with Ram Rajya (as well as from new political groups), as they "reinvent" the concept to meet political expediencies.

Conclusion

Academic discourses have, by building "essences" into their descriptive metaphors, given the impression that India is a land dominated by "mysticism," "arcane systems," and "vague imagination." Anthropologist/historian Ronald Inden states:

> Certain metaphors appear in [these] Indological texts as constitutive of India and the West. The most important of these, from the standpoint of trying to understand how these . . . texts do their work, is the metaphor used to depict Indian thought itself. That metaphor, implicit in the text of Renou and other Indologists and used again and again, is the metaphor of the Other as a dreamer, as a neurotic, insane or madman, one whose own representations of reality are made by his imagination rather than his reason . . . orientalists from Hegel onward have constructed Indian thought as a dream.
>
> (Inden, 1990: 40)

The representation of Indian thought-as-dream according to Inden is a mechanism by which Europeans have constructed the "Self" from the Indian "Other": "the essence of Indian thought is a dreamy imagination, while that of Western thought is practical reason" (Inden, 1990: 3).

References to India as a land dominated by the "dreamy imagination" and not practical reason occur in representations of the BJP. These representations accuse the BJP of being based on theatrics (Austin and Lyon, 1993: 36), and are full of images of religious mobs out of control, of BJP leaders accepting blood sacrifices from supporters, and of the employment of astrology to determine political events (Cook, 1993: 14). Many of these same images blur into the BJP's desire to establish Ram Rajya by stating that the party consists of "fundamentalists" who desire to establish a Hindu "theocracy" in India (Cook, 1993). For example, Ram Rajya is depicted as a dream:

> The BJP is at the confluence of several streams of Hindu revivalist thought and action extending back to the Hindu Mahasabha, the Rashtriya Swayamsevak Sangh, the Vishwa Hindu Parishad, the Jan Sangh and the Janata and Swatantra parties. Each carried dreams of a restored past . . . At its most poignant, the dream has been of Ram Rajya – the kingdom of Rama.
>
> (Austin and Lyon, 1993: 38)

Metaphors depicting the essence of India being the "dreamy imagination" have had a great effect on the representation of Ram Rajya in the press. According to sociolinguist Roger Fowler, in *Language in the News: Discourse and Ideology in the Press*:

> News is socially constructed ... Both "selection" and transformation are guided by reference, generally unconscious, to ideas and beliefs ... Thus news is a practice: a discourse which, far from neutrally reflecting social reality and empirical facts, intervenes in what Berger and Luckmann call the social construction of reality.
>
> (Fowler, 1991: 2)

Fowler continues, stating that this social construction treats both mysterious and unclear events as newsworthy if they can be related to cultural stereotypes (Fowler, 1991: 14). These stereotypes, in turn, are designed to reinforce the social construction of reality from which they are derived:

> Now, it is of fundamental importance to realize that stereotypes are creative: they are categories which we project onto the world in order to make sense of it. We construct the world in this way ... the formation of news values, is in fact a reciprocal, dialectic process in which stereotypes are the currency of negotiation. The occurrence of a striking event will reinforce a stereotype, and reciprocally, the firmer the stereotype, the more likely are relevant events to become news.
>
> (Fowler, 1991: 17)

Press representations which depict Ram Rajya as a mythical place and time to which the BJP actually wishes to return are based on cultural constructs which place the characteristics of the "East" in opposition to those of the "West." These constructs, which parallel Indology's "essences," employ metaphors that depict India as a land based on dreams, mysticism, and imagination, not practical reason. Not surprisingly, these same metaphors occur in press representations of Ram Rajya. These representations do not give critical insight into the reality of the BJP as a powerful, contemporary political party, but simply reinforce particular social constructions largely created by the "West" as a way to maintain its superiority over the "East", and "the twain shall never meet." As such, they do little to explain the potential harm or benefits that the BJP might bring to India. More yet, the representations simply continue a tradition of writing that binds itself to substitute stereotypical constructs for critical analysis.

Notes

1 The use of the label "traditional" here should not be misunderstood as refer- ring to a crusty old text that only Sanskritists can read. To the contrary, *The Ramayana* and its themes are quite "alive" in contemporary India. For example, a professor once described at length that every Sunday morning came to a standstill for an hour while a TV serial based on *The Ramayana* was shown. Furthermore, comic books depicting stories from *The Ramayana* are widely available. An Indian friend once said, as he handed me a pile of comic books based on *The Ramayana*, "these were what I was raised on."

2 The relationship between tradition and change is located in a history of binary relations created in Western discourse. In these binaries, "Us" (or the West) always occupy positions associated with change, while everyone else (the "them") occupy positions associated with changelessness. Tonnies' theory of *Gemeinschaft* and *Gesellschaft*, Durkheim's Mechanical and Organic Solidarity, and Sapier's Genuine and Spurious Culture exemplify this concept. These theories describe social phenomena by assigning juxtaposing cate- gories, like homogeneous/heterogeneous, traditional/modern, agrarian/ industrial, static/dynamic, etc. By arranging descriptive categories in binary opposition, these theories produce the impression that a phenomenon can only be associated with one of two sides of the binary: either "Us," or "them." Since tradition is usually not associated with the "modern" Western world (the "Us"), it becomes associated with the "them" and its descriptive cate- gories. These categories, since they are not associated with modernity, are assigned meanings that are allegorical with lack of change.

3 This statement holds despite the coming to power of the Janata Party from 1976 to 1980 and the National Front from 1989 to 1990: Both these groups consisted largely of former Congress politicians.

4 This argument is reflected in an Nov. 15, 1993 article in *India Today* which states, "But on religion the BJP is leaving it to its allies. While the party's pub- licity will avoid any religious or communal appeal, the VHP's audio cassettes of Rithambara and Uma Bharati and video films on the killing of *kar sevaks* in 1990 and the events of December 6 will drill home the *Hindutva* appeal for the BJP. The RSS is propagating the same through a thousand '*dharm sabhas*' in Rajastan where Sadhus appeal to voters to bring the '*Ram Bakts*' to power. In Madhya Pradesh, RSS volunteers used *Dussehra* to reemphasize the party's affiliation to *Ram*. Obviously, the BJP wants to garner a more secular and responsible image for itself."

5 For more information on these differences refer to my paper (Cook, 1993).

6 During the 1991 general election an actual BJP slogan was, "You've tried the rest, now try us."

7 L.K. Advani, BJP president, illustrated the party's relationship to "neo- Gandhian" groups by stating, "I think I am a Congressman, as the BJP has inherited the real tradition of the Congress – the tradition of Sardar Patel and Gandhiji" (Advani, 1993: 12). For more information on the BJP relation to Gandhian philosophy, refer to Graham (1987).

References

Advani, L.K. 1993. "Voices." *India Today* (Oct. 31, 1993): 12.

Austin, Dennis and Peter Lyon. 1992. "Bharatiya Janata Party." *Government and Opposition* 21 (1): 36–50.

Bhandare, Namita and Louise Fernandes. 1993. "In Search of Ram." *Sunday* (Feb. 21–27, 1993): 24–30.

Clifford, James. 1986. "On Ethnographic Allegory." In *Writing Culture*, eds. Clifford and Marcus. Berkeley: University of California Press.

Clifford, James and George Marcus, eds. 1986. *Writing Culture: the Politics and Poetics of Ethnography*. Berkeley: University of California Press.

Cohen, Bernard. 1987. *The Anthropologist Among the Historians and Other Essays*. Oxford: Oxford University Press.

Cook, Geoffrey. 1993. "Opposing Fascism." *India Currents* 7 (7): 24.

Cook, Matthew. 1993. "Journalistic 'Fictions': a Critique of the Categories 'Fundamentalist' and 'Nazi' in Journalists' Writing on the Bharatiya Janata Party." Thesis, Anthropology department, UC Santa Cruz.

Dasgupta, Swapan. 1993. "Emerging Rashtra." *Sunday* (Feb. 7–13, 1993): 8–9.

Desmond, Edward. 1991. "Mahatma vs. Rama." *Time* (June 24, 1991): 35.

Dirks, Nicholas. 1992. *Colonialism and Culture*. Ann Arbor: University of Michigan Press.

Dubashi, Jay. 1992. *The Road to Ayodhya*. New Delhi: Voice of India.

Dundes, Alan. 1969. "The Devolutionary Premise in Folklore Theory." *Journal of the Folklore Institute* 6 (1): 5–19.

Embree, Ainslie T. 1980. *India's Search for National Identity*. Delhi: Channakya Publications.

Fowler, Roger. 1991. *Language in the News: Discourse and Ideology in the Press*. London and New York: Routledge.

Graham, Bruce. 1987. "The Challenge of Hindu Nationalism: the Bharatiya Janata Party in Comtemporary Indian Politics." *Hull Papers in Politics*, no. 40. Hull: University of Hull Press.

Hall, Stuart. 1990. "Cultural Identity and Diaspora." In *Identity: Community, Culture, and Difference*, ed. Jonathan Rutherford. London: Lawrence and Wishart.

Handler, Richard and Jocelyn Linnekin. 1984. "Tradition, Genuine or Spurious." *Journal of American Folklore* 97 (385): 273–90.

Hobsbawm, Eric and Terence Ranger. 1983. *The Invention of Tradition*. Cambridge: Cambridge Univesity Press.

Inden, Ronald. 1990. *Imagining India*. Oxford: Blackwell.

India Today Staff Writer. 1992. "Politics: Slowdown." In *India Today: 1991 Year of Destiny*. Living Media: New Delhi.

Kohli, Atul. 1988. *India Democracy: an Analysis of Changing State-Society Relations*. Princeton: Princeton University Press.

Kroeber, A.L. 1948. *Anthropology*. New York: Harcourt, Brace.

Ludden, David. 1992. "India's Development Regime." In *Colonialism and Culture*, ed. Nicholas Dirks. Ann Arbor: University of Michigan Press.

Manor, James. 1988. "Parties and the Party System." In *India Democracy: an Analysis of Changing State-Society Relations*, ed. Atul Kohli. Princeton: Princeton University Press.

Naipaul, V.S. 1976. *India: a Wounded Civilization*. New York: Vintage Books.

Pelikan, Jaroslav. 1984. *The Vindication of Tradition*. New Haven: Yale University Press.

Prakash, Gyan. 1992. "Writing Post-Orientalist Histories of the Third World: Indian Historiography Is Good to Think." In *Colonialism and Culture*, ed. Nicholas Dirks. Ann Arbor: University of Michigan Press.

Shils, Edward. 1981. *Tradition*. Chicago: University of Chicago Press.

Singh, N.K. and Yubaraj Ghimire. 1993. "Joshi vs. Advani." In *India Today* (June 15, 1993): 38–9.

Stock, Brian. 1990. *Listening for the Text: On the Uses of the Past*. Baltimore: Johns Hopkins University Press.

Thompson, Jennifer. 1993. "The Construction of Nationalism in the Jawaharlal Nehru Museum." Thesis, Anthropology Department, UC Santa Cruz.

Tierney, Ben. 1991. "Hindu Nationalism On the March." *World Press Review* (Jan. 1991): 35–6.

4
The Politics of Paradise: Islam, Identity, and Politics in India

Dhirendra K. Vajpeyi

India's cultural, religious, and ethnic diversity is so vast and complex that despite a great deal of intellectual scholarly efforts – from Marxist to non-Marxist – no single dominant paradigm has yet emerged to satisfactorily analyze India's post-independence experiments with secularism, national integration, and democratization. India's two major religious communities – Hindus and Muslims – have uneasily coexisted with each other for centuries but have failed to come to terms with each other's religious and cultural "uniqueness," and seem to have a death-wish to destroy both each other and the sociopolitical system in which they have willingly or unwillingly found themselves. It is often observed that in a traditionally religious society where a vast majority of the people have not yet internalized the real meaning and substance of democracy, cultural, religious, and ethnic pluralism, state-sponsored "secular-nationalist ideology" is doomed to fail. India is cited as one such society. Despite the "mystique" of unity in diversity, India has a history of a bitter communal relationship between a predominant majority (82 percent Hindus) and a large minority (11-plus percent Muslims). According to Muslims, Hindus view Muslims not only as hateful and alien, but to be dominated and ruled and made politically impotent. Islam is seen as an alien religion which has neither sprung from the Hindu fold nor can be assimilated into it. Hence, Hindus talk about Indianizing Muslims and, as a consequence, "Muslims Islamise themselves more and more" (Engineer, 1991: 1038).

On the other hand, nationalist Hindus believe that "pseudo-secularism has weakened national unity. It has undermined the unifying ingredient of nationalism which is Hinduism" (Advani, 1991: 7). The Hindus blame Muslims for "refusing to join the mainstream ... Some Muslims are still trying to lord over us. A section of the Muslims still take pride in the fact that they were once the rulers. This vitiates the atmosphere" (Vajpeyi, 1991: 14); "Muslims have extra-territorial loyalty" (Goradai, 1991: 7); "Muslim minority rights have turned political and destructive of national integration and ethos" (Sheshadari, 1991: 9).

The Islamic worldview and politics

For a proper understanding of Islamic resurgence in India and elsewhere it is essential to examine the Islamic worldview, the duties of individuals (*farz al-ain*) in the Islamic community (*umma*) and the relationship between religion and politics. The Islamic creed – there is no God but Allah and Muhammad is His last messenger and prophet (*Paigambar*) to whom the actual and literal living word of God (*Quran*) was revealed – in a clear and definitive manner lays down a Muslim's obligations and duties by demanding total submission (*islam*) to the will and command of Allah. Man as his representative (*Khalifa*) must actively wage "*Jihad*, the struggle against the ungodly" as part of "the historical mission of Islam. The intended premise surrounding the entire episode is that the Islamic way of life is incompatible with that of unbelieving mundane societies. The two are by definition in a state of war with each other because they are diametrically opposed. From the Islamic point of view, however, the conflict between *dar al-Islam* (realm of Islam) and *dar al-harb* (realm of war) is not conducted by the Muslims for glory or booty or revenge but to spread Islam in the world. The *umma* seeks to enlighten its adversaries, though it cannot compromise with them. Ideally, victory should be followed by the conversion of the vanquished" (Taylor, 1988: 16). Islam also posits that religion (*din*) and the world, the holy law (*Sharia*), and government (*dawla*) are not separate. God is one (*tauhid*). He is the center around which all other beliefs form a circle. The political state is the "outward expression of man's acceptance of '*tauhid*' as the centre of Muslim life" (Azad, 1958: 36). "True government and conformity with the will of God is that which the *Sharia* has itself brought into being" (Azad, 1958: 36). Muslims as individuals and as members of a group/community must conduct themselves towards other Muslims "in conformity with the virtues of brotherhood (*ukhwa*) and mercy (*rahma*)" (Taylor, 1988: 17), and faithfully follow the Quranic and *Sunna*-based law (*Sharia*). Even minor deviation from the prescribed unique and divine right path is impious, ungrateful, and needs to be eliminated by reaffirming the authenticity and uniqueness of the holy law through renewal of the teaching of the

Prophet (*tajdid*) and reform (*islah*) and return to the Quran. "Islamic law . . . remained the ideal blueprint of Muslim Society. The basic criterion for the legitimacy of Muslim governments was the ruler's commitment to *Sharia* rule. Thus to be a Muslim was to live in an Islamic state, governed by Islamic law, pursuing a divinely mandated mission. The traditional Islamic worldview provided a holistic approach toward life, a life in which religion was intimately and organically related to politics, law, and society" (Esposito, 1983: 5).

Muslim communalism and separatism in India

Muslim demand for a separate homeland – Pakistan – in India was dictated as much by political considerations as it was by ideological/religious considerations. A non-Islamic secular state and the

> politics and ideology of liberal representation were found to be unacceptable because of fundamental Muslim assumptions about the nature of political consensus, the pivotal role of the communal group and its exclusive claim to individual loyalties, and the organization of power in society . . . Exposed over many centuries to a radically different set of political values, Indian Muslims found unacceptable the liberal emphasis upon the representation of the individual and his interests, its separation of man's religions from his political dimensions, and its resort to forms of arithmetical democracy as the sole basis for a system of representation.
>
> (Shaikh, 1986: 74–5)

The main ideological/theological justification for an Islamic state in India was that the Muslims had their own separate identity or nationality. They were bound together not by geography, race, language, mutual economic and political ties but by their commitment to Islam. It has been argued that Islam and nationalism are polar opposites, that Islam is transnational in nature, and that all Muslims wherever they live owe their allegiance to God and His law (Sharia) revealed to Prophet Muhammad. Nationalism has been viewed as an alien concept "to shatter the religious unity of Islam in pieces" (Shamloo, 1948: 224). Both Maulana Maududi and Muhammad Iqbal called for the formation of a separate homeland (Pakistan) for Indian Muslims where they could tailor their lives without any impurities and interference, and establish the haven of Islam (*dar-al-Islam*) based on Quranic laws. Both asserted that a secular state was unfavorable to Islam. The creation of Pakistan, therefore, should have provided Indian Muslims with an ideal place to fulfill their spiritual destiny by "people of the practice of the prophet and of the community" (ahl al-Sunna Wa'l Jama'a) without a Hindu-dominated secular (*la-dini*, literally meaning *religionless*) political system. In fact the partition of India and the foundation of Pakistan resulted in a very emotionally and politically precarious situation for a majority of the Indian Muslims, and despite brutal riots and insecure conditions which prevailed after partition, most Muslims did not rush to Pakistan. They were left in a dilemma. The partition was followed by an almost total exodus of prominent Muslim political leaders, fanatic Mullahs, and other champions of Muslim masses to Pakistan. Leaderless and faced with new pressures in a secular state, Muslims found themselves as a minority which lacked political power, dependent on non-Muslims for their security and survival. Any mention of Islamic "uniqueness"/distinctiveness was out of the question. It would be even considered antinational, anti-India. Both nationalist (Azad, Kidwai, Zakir Hussain) and communalist (Aizaz Rasul, Khaliquzzaman) Muslim leaders who remained in India faced a formidable problem in evolving a logical and effective approach to the changed political conditions. The communalists/separatists could not disassociate themselves from the stand which they had taken before partition. Their past communal politics came to haunt them. They felt immobilized and confused. The fact that a large population of Muslims stayed on in India posed a practical and ideological dilemma for these Muslim leaders. Islamically a predominantly non-Muslim India could not be considered as *dar-al-islam* (a haven of Islam) or a zone of peace, but the practical consequences of regarding it as a zone of war could be terrible.

> The question of political power and social organization, so central to Islam, has in the past always been considered in yes or no terms. Moslems have either had political power or they had not. Never before have they shared it with others . . . The Muslims of India, in fact, face what is a radically new and profound problem, namely, how to live with others as equals . . . it is a question on which the past experience and doctrines of Islam offer no immediate guidance.
>
> (Smith, 1959: 287–9)

Norman Brown seems to share the above interpretation of W.C. Smith about the Islamic dilemma of sharing political power with non-Muslims:

It is a general Islamic dogma that Muslims should be governed only by Muslims; Hinduism has no such religious criterion of rulership ... [traditional Hindus] do not regard it as divine will that all people should be Hindu under a single rule. To the traditionally educated Hindu the Muslim theory that state and religion are identical is illogical and untenable.

(1972: 133–4)

The politically active communal Muslims, who had demonstrated their overwhelming loyalty to the League's doctrine of two nations, found it difficult to adjust their ideas to suit the new reality. Shortly after partition, a group of Muslim Leaguers went to see Maulana Azad.

They felt that Jinnah had deceived them ... These men had formed a picture of partition which had no relevance to the real situation ... they felt that once Pakistan was formed Muslims, whether they came from a minority or a majority area province, would be regarded as a separate nation ... It was now clear to them that their position as a minority was much weaker than before.

(Azad, 1958: 208)

These feelings of bitterness and frustration were reflected in a letter written on September 10, 1947 by Suhrawardy, a prominent Muslim League leader of Bengal, to Khaliquzzaman of UP:

"Personally, I think that Pakistan has provided a homeland for the Muslims living in those majority areas, but not a homeland for the Muslims of India. The Muslims in the Indian Union have been left high and dry and must shape their own destiny ..." He continued, "The Quaid-i-Azam and the Muslim League, in general, are too busy with doing nothing in Pakistan."

(Khaliquzzaman, 1961: 398)

In his letter, Suhrawardy further discusses the dilemma of the precarious situation of Muslims in India after partition. He observed that a Muslim could (1) adopt "an attitude of complete aloofness and hold on to the two nation theory," but this would expose him to the Hindu community's indignation; (2) accept common citizenship and remain on friendly terms with the Hindus; or (3) accept complete subservience and submergence. The only viable and honourable option was to accept common citizenship and stay friendly with the Hindus, but it posed two problems: first, would the Hindus accept the Muslim as an equal or would they assert their numerical superiority; and second, would they treat the Muslims with cordiality. Khaliquzzaman responded that he

> doubted the utility of the two-nation theory, which to my mind also had never paid any dividends to us. But after partition it proved positively injurious to the Muslims of India, and on a long view basis for Muslims everywhere. Many of the queries in Mr. Shaheed's letter are only off-shoots of the first question covering the two-nation theory.
>
> (Khaliquzzaman, 1961: 400)

In 1987, forty years after the creation of a Muslim homeland, similar frustrations were expressed by Khalid Sultan, a leading member of the Muhajir Qaumi Mahaz:

> When Pakistan was made, we all meant it to be one nation. But when our parents came here, they found Punjabis, Sindhis, Pathans and Baluchis. The only Pakistanis seemed to be Muhajirs.
>
> (Puri, 1987: 126)

The assertion of other Muslim ethnic groups made these Muhajirs more aware of the shattered utopian concept of Pakistan. To again quote Khalid Sultan,

> We have a separate cultural, historical and linguistic identity from other nationalities of Pakistan
>
> (Puri, 1987: 126)

In Naipaul's *India: a Million Mutinies Now*, Amir, a young Muslim from a prominent old Shia family of UP (Raja of Mahmoodabad), which actively participated in the creation of Pakistan, vents his frustrations:

> After two months I was glad to leave [Pakistan]. I felt relief to be back in India, after the claustrophobia of an Islamic society . . . I felt relief to be back here. That sense of belonging, which I had in India, I knew I couldn't find anywhere else . . . The creation and existence of Pakistan has damaged a part of my psyche. I simply cannot pretend it doesn't exist.
>
> (Naipaul, 1990: 387)

Another factor which certainly did not help Muslims in India was the Pakistani pretension of being the protector and defender of all Muslims in South Asia including India. One observer noted that the anti-Indian posture adopted by Pakistan after partition had been an important source of much difficulty for Indian Muslims. "Next to Hindu communalism the most conspicuous factor in the continuing insecurity and distress of the Muslims of India has been the behavior of Pakistan" (Smith, 1959: 269).

The Muslims of Pakistan have contributed strikingly to the dislocation of the Indian Muslims' lives. By the simple fact of Pakistan's establishment the Indian Muslims could more easily have adjusted themselves had it not been for that Islamic nation's subsequent activities. Smith points out the incapacity of Pakistan to approach the question of communal riots from a rational angle. "Pakistan, on the other hand, seems not to have had the freedom from prejudice and the moral sensitivity and courage to acknowledge its roughly equal guilt"; and "rather than coming firmly to terms with the realization that the position of India's Muslims depends primarily on two things, their aspiration towards Indianness and India's aspiration towards secularism, Pakistan has tended to deride that secularism and to presume and encourage a disloyalty of Indian Muslims to the state." "Pakistan's Muslims have had so heavy a psychological investment in the conviction that Indian Muslims are mistreated, that at times one cannot but detect a morbid welcoming of adverse news, and a resistance to awareness of Indo-Muslim welfare" (Smith, 1959: 270). Statements from Pakistani religious and political leaders have added an extra responsibility on Indian Muslims to prove their loyalty to India. Responding to a question, "What will be the duty of the Muslims in India in case of war between India and Pakistan?", Maududi said, "Their duty is obvious and that is not to fight against Pakistan or to do anything injurious to the safety of Pakistan" (Munir, 1980: 67). Pakistani behavior has not changed over the years. In an article M.H. Askari, a spokesman for the Pakistan government, has underlined how the Muslims in India have strong emotional ties with Pakistan and could constitute an integral element of Pakistan's foreign policy (*Pakistan Times*, Dec. 25, 1985). The post-partition psychological shock to Muslims in India made their adjustment difficult to structural and social changes launched by independent India. Even before independence, Muslims, in comparison to other minority communities, i.e., Sikh and Christians, were backward and lagged behind in education and economic activities. Paul Brass in *Language, Religion and Politics in*

North India (1974: 140) strongly refutes the "myth" of Muslim backwardness in UP/India. He asserts that the myth was "articulated by the Muslim aristocracy of North India, in an effort to retain their dominance in the area of the subcontinent where Muslims generally were not advanced . . . Thus a myth originated in yearnings by an upper class for the maintenance of aristocratic privilege, entirely anti-democratic in content."

There is the complex economic situation, in whose evolution for 75 years the Muslims have, as a group, been disfavored, since their community has throughout produced fewer than its due share of individuals and groups adjusted to or able to take advantage of new opportunities and necessities. This disadvantage, this communal lag behind constantly developing circumstances, has operated to depress the economic level of individuals and groups, with all the consequent psychological and emotional disturbances. The modernization of India has in substance been gathering momentum for long, but in form had been held back by British control; it made a forward spurt after 1947. In doing so it has left Muslim feudal institutions unprotected in an industrial/technologically changing society. The abolition of *zamindari* and the deprivileging of native princes have been two of the most striking achievements of modern India; they must be regarded as major steps of progress; that they have spelled hardship for Indian Islam reveals the backwardness of that community (Smith, 1959: 276). The Muslims "have relied all these years, as in the past, on communal bodies and on the knights and Khan Bahadurs of the day – the Sarkari Musalmans – both of whom have a vested interest in Muslim discontent" (Noorani, 1990: 2417).

While the impact of modernization has somewhat percolated down the Muslim society in general, there is no doubt that the Muslims have not been able to keep up with the tempo of change. While the contribution of non-agricultural sectors, like industry and manufacturing services, and professions – trade and commerce – to the national income of India has been steadily rising, the Muslim's share in these new activities has been very limited. Another important factor contributing to Indian Muslims' backwardness has been their rigid adherence to oftentimes outdated ideological/theological doctrines. There has been virtually no worthwhile renaissance in Muslim society. The Muslims continue to be fanatically devoted to religion at the cost of nationalism and modernization. The Muslim masses, in spite of their secularized rulers and environment, have turned deaf ears to the message of secularism and democracy, and have remained constant in their belief in

God, the Prophet, and the Quran. They abide by values and religious advice of their Mullahs and refuse to come to terms with sweeping changes taking place around them. "There is a closure to self-criticism and opposition to reformism within Islam even among Muslims completely nontraditional in their own ways of life" (Dutta et al., 1990: 2489).

Communal politics has been practiced by the Muslims for such a long time that after partition they were faced with the problem of adjusting themselves to secular politics. The political future of the Muslim community also depended much on the extent and style of their participation in politics. Even during the freedom movement, the Muslim participation was much less than that of Hindus and Sikhs. The Muslim problem was also partly due to the virtual withdrawal of formerly active Muslims from politics, the sudden disappearance of the only political party, the Muslim League, which claimed to have represented Muslim interests in India.

Formation or support of a new Muslim party in post-independent India, however progressive and secular, would have been unwise and strategically suicidal for two reasons: such a step would have provided extra fuel and impetus to growing Hindu communalism and its demand for a Hindu India, and it would have been impractical because not many Muslim leaders of the caliber of Azad were willing to associate themselves with such a party. Most of the nationalist Muslim leaders had stayed with the Congress even at the peril of being labeled *Kafirs* and "traitors" by the Muslim League. They had all along believed in a secular, democratic nation and were eagerly looking forward to playing a prominent role in noncommunal politics. Even those Muslim Leaguers who stayed in India were not willing to be part of a new Muslim party. Most of them joined the Congress Party. The right-wing political parties were incapable of accommodating Muslims. The situation changed only in 1959 when the Swatantra Party was founded with an express conservative platform. Even then the accommodation of Muslims on language and other issues was a divisive and sore point in some areas, namely UP, Bihar, and Madhya Pradesh. The extreme left – the Communist parties – were by definition Godless (atheistic) and unable to promote Muslim interests as such. The socialist parties, likewise, were averse to communal politics and too feeble to be of any great advantage to Muslims. Indeed, it was a dangerous liability for any party to be heavily manned by the former Muslim Leaguers, or Muslims. It was only in South India, particularly in Kerala, where pre-independence communal politics did not have the sting of the North Indian heartland, that the Muslims continued to find an outlet through a local Muslim League.

Hence the Muslims turned to the Congress Party for various reasons: (1) there were Muslim leaders such as Azad, Kidwai, and Zakir Hussain, who had a nonsectarian, noncommunal image and had tremendous influence on both Nehru and in the Congress Party itself; (2) the Congress Party was more than eager to accommodate Muslims due to ideological (secular, democratic) and practical (votes) reasons; (3) the Congress Party was a strong party which had "developed a machinery for dealing with diverse interests and reconciling them; the Congress Parliamentary Board which selects candidates for election tries to balance the party tickets with sufficient numbers of, for example, Muslims, other minorities, women, untouchables . . ." (Weiner, 1960: 129); (4) Nehru was the biggest guarantor of secularism, therefore, minority interests were safe as long as he was in power.

The Muslim decision to align with Congress paid rich dividends. While government did not hesitate to interfere in Hindu religious affairs (rights to Harijans to enter Hindu temples, passage of Hindu Marriage Act), Muslim personal law was left intact. Nehru never spared Hindu communalism, but was not always quick to criticize Muslim communalists. Speaking at the AICC session on May 11, 1958 Nehru observed that "Communalism of the majority is far more dangerous than the communalism of the minority" (Noorani, 1990: 2417). By and large, Muslims stood by Congress. They provided much-needed votes to Congress and reaped advantages from the Congress for their support. They were adequately represented in the Parliament, State Legislatures, Cabinets, and Civil Services. The Indian Constitution provided them security; the adult franchise, the political clout. Only in the post-1975 (emergency) period did Muslim support from the Congress Party started to shift for a short while. Their disappointment with the Janata government, however, brought them back to the Congress fold. But the Muslims were not as happy with the Congress as in the Nehru era. They felt that they were being used in the electoral politics but were denied due access to political, social, and economic resources, were not treated equally/at a par with other groups, were less represented in the army, the police, and public services. They were being denied the right to develop their culture, promote their language and religion, and above all they expressed anxiety and fear about being engulfed by the Hindu majority. A study (Saxena, 1983: 61–5) which surveyed 45 districts in 12 states in India pointed out that:

1. At the High School and Intermediate levels, which are crucial for employment purposes, the percentage of Muslims is roughly one-fourth to one-third of what it should be in proportion to their population;
2. The drop-out rate of Muslim students keeps going up progressively as they move up in educational level compared to the non-Muslim students;
3. Muslim students did better in nondenominational schools than in Muslim-managed schools;
4. The number of first divisioners among Muslim students is very low.

The study also provided the data on Muslim representation in the IAS, central services, state judiciary, and public sector undertakings (Tables 4.1 to 4.4)

Some of these grievances are genuine, while others are the product of a frustrated minority which has failed to accept its own failure. A.R. Sherwani notes that "the reason for the poor representation of Muslims in the IAS is not that they are discriminated against but that too few of them compete" (*Hindustam Times*, March 11, 1983). Another Muslim observer points out that the educational backwardness of Muslim

Table 4.1 Muslim representation in the IAS, other central services, and public sector undertakings (1980)

IAS	IPS	Directors	Senior officers
2.9%	2.85%	4.2%	2.32%
(116)	(50)	(21)	(321)

Table 4.2 Muslim students enrolled in educational institutions in relation to their total population in the surveyed districts

Elementary school	High school	Intermediate	Engineering	Medical
12.39%	4% (Muslim population 12%)	2.49% (Muslim population 12.44%)	3.41% (Muslim population 12.44%)	3.44% (Muslim population 9.55%)

Table 4.3   Muslims in State Judiciary (1981)

State	Total Muslims	Percentage
Andhra	327	9.48
Assam	155	20.00
Bihar	1,060	8.74
Gujarat	412	8.74
Haryana	32	6.25
Karnataka	223	7.17
Kerala	249	7.63
Maharashtra	614	3.09
Orissa	264	0.76
UP	1,144	5.59
West Bengal	418	3.11

Table 4.4   Muslims' performance in competitive examinations held during 1978–80 (percentages)

State Commission	Muslims who took the exam	Called for interview	Selected
Andhra	4.27	3.37	3.06
Tamil Nadu	3.95	3.91	4.63
UP	8.46	1.21	2.46
Bihar	4.54	6.36	7.30
MP	2.89	1.77	1.70

students is not due to any discrimination, but because "the attitudes of Muslim parents and guardians and their approach to education make a real difference. The children are not inspired to aspire for higher academic standards and are not reminded of their present tasks and future target" (Zaidi, 1986). Salman Khurshid presents yet another explanation: "when you fail in a secular society, it is not because the state discriminates consciously but because internal weaknesses become a fertile recipient for unconscious failures to provide for a minority. You fail because you are taken for granted" (1986: 4).

These real/imaginary grievances have resulted in increasingly frequent Hindu–Muslim frictions and communal riots (Raju, 1987: 16–17), and the recent rise in fundamentalism among Muslims (Table 4.5). The emergence of Muslims' *senas* (armies) in Delhi and other parts of India is indicative of rising Muslim assertiveness. "The purpose of our *senas*

Table 4.5 Number of communal incidents and persons killed and injured in these incidents, 1954–85

Year	Number of incidents	Persons killed	Persons injured
1954	84	34	512
1964	1,070	1,919	2,053
1974	248	87	1,123
1985	525	328	3,665

is to unite Muslims, wherever they are, and check the *trishul gardi"* (menace of Hindu *sena's* symbol), declared old Delhi's Rafiullah Khan, a self-avowed popular Muslim leader (*India Today*, Oct. 15, 1986: 33). Muslim politicians and other community leaders, including Syed Shahabuddin, have so far refused to associate with these *senas* and view their formation with distaste. "This is really a very bad trend," said Kalimuddin Shams, deputy speaker of the West Bengal Assembly. "People with no following are creating these stunts for cheap publicity without realizing what impact it would have on our suspicion-ridden society" (*India Today*, Oct. 15, 1986: 33).

The Hindu reaction to increasing Muslim militancy has manifested itself in several ways, including attacks on minorities, "liberation" of Hindu places of worship, and reconversion of those Hindus who had embraced either Islam or Christianity (Malik and Vajpeyi, 1989: 318). On December 6, 1992, 3,000,000-strong Hindu militants destroyed the Babri Mosque in Ayodhya in one of the worst outbreaks of communal violence in India since partition. It is reported that more than 1,700 persons were killed and 5,500 injured. The incident raises serious doubts about the capacity of the Indian political system to cope with communal violence and adhere to its secularism. Such incidents and the inability of India's political elites to effectively defuse them will have far-reaching consequences for almost every aspect of national life.

Several external factors, such as the "oil revolution and the humiliating defeat of Egypt and Syria at the hands of Israel in the 1967 war . . . and a great deal of beating" that Muslims in India "had taken in communal riots throughout the sixties . . . , the breakup of Pakistan in the early seventies" (Engineer, 1991: 1037), and the post-1973 resurgence of Islamic fundamentalism in general and in the Middle East in particular, were also responsible for Muslim assertiveness in India. Akeel Bilgrami points out "that a good deal of Islamic revivalism in various countries in West Asia, South Asia, and Northern Africa, not to mention some of the northern cities of England, is the product of a long colonial and post-colonial history, which has shaped a community's perception of itself in terms of the other" (1992: 1073). Ayatollah Khomeini's call to reject both eastern and western political paradigms, and return to real Islam, have rekindled Muslim hopes to revive their religious and cultural visions. The Middle Eastern economies were propeled to great prosperity due to sky-high oil prices. Unprecedented economic rejuvenation programs were launched in these erstwhile poor and underdeveloped Middle Eastern countries. This opened the doors to a large number of unskilled and semiskilled labor forces from the Third World and especially from Muslim countries such as Pakistan, India, Bangladesh, and Indonesia. In 1987 there were about 122,000 skilled and unskilled Indian workers in the Middle East (Naidu, 1991: 349). Most of these workers were Muslims (*Times of India*, March 21, 1988). They came in contact with their co-religionists from other countries, mainly conservative and predominantly Muslim. The transnational connection was made.

A study of 125 Muslims of UP who had worked a minimum of two years in the Middle East found that most of these Muslims (Gulfis) were an uneducated lot, and had hardly any concept of Islamic doctrine prior to their departure to the Middle East. Being away from home and family religion brought them closer. Their leisure time was spent in discussing "commonality" – their Islamic heritage. When they returned to India they not only brought money, watches, and expensive transistor radios (boom-boxes/ghetto blasters), they also had a new awareness and the assertive spirit of *din-e-ilahi*. The new money gave them confidence, new mosques, and new madrasas for religious education to children who were deemed necessary to thank Allah (God) for their prosperity. It also generated increased social, religious, and political consciousness, and naturally brought them into a direct collision course with other communities (Vajpeyi, 1986–8, Table 4.6). "Hindus tend to raise their eyebrows at the assertion of equal status by a community they are used to looking down upon as their inferiors in the post-independence era" (Hasan, 1989: 45).

Similar attitudinal changes were reported by Muslim workers from Kerala (Prakash, 1978: 1107–11; Thomas, 1979), and other rural (both non-Muslim and Muslim) migrants elsewhere (Joshi, 1989). The political environment in India also contributed to the militancy. Despite 46 years of independence and efforts by ruling elites to placate the anxieties and fears of minorities in India, they have not succeeded in the national and emotional integration of these groups, economic and

Table 4.6   Changes in religious attitudes of Gulfis (125)

A. Changes in the degree of religious consciousness

Before going to the Middle East			After returning from the Middle East		
High	**Medium**	**Low**	**High**	**Medium**	**About the same**
5 4%	50 40%	70 56%	56 44.8%	33 26.4%	46 36.8%

B. Attitude towards other religious groups in the community

TOLERANCE					
Before			**After**		
More	**Moderately**	**Low**	**More**	**Moderately**	**Low**
11 8.8%	86 68.8%	38 30.4%	13 10.4%	41 32.8%	71 56.8%

C. Change in the degree of religious assertiveness

Before			After		
High	**Moderate**	**Low**	**High**	**Moderate**	**Low**
21 16.8%	83 66.4%	21 16.8%	78 62.4%	40 32%	7 5.6%

D. With your new money have you acquired better/improved status in your community (among non-Muslims and among Muslims)?

Improved status/respect				
Among Muslims		**Non-Muslims**	
Yes	**No**	**Yes**	**No**
91 72.8%	34 27.2%	24 19.2%	101 80.8%

Table 4.6   Continued

E. Financial support to causes/projects

Mosques	Madrasas	Political candidate (Muslim)	Political cause (Babri Masjid)
90	80	33	70
72%	64%	26.4%	56%

political gains by minorities notwithstanding. Sikhs are a good example of the sad story. Somehow short-range political gains have overshadowed national interests. "In India, often fully secular, even anti-religious Muslim politicians get access to power in the name of their Muslim origins which they themselves see in purely instrumental terms" (Nandy, 1985: 17). In the context of Islamic fundamentalist movements, it has been observed that often religion becomes a "mere appearance; people are not really concerned with the substance of religion, religion having become a sign of their being distinct" (Lannoy, 1971: 22–3), and, therefore, "these [fundamentalist] movements generally involve persons marginal to – and not to be confused with – the cultural mainstream. Precisely because of their marginality, these groups and their leaders typically lack the broad political credibility necessary to convert sparks into fire" (Demerath, 1991: 33). Also, "the need for a sense of identity is an irreducible need, and a fundamental commitment to religion (or nation) often fulfills that need" (Cohen, 1989: 54–5).

The return of Mrs. Gandhi to power in 1980 and her determination to hold onto power and promote her own dynasty led her to opportunistic politics. Ideological concerns took a back seat to political interests. Votes became new gods. Mrs. Gandhi exploited religious and ethnic grievances to the hilt (Noorani, 1990: 2417–23). Her authoritarian style, and her exploitation of one group against the other created a political environment of paranoia. "The last phase of the Indira Gandhi era witnessed an unprecedented spurt in religious fervor and a marked polarization of Indian society on communal and sectarian lines. Nearly 4,000 people were killed in communal violence" (Hasan, 1989: 45). According to one Muslim observer "there was no secular alternative for them [Muslims] and they could only think of increased assertion of their religious identity . . . The assertion of religious identity in the process of democratization or even modernization for that matter, should not be seen only as religious fanaticism or fundamentalism; it should also be seen as the best available way for these deprived communities in a backward society for realizing a greater share in power, in government jobs and economic resources" (Engineer, 1991: 1038). The Shah Banu case is cited as one of the examples which achieved unprecedented support from almost all walks of Indian Muslims as a result of Muslim frustrations on other issues (Kozlowski, 1990: 88–111; Shourie, 1986; Khurshid, 1986: 66–76).

The rise of a Bhinderwale and the Sikh militancy in Punjab, and the Hindu backlash in North India provided ample opportunities to other groups to throw away their cautious approach. The rise of Muslim assertion at this point could be attributed partly to the above factors. The Indian political system has been under siege from within for quite a while. Muslim militancy is not an isolated case. The militant Sikhs' call to arms and their demand for Khalistan have posed the single most important threat to Indian security and stability and challenge to India's secularism since independence. Demands for a Gorakhaland in Northeast India, and a Tribal homeland in Bihar, as well as disturbances in Kashmir, are part of the general malaise.

The Indian political system's response to these movements has been a confused bandaid approach. Rajiv Gandhi, despite his good intentions, was unable to provide strong leadership. His "laissez-faire" approach and appeasement/"abject surrender" to powerful fundamentalists on the Shah Banu case did as much damage to Indian secularism as his mother's (Mrs. Gandhi's) abject and cynical manipulation of fundamentalists to further her narrow political interests. Rajiv Gandhi's successors (V.P. Singh and Chandra Shekhar), proved to be of the same ineffective mold. There is no doubt that the "religious dedication of those in or led by modern resurgence movements is an expression of the reoriented anger of abused, disaffected, and disillusioned elements in respective countries of the area. The desire to address grievances underlies the interest in the sanctification of Islamic communities" (Taylor, 1988: 26) but at the same time these psychological and social problems do not bestow upon a community unbridled license to use extra-constitutional means and the "doctrine of purification as a political tool" to disrupt the political process. One of the main problems with Indian Muslims has been that they have not been able to reconcile Islamic beliefs in their "uniqueness," transnational loyalties, and an outdated system of law to the challenges of modernization. Also "the very fact that the Muslims who have stayed back or who have been born and are living in India harbor Pan-Islamic feelings is perhaps a pointer to the view that Indian Muslims have made this country their home but they look outward if something happens somewhere in the Islamic crescent" (Hassan, 1980: 11).

Democratization and politicization have failed to eliminate communalism in India. In fact they have given xenophobic and antidemocratic forms of religion new power and salience (Nandy, 1985: 17).

After the achievement of independence, two formations emerged in the subcontinent (Khan, 1983: 11–15). In India, triumphant nationalism with secular overtones continues to battle against irrepressible communalism, while in Pakistan triumphant communalism with Islamic orientation is choking the prospect of a secular nationalism. The Indian Muslims have these two examples to choose from. As a minority, they would like to live in a secular, democratic system where they not only have their freedom to practice their religion without interference from state, but also enjoy their democratic rights (Indian model). As Muslims, however, they would like to have their own laws and care less for other religious groups by asserting their uniqueness (Pakistani model). In short, they want to have their cake and eat it too. That is the problem. Madan's observation about the behavior of India's minorities expresses this contradiction. "Secularism is the dream of a minority which wants to impose its will upon history but lacks the power to do so under a democratically organized polity" (Madan, 1987: 748–9). The Muslims of India expect Hindus to be secular and the state to be secular where Muslim interests and personal laws are concerned, but they talk of discrimination when Hindus behave in a nonsecular, sectarian fashion. This continuing tussle between nationalism, secularism, and communalism remains a major challenge to the process of nation-building in India. These challenges can be met only if (1) the Indian state remains strong and viable, secular and democratic – only if it can manage external and internal pressures, and (2) it carries out the long-expected secularization of the population through education, modernization, and political development, expansion of economic resources, and national integration. These objectives are not easy to achieve. India made a good start in 1947. It has yet to be seen how it makes it to the finish line.

There is no doubt that the process of modernization produces tensions and frustrations (Huntington, 1968: 55). It opens the door to opportunities for the erstwhile "silent majority" by raising their political and social consciousness and hence assertion of religious/ethnic identity to obtain a greater share of power, government jobs, and economic resources. "The struggle for mandir and masjid is nothing but a struggle for greater power between Hindus and Muslims. These religious places have become an integral part of political discourse in contemporary India" (Engineer, 1991: 1038). "Cultural power is the capacity to use cultural resources to affect political outcomes. These resources include symbols, ideologies, moral authority and cultural meanings. They can be used to legitimate or delegitimate political outcomes or actors, to keep some issues public and political and others out of the public eye altogether, and to frame the terms with which issues are discussed when they are public . . . religious revivals are frequently direct responses to secularization itself. Every retreat into the past is inevitably a dialectic with the present" (Demerath, 1991: 31–3).

In view of the above discussion, the question arises as to what really went wrong in the Indian situation. Was it the failure of an alien – democratic, secular – ideology, or is the blame to be placed on the elite who failed to realize the severe demands such an ideology places on a backward society still struggling to sort out ethnic, religious, and cultural identities? In the Indian case, both ideology and the elites have been blamed. In 1966 E.M.S. Namboodripad (1966: 343) observed that "the dominant ruling group at the center tried to establish a fake unity of the nation by denying the right of every nationality and social group to have equality of opportunity and status in a democratic set up . . . the so-called struggle between nationalism and the fissiparous forces – the struggle in the name of which the leaders of the ruling party are trying to beat the opposition forces into submission – is a fake struggle." "The failure of secularism in India is hardly the failure of an ideology. It is essentially the failure of a ruling class that used secular ideals as a means of seeking legitimacy, but which largely ignored the social tasks associated with the development of a secular society" (Kumar, 1989: 2473). The right-wing politicians, on the other hand, have cursed both ruling elites and the ideology itself.

The need is to properly understand the role and meaning of secularism in a multireligious, multi-ethnic, and multicultural society in defining the role of the individual and the state in politics and religion. State-sponsored secularism is bound to flounder as did Marxism-Leninism in the Soviet Union and Eastern Europe. It is to be recognized that homogenization of minorities is not secularism, while minorities' insistence and assertion of their "uniqueness" or "purity" (Khalis/Pak) in relation to the majority is neither democratic nor secular. In a society such as India multiple identities (Hindu-Indian, Muslim-Indian, Sikh-Indian, and so on) have to be accepted, partly shared with others and partly exclusive. God must be liberated in India from the Babri Masjid, Ramjanmabhumi, and the politics of paradise eschewed in favor of a culturally and ethnically plural yet politically united, secular, and modern India.

References

Advani, L.K. (1991). "Pseudo-Secularism has Weakened National Unity." *Organizer*, May 5.

Ahmad, Aziz and G.E. von Grunebaum, eds. (1970). *Muslim Self-statement in India and Pakistan 1857–1968*. Wiesbaden: Otto Harrassowitz.

Azad, Abul Kalam. (1958). *India Wins Freedom*. Calcutta: Orient-Longman.

Bilgrami, Akeel. (1992). "What is a Muslim? Fundamental Commitment and Cultural Identity." *Economic and Political Weekly*, May 16–23.

Brass, Paul R. (1974). *Language, Religion and Politics in North India*. London: Cambridge University Press.

Brown, W. Norman. (1972). *The United States and India, Pakistan, and Bangladesh*. Cambridge: Harvard University Press.

Cohen, G.A. (1989). "Reconsidering Historical Materialism in Marxist Theory," in A. Callinicos (ed.), *Marxist Theory*. Oxford: Oxford University Press.

Demerath, N.J. (1991). "Religious Capital and Capital Religions: Cross-Cultural and Non-Legal Factors in the Separation of Church and State." *Daedalus*, Summer.

Dutta, Pradeep, et al. (1990). "Understanding Communal Violence." *Economic and Political Weekly*, Nov. 10.

Engineer, Asghar Ali. (1991). "Remaking Indian Muslim Identity." *Economic and Political Weekly*, April 20.

Frankel, Francine. (1978). *India's Political Economy 1947–1977: the Gradual Revolution*, Princeton: Princeton University Press.

Goradai, Prafulla. (1991). "Value of Hindutva to Modern India." *Organizer*, May 19.

Hasan, Zoya. (1989). "Minority Identity, Muslim Women Bill Campaign and the Political Process." *Economic and Political Weekly*, Jan. 7.

Hassan, Syed Majeedul. (1980). "Indian Muslims: Have they Transnational Loyalties." *Illustrated Weekly of India*, March 30.

Huntington, Samuel P. (1968). *Political Order in Changing Societies*. New Haven: Yale University Press.

Joshi, Chittra. (1989) "Bonds of Community, Ties of Religion"; NMML Occasional Paper no. 16 quoted in Alok Rai, 1989, "Addled Only in Parts, Strange Case of Indian Secularism," *Economic and Political Weekly*, Dec. 16, p. 2772. [In her research of Kanpur (UP) industrial labor, Chittra Joshi points out the "manner in which the dissolution of the rural communities at one level in the lives of the migrants was matched at other levels by an integration of their religious and cultural identities within the new environment. The mohalla, the social milieu, the recruitment system, the nature of the labor market, all in many ways sustained past traditions and customs, religious and community ties among the workers."]

Khaliquzzaman, Chaudhary. (1961). *Pathway to Pakistan*. Calcutta: Orient-Longman.

Khan, Rasheedudin. (1983). "Problems of Nation-Building." *World Focus*, Sept.

Khurshid, Salman. (1986). *At Home in India – a Restatement of Indian Muslims*, Delhi: Vikas.

Kozlowski, George C. (1990). "Shah Banu Case, Britain's Legacy and Muslim

Politics in Modern India," in Yogendra Malik and Dhirendra Vajpeyi (eds), *Law, Politics and Society in India*. Delhi: Chanakya.

Kumar, Krishna. (1989). "Secularism: its Politics and Pedagogy." *Economic and Political Weekly*, Nov. 4–11.

Lannoy, Richard. (1971). *The Speaking Tree: a Study of Indian Culture and Society*. London: Oxford University Press.

Madan, T.N. (1987). "Secularism in its Place." *Journal of Asian Studies*, Nov.

Malik, Yogendra and Dhirendra Vajpeyi. (1989). "The Rise of Hindu Militancy: India's Secular Democracy at Risk." *Asian Survey*, March.

Munir, Muhammad. (1980). *From Jinnah to Zia*. Lahore: Vanguard Books.

Naidu, K. Lakshmaiah. (1991). "Indian Labor Migration to Gulf Countries." *Economic and Political Weekly*, Feb. 16.

Naipaul, V.S. (1990). *India: a Million Mutinies Now*. New York: Viking.

Namboodripad, E.M.S. (1966). "Nationalities and Nation-Building," quoted in Pran chopra (ed.) (1986). *Future of South Asia*. Delhi: Macmillan India.

Nandy, Ashis. (1985). "An Anti-Secularist Manifesto." *Seminar*, Oct.

Noorani, A.G. (1990). "Indira Gandhi and Indian Muslims." *Economic and Political Weekly*, Nov. 3.

Prakash, B.A. (1978). "Impact of Foreign Remittance: A Case Study of Chavakkad Village in Kerala." *Economic and Political Weekly*, July 8.

Puri, Balraj. (1987). "Ethnic Dimension of Subcontinental Muslims." *Economic and Political Weekly*, Jan. 24.

Rajgopal, P.R. (1987). *Communal Violence in India*. New Delhi: Uppal Publishing House.

Raju, V.P. (1987). *Communal Violence in India*. Delhi: Uppal Publishing House.

Saxena, N.C. (1983). "Public Employment and Educational Backwardness among Muslims in India." *Political Science Review*, 23, nos. 2–3, April–Sept.

Shaikh, Farzana. (1986). "Islam and the Quest for Democracy in Pakistan." *Journal of Commonwealth and Comparative Politics*, March.

Shamloo, K., ed. (1948). *Speeches and Statements of Iqbal*. Lahore: Al-Manar Academy.

Sheshadari, H.V. (1991). "Perversions of Secularism." *Organizer*, Feb. 3.

Shourie, Arun. (1986). "We Want Shariat." *Illustrated Weekly of India*, Jan. 5, 12, and 19.

Smith, W.C. (1959). *Islam in Modern History*. New York: New American Library.

Taylor, Alan R. (1988). *The Islamic Question in the Middle East Politics*. Boulder, Colo.: Westview.

Thomas, V.J. (1979). "Gulf Booms in Kerala." *Hindustan Times*, July 26.

Vajpayi, A.B. (1991). "Muslims Refuse to Join the Mainstream." *Organizer*, Feb. 10.

Vajpeyi, Dhirendra. 1986–8. Based on 125 interviews in August 1986, June 1987 and 1988, in Lucknow, Hardoi, Barabanki, Allahabad, and Delhi.

Weiner, Myron. (1960). "The Congress Party," in G. Almond and James Coleman (eds), *Politics of the Developing Areas*. Princeton: Princeton University Press.

Zaidi, Naseem A. (1986). "Muslims in Public Services: No Bias." *The Times of India*, May 8.

5

The Case for a Divorce between Religion and Politics

Subhash C. Kashyap

A special session of the Parliament of India was convened on June 13, 1994 to amend the Representation of the People Act and the Constitution itself in order to implement some electoral reform proposals.[1] These *inter alia* included certain provisions seeking to ban the use of religion for political purposes, mainly for influencing voters in electoral battles. The two bills evoked very strong responses from the media, the people, the political parties, and the intellectuals.

While finally the Constitution Amendment Bill could not be introduced and the Lok Sabha was abruptly adjourned *sine die* on June 14 itself, the Bill to amend the Representation of the People Act was introduced on June 13. It stands referred to the Standing Committee on Home Affairs which deals with law and justice. The Bill can be taken up for consideration by the House during the next session if the government feels confident of majority support for the Bill.

Earlier, in August 1993 the government also had to beat a hasty and humiliating retreat on two bills seeking to delink religion from politics. This was just as well, inasmuch as the bills were conceived in haste, badly drafted, and incapable of implementation.

The present bill seeking to amend Section 29A of RPA *inter alia* provides that "no association or body shall be registered as a political party" if it "bears a religious name" or its memorandum or rules and regulations do not contain a specific provision declaring "true faith and allegiance to the Constitution of India as by law established, and to the principles of socialism, secularism and democracy . . ." If already registered, such a party would be deregistered under a new Section 29B. Registration of a party would also be canceled if it were found promoting or attempting to promote "on ground of religion, disharmony or feelings of enmity, hatred or ill will between different religious groups."

The term "secular," although used in the Preamble, has not been defined by the Constitution, the Representation of the People Act, or any other law. The normal definitions given to the term in dictionaries and encyclopedias do not seem to apply to the Indian concept of secularism.

As Justice Desai put it, a secular state deals with the individual as a citizen irrespective of his religion, is not connected to a particular religion, nor does it seek to promote or interfere with religion. A secular state must have nothing to do with religious affairs except when their management involves crime, fraud, or becomes a threat to the unity and integrity of the State.[2]

Delivering his judgment in *Ziyauddin Burhammudin Bukhari* v. *Brijmohan Ramdass Mehra and Bros.* (1975 Suppl. SCR 281), Justice M.H. Beg said:

> The Secular State, rising above all differences of religion, attempts to secure the good of all its citizens irrespective of their religious beliefs and practices. It is neutral or impartial in extending its benefits to citizens of all castes and creeds. Maitland had pointed out that such a state has to ensure, through its laws, that the existence or exercise of political or civil right or the right or capacity to occupy any office or position under it or to perform any public duty connected with it does not depend upon the profession or practice of any particular religion.
>
> Our Constitution and the laws formed thereunder leave citizens free to work out happy and harmonious relationships between their religions and the quite separable secular fields of law and politics. But they do not permit an unjustifiable invasion of what belongs to one sphere by what appertains really to another. It is for courts to determine, in a case of dispute, whether any sphere was or was not properly interfered with, in accordance with the Constitution, even by a purported law.[3]

Anything that is pernicious and exploitative cannot be allowed to remain outside the control of law simply because it is paraded under the banner of religion.[4]

Justices Gajendragadkar, Dhawan, and Beg found secularism practiced by ancient Hindu society and equally traceable to Islamic jurisprudence. Justice Beg suggested that "a happy harmony and synthesis of the best in secularism and religion" was possible. A theory of secularism could be built on ancient jurisprudence. In the *Kesvananda Bharti* case, quoting from Manu and Parashara, Justice Beg said:

> Even our ancient jurists recognized the principles that one genera-
> tion has no right to tie down future generations to its own views or
> laws even on fundamentals. They not only differ between one society
> and another but also as between one generation and another of the
> same society or nation.[5]

Balraj Puri has made certain interesting points. He says that "religion is more important factor in the politics of the West than it is in India. The religious lobbies even in the most secular Western country, USA, influence major public issues.[6] India has never witnessed serious clashes on religious issues; even in the worst communal riots, issues involved have not been religious. Scriptures were not cited by Jinnah in support of Pakistan. The Ayodhya issue is a dispute over real estate. Neither do Hindus oppose a masjid in Ayodhya nor have Muslims ever shown disrespect of Ram or opposed a Ram temple there. Actually, it is the social role of religion that has become a vital factor in politics. Reli-gious communities have got politicized. The question that needs to be debated is what is the legitimate field of religious identities and how they should be related to each other and to the national identity?"[7] One may add that a parallel question that needs equal attention is that of defining and delimiting the scope and role of politics *vis-à-vis* religion and individual lives and private beliefs of citizens or groups thereof. Religious communities should not be politicized and national politics should not be communalized.

Communalism, as S.N. Mishra puts it, is not the progeny of the surfeit of religion but of the very lack of it. Religion does not divide, it unites. A true votary of a religion can never come into conflict with the true votary of another religion. The real trouble is not between religion and politics but between the unreligious aspect of religion and the unsecu-lar aspect of politics. He adds: "What we call religious differences pertain to forms and not to substance, to rituals and religiosity and not to reli-gion as such . . ."[8]

Religious tolerance in India is rooted in our own past history and culture, a very likely response to her pluralism or the desire of the found-ing fathers to be just and fair to all communities irrespective of their numbers. Very often, in our common parlance, the term "secularism", therefore, is used merely as a opposite of "communalism." "Commu-nal" has come to be regarded as a term of abuse. No individual and no party is prepared to accept the communal label and every individual and every party considers itself to be secular or even more secular than others.

After the storming of the disputed Mandir-Masjid structure in Ayodhya, followed by communal riots in various places, and finally the gruesome blasts in Bombay, communal harmony, national integration, and constitutional objectives of secularism once again become burning issues. But neither the problem nor the suggested remedy were new.

At least twice in the Constituent Assembly efforts were made in vain to make a specific mention of the principle of secularism in the Constitution. For example, a motion for amendment had sought to ensure that no law could be made which discriminated between man and man on the basis of religion or applied to adherents of any one religion and left others untouched. An amendment to introduce the word "secular" in the preamble was moved but negated. While speaking on the Hindu Code Bill in Parliament later on, Ambedkar made it amply clear that he did not believe that our Constitution was "secular" inasmuch as it allowed the state to extend different treatment to various communities and provided for discrimination on grounds of religion and caste and for legislatures framing separate laws for them.

In the Constituent Assembly (Legislative) a resolution was moved on April 3, 1948 by Ananthasayanam Ayyanager to ban communal parties. Ayyanagar said that the time had come to separate religion from politics, that for the proper functioning of democracy and for national unity and integrity it was essential to root out communalism from the body politic of India. Any political party the membership of which was dependent on religion, caste, etc., could not be allowed to engage itself in any activities except those connected with the religious, cultural, social, and educational needs of the community.[9]

The resolution was generally supported by the members. Prime Minister Jawaharlal Nehru in his intervention in the debate welcomed the resolution and indicated the attitude of his government in the matter. He said that they wished to do everything in their power to achieve the objective behind the resolution. Nehru added that the combination of politics and religion in the narrowest sense of the word, resulting in communal politics, was "a most dangerous combination and must be put an end to."[10] However, so far as the actual implementation of the resolution was concerned, Nehru warned that the matter would have to be examined in depth and, in any case, government would have to come before the House with appropriate legislation.

Dr. Shyama Prasad Mookerjee emphasized that it was "no use passing a pious resolution; if we are really anxious to uproot communalism from the political sphere in India altogether, we shall have to see that there is no place for communalism of any kind whatsoever in the Constitution of our country. You cannot justify reservations on grounds of religion or caste and in the same breath say that you want to banish communalism from the political life of India."[11] Tajamul Hussain considered providing for reservations even for depressed classes as communal.[12] Syed Karimuddin warned:

> India has been declared a secular state. It is in the interest of the minorities of the country that this secular state should exist. If any community wants to say that there should be communalism or that communal activities should be allowed to be practised, then the majority cannot be prevented from preaching communalism which will go to the great detriment of the minorities in this country.[13]

Speaking in the Constituent Assembly, Jawaharlal Nehru said: "A nation lives by the things of the spirit." Dr. S. Radhakrishnan spoke of Ashoka's wheel in the middle of the national flag and said, "Truth can be gained only by the pursuit of *Dharma*." Md. Saadulla, who was later a member of the Constitution Drafting Committee, said: "By the *Dharma Chakra* we should be reminded at all times that we are here not only for our material prosperity but also for our spiritual advancement. This *Chakra* was a religious emblem and we cannot dissociate our social life from our religious environment."[14]

With such an importance given to *Dharma Chakra* in our national flag and with such perspectives expressed by the founding fathers of religion and matters of the spirit, it is obvious that secularism in the context of our Constitution cannot be irreligious.

Nehru, who waged a relentless war to inculcate among his compatriots a spirit of tolerance for other faiths, said: "We have laid down in our Constitution that India is a secular state. That does not mean irreligion. It means equal respect for all faiths and equal opportunities for those who profess any faith."[15]

The original text of the preamble as adopted by the Constituent Assembly did not contain the word "secular." Like the word "socialist," it was also inserted as an additional adjective before "republic" by the 42nd Constitutional Amendment Act during the Emergency. It is entirely likely that the motivation for the addition of the word "secular" was purely political. The meaning sought to be given to the term has been that of *Panth-Nirpeksh* or *Sarva Dharm Sambhava*; i.e., treating all religions alike or giving equal respect to all religions, instead of *Dharma Nirpeksh*, i.e., state neutrality in matters of religion.

Secularism in our context only means that ours was a nontheocratic state, that the state as such does not have its own religion, that in its eyes all religions are equal and that it would make no distinction between citizens on grounds of religion. Dr. Radhakrishnan also emphatically asserted that Indian Secularism did not mean irreligion, atheism, or indifference to religion, or even stress on material comforts; it meant that we respected all faiths and religions and that the state did not identify with any particular religion.

Justice Gajendragadkar defined secularism of the Indian Constitution to mean equality of rights to all citizens as citizens with their religion being entirely irrelevant in the matter. "The State," he said, "does not owe loyalty to any particular religion as such; it is not irreligious or anti-religious; it gives equal freedom to all religions."[16] Indian Secularism sought to establish a rational synthesis between the "legitimate functions of religion and the legitimate and expanding functions of the State."[17] M.C. Setalvad also believed that under a secular state all citizens are to be treated alike and not discriminated against on account of their religion.[18]

Before the 42nd Amendment, the only mention of the word "secular" in the Constitution was in article 25(2), wherein the state had been empowered to regulate or restrict any "secular activity" associated with religious practice. Obviously, here the connotation of "secular" was "nonreligious" or "pertaining to matters other than purely religious." In the *Kesavananda Bharti* and *Minerva Mills* cases, secularism came to be mentioned as a basic feature. Also, it was inherent in the guarantee of freedom of religion as a fundamental right. In *St. Xavier College Society v. State of Gujarat*, it was held by the Supreme Court in 1974 that even though the Constitution did not speak of a secular state there could be no doubt that the Constitution-makers wanted to establish such a state. The Supreme Court said:

Secularism is neither anti-God, nor pro-God; it treats alike the devout, the agnostic and the atheist. It eliminates God from matters of the State and ensures that no one shall be discriminated against on the ground of religion. The Constitution at the same time expressly guarantees freedom of conscience and the right freely to profess, practice and propagate religion. The Constitution makers were conscious of the deep attachment the vast masses of our country had towards religion, the sway it had on their minds and the significant role it played in their lives. To allay all apprehensions of interference by the legislature and the executive in matters of religion, the rights mentioned in articles 25 to 30 were made a part of the fundamental rights and religious freedom contained in these articles was guaranteed by the Constitution.[19]

But, apart from using the word "secular" in the preamble, our Constitution does not anywhere categorically say that religion and politics would not be allowed to be mixed, or that religious issues or funds and places of worship would not be allowed to be exploited for political ends by "power mongers and communal groups masquerading as political parties."[20]

Notwithstanding anything, the only operative interpretation of the term "secular" in Indian Constitutional Law now would be what can be gathered from the different provisions of the Constitution, for example, articles 14, 15, 16, 19, 25 to 28, 44, etc. The preamble itself, even in its original unamended form, contained the concept of liberty of belief, faith, and worship. In other words, it stood for a solemn commitment to religious freedom for all. This was reinforced by the principles of equality of status and opportunity and of fraternity among all the people of India. The fundamental rights specifically guaranteed to all persons freedom of religion – right to profess, practice, and propagate any religion of one's choice and prohibition of any discrimination on grounds of, for instance, religion, race, caste, etc. Religious freedom also covered freedom of any person who did not have or did not believe in any religion at all. No one could be compelled to pay for the promotion or maintenance of any religion or to take part in any religious instruction; wholly state-funded institutions were barred from imparting any religious instruction (arts. 27 and 28). The language, script, and culture of minorities were protected. No citizen was to be denied admission to any educational institution on the ground only of religion, etc. (art. 29). Articles 14, 15, and 16 commanded the state not to discriminate against any citizen on the ground of race, religion, caste, place of birth, or sex. Articles 25 and 26 guaranteed freedom of conscience and of profession, practice and propagation of religion, as well as the freedom to manage religious affairs. Citizenship of India under the Constitution and the Citizenship Act was not in any way related to any considerations of religion. The state had to deal with every citizen as a citizen irrespective of his religion (or no religion), with freedom of religion guaranteed to every individual.

The vision of the founding fathers was that of a nation transcending all diversities of religion, caste, and creed. They were not hostile to religion but they hoped that it would be possible to forge political unity and that religious differences would not hamper nation-building. The Constitution envisaged a new social order free from communal conflicts and based on Justice – social, economic, and political. It visualized a polity under which laws would not discriminate between citizens on grounds of religion, caste, or the like. The Constitution sought to establish a "secular" order under which the majority of the population did not enjoy any special privileges or preferential treatment at the hands of the state. The "religious" rights of the minorities were protected in different ways. But what happened during the decades following the commencement of the Constitution – the way the Constitution was amended and operated – was different and far removed from the intentions of the founding fathers. The Constitution was amended to allow discrimination along communal and caste lines.

The Indian State continues to recognize various religions and religious organizations. It can extend financial assistance to religious institutions. It can change, regulate, and end certain religious practices. It legitimizes distinctions on the basis of community and caste in the matter of services under the state and permits public celebration of religious functions. The holders of the highest offices of state and top political dignitaries publicly participate in religious festivals, visit religious places, and pay obeisance to religious leaders at open public gatherings. Thus, religion and politics have become interlocked. Laws exist to prevent misuse of religion during elections. But these are hardly ever enforced. The working of the Constitution during the last four decades and more has shown that there is increasingly greater emphasis on religion, community, and caste than ever before.

> Political parties, some of the State Governments and the superior judiciary, all of them have to share responsibility for this – politicians for mixing religion and caste with politics for electoral gains, the governments by making caste the basis for reservation of appointments and posts as well as seats in educational institutions, and the judiciary by recognising "caste" as a relevant factor for identifying backward classes for the purposes of reservation.[21]

As a senior out-of-power politician bemoans, the devil of elections has supplanted all other issues and made communalism acceptable in varying degrees. Recalling Maulana Azad's memorable words, he says:

The palm of almost every politician bears the blood stains of a bleeding secularism. With the process of deideologisation nearing completion, casteism and communalism are bound to step in as successors, no matter how illegitimate they are . . . Now no party can think of setting up a candidate without any caste and communal considerations. In fact the spirit of nationalism has waned so precipitously under the impact of competitive politics of elections that all kinds of particularistic trends are on the rise and Indians without denominational labels are a dying species.[22]

The *Shah Bano* case marked a turning point in Hindu–Muslim politics. In that case, unfortunately, the law-makers yielded to the pressure of fundamentalist Muslim opinion and much against the letter and spirit of the constitutional precepts of secularism or equal justice for all, the Muslim Women (Protection of Right of Divorce) Act, 1986, was brought in to nullify the Supreme Court judgment.[23] Actually, the state was guilty of appeasing all forms of communalism, whether of the majority or of the minority.

Soon after the reversal of the Supreme Court judgment in the *Shah Bano* case, the doors of the disputed structure in Ayodhya were opened, perhaps as a balancing act to appease Hindu sentiment. Professor C.P. Bhambri concludes his analysis of the theme by pointing out the moral that "the State can fight against communalism if it does not make compromise with any kind of communalism." Since in the 1980s, the state has not been equally firm against the aggressive communalism of Hindus, Sikhs, and Muslims, the whole of North India was communalized. He adds:

> Further, a contribution has been made by weak centrist and secular parties by playing the vote bank games around communities. How can a so-called centrist party protect and promote secular politics if it wins elections on the basis of appeasement of a community?[24]

To quote Asghar Ali Engineer:

> By adopting an aggressive posture on the *Shah Banu* judgement the Muslim leadership alienated even the progressive, secular Hindus who are quite sympathetic to the Muslim cause . . . one can say that the Ramjanmabhoomi–Babri Masjid controversy is a fallout of the *Shah Banu* agitation.[25]

As has been stated elsewhere:

> Where there is a discrimination between man and man on the grounds of religion, where governors, ambassadors, Ministers and other high functionaries are appointed or not appointed because of the community or caste to which they happen to belong by the accident of birth, where even for the highest office of the Head of the State caste and communal considerations are seriously and shamelessly discussed, where there are separate laws and codes for different communities, where the administration of places of worship can be entrusted to Government officers, where under a 1925 Sikh Gurudwara Act, State Government spends lakhs of rupees for conducting elections to the Shiromani Gurudwara Prabandhak Committee and this Committee controls the huge gurudwara funds and runs the Akali politics, where no government has the courage to enforce the laws in regard to misuse of religion during elections, where parties with communal denominations not only exist but participate in elections, where even fundamental rights are demanded and conceded on grounds of communities, it is a cruel joke to talk of separating religion from politics.[26]

Unfortunately the concept of secularism has got mixed up with the problem of religious minorities and more particularly differences between the Hindu and Muslim fundamentalists. Political parties have sought to convert religious communities into political communities. Also, secularism itself has become a political weapon and a mere slogan for catching votes rather than any matter of ideology or belief. Political parties have failed to promise that they would not hob-nob with communal forces or not mix religion with their strategies of building vote banks.

Nobody has questioned the ethicality of "inverted communalism" passing itself off as secularism, as well as the danger of encouraging minority communalism as a countermeasure to majority communalism. The police–criminal nexus and political parties playing the communal card are by now well-known to be behind the communal riots. The police force is also said to be highly politicized and communalized.[27] One is tempted to pose the question: What has been done to break the unholy alliance between communal criminals and politicians, to stop political interference in law enforcement, and to make district administration accountable for communal riots?

Certain other specific questions in the field of secularism/communalism have been raised and brought to the fore during recent years. At least some of these questions are reported to have caught, rightly or wrongly, the imagination of large sections of the urban and rural populations. Thus, it is asked what would happen to our concepts and values of secularism if majority and minority ratios are reversed, as in Pakistan, and the majority community becomes a minority in some states, like Assam. Are there any Muslim majority states that are secular?

Minorities must be protected and their interests promoted in all civilized societies. But, the question remains whether it is not anachronistic for a secular constitution to recognize religious immunities in the political system or to provide for any special political privileges on grounds of religion under the guise of protecting them. As such, can religious minorities be allowed to be converted into political groups, or what have been called vote banks?

Some of the more fundamental questions were candidly raised by no less a person than Jawaharlal Nehru himself, as early as 1948, during his convocation address at the Aligarh Muslim University. He said, "You are Muslim and I am a Hindu. We may adhere to different religious faiths or even to none; but that does not take away from the cultural inheritance that is yours as much as it is mine." Nehru pointedly asked the students: "Do you believe in a national State which includes people of all religions, and is essentially secular . . . or do you believe in a religious, theocratic conception of a State which regards people of other faiths as somebody beyond the pale?" Even earlier, Nehru had once said that a minority cannot be allowed to dominate or override the majority. After all, the majority also has some rights.[28]

Is it just and proper or in keeping with the principles of secularism to allow state assistance to some institutions imparting religious instruction which are administered and controlled by members of minority communities, while the same facility and rights are not conceded to institutions run by the majority, thereby driving, for example, a body like the Ramakrishna Mission to declare itself non-Hindu? Is there any justification for the government taking over and managing temples and their funds while leaving the churches and mosques undisturbed or for amending the Hindu personal law or implementing the constitutional directive of a uniform civil code? Also, is the so-called appeasement of Muslims merely an effort to win over the fundamentalist fringe without any regard for the sentiments or welfare of the Muslim masses whose needs and concerns basically are much more of economic development? Enlightened Muslims demand justice and equality and not appeasement. As Iqbal Khan, the editor of *Mashal* (Pakistan), significantly remarks:

> Modern politics is a game of numbers, power belongs to those who command the highest number of votes. In a backward society where people's behaviour is governed by emotions and prejudices rather than reason, and where society is fragmented into numerous groups on religious, ethnic, tribal, casteist, biradari, etc. lines, it is not surprising that politicians win votes by playing off one group against another.[29]

According to Iqbal Khan, it is the mischievous politicians who don the cloak of religious piety to (among other things) give rise to a persecution complex, encouraging a community to believe that their lives or religion or rights are under threat from this or that community and that their best defense is aggression. Religious extremism and communal hatred are often stage-managed and rarely the result of spontaneous behavior of the masses. Sometimes the parties in power play this dirty game when they feel insecure. Instead of serving the country they become busy in the effort to survive in power. They court and strengthen parties with the greatest potential to divide, which means encouraging religious and communal movements.[30]

Today, more and more people are asking whether it is not a fact that just as some parties use religion to foster separate identities for seeking votes and getting to power, others use the secularism slogan to create a divide between the majority and minority communities and between different castes. There has been a general politicization of religious communities and an equally general communalization of secular politics.

On the other hand, the apprehensions of some religious minorities of insecurity, of losing their identity and being submerged, of discrimination, of distrust, of being kept poor, backward, and deprived of their due share in education, business, the civil service, etc., have to be understood, appreciated, and allayed.

If the objective of the bill now before Parliament is to prevent the misuse of religion for electoral purposes, it is hardly possible to disagree with it. But, unfortunately, the motivations behind the proposed moves are neither honest nor clean. It is not as if we have developed a new love for secularism or for the first time realized the damage done to our body politic by the use of communal cards in electoral battles. The hard facts are that for the first time since Independence, the ruling Congress Party today stands convinced that the use of religious identities, slogans, and issues is getting more detrimental to its interests. It seems that the new enthusiasm to outlaw communal parties comes from the ruling Congress Party's perception of the BJP being the only opposition and the only threat left to Congress monopoly of a divided left and a dying Janta party. No amount of hypocrisy, make-believe, or preaching of righteousness and high principles of secularism, patriotism, democracy, and national integration can hide from the people the hard truth that the bringing forth of the bill at present is motivated more by the desire to eliminate the BJP than any commitment to fight communalism or misuse of religion.

Indians at large are a highly religious people, at least that is what the outer trappings of their behavior patterns indicate. Religious codes are all-pervasive and cover all aspects of life. It is difficult to separate the religious from the secular. As S. Nihal Singh put it, "Religion in politics is here to stay; sagacity lies in defining what the relationship should be."[31] Also, the word *Dharma* has such a connotation that it would be difficult for an average Indian to think of divorcing public life from *Dharma*, which appears almost as an equivalent of righteousness, duty, or rule of law. Even the Speaker of Lok Sabha and the members of the House are enjoined to work according to *Dharma*. The inscription overlooking the Speaker's Chair in the Lok Sabha Chamber reads "*Dharmchakra Pravartanaya*," i.e., is for establishing the rule of the wheel of righteousness or the rule of law.

In the actual game of power politics, almost all the political parties have been guilty of using caste and communal identities for selecting candidates and garnering support and building their vote-bank bases. The Congress and the Janta Dal perhaps have been more responsible for dividing Indian society on caste and communal lines to win the battles of the ballot. None of the parties have done anything substantial for ameliorating the communities. They have been more concerned with raising appropriate slogans, bribing the "creamy layers," and serving their own selfish ends in the power game.

It is well known that just as the Congress in the name of secularism used the minority card for the near monopoly of power for some four decades, V.P. Singh tried the Mandal card, and Advani the *Rath Yatra* and the *Ram Janmabhoomi*. They are all in similar glass houses. The interests of the nation and of the people are nobody's concern. Every party is for power by whatever means. If religion and caste come in handy and deliver votes, why not, and who would not, use them?

However unexceptionable in principle, the proposed legislation is incapable of being implemented in practice. What was most essential was first to define terms like secularism, religion, etc., but it has not been done. Even in the secular western democracies, there are parties with religious names like the Christian Democratic or Christian Socialist Parties in Europe. Jews are a major force in US politics. Not only domestic but even foreign policies are greatly influenced by Jewish lobbies. A Catholic President becomes a big exception. Abortion is paraded as a major religious issue in politics. The question is how to define or determine a party with a religious name, and how under the sun to prevent any party from using religion to influence votes? If the religious names of parties can influence votes, what about the religious names of the candidates themselves? After all, irrespective of the parties from which they contest, Shiv Shankar, Shankaranand, Narasimha, Arjuna, Balram, Ghulam Nabi, Sitaram, Madhav, Man Mohan, Kamalnath, Jagdish, Ramashwar, Krishna, Venkataswamy, and others are religious names. They symbolize and convey the religion of the person.

The National Flag has the *Dharma Chakra* in its middle. Also, the Constitution allows an oath in the name of God to be taken by legislators and holders of high office.

It would be difficult to imagine Gandhiji's "Ramdhun" and "Ramrajya" outlawed from politics. After all, did not Gandhi, Tilak, Maulana Azad, Lajput Rai, Malviya, and other leaders of the Independence Struggle mix religion with politics and did they not use religious names and symbols? It is a hard fact of history that the dominant role of religion in Indian politics really began with Gandhiji's leadership of the Khilafat movement and the use of Muslim *ulema* and fundamentalists against the more liberal and secular Muslim leadership.

The proposed measure would give to the government of the day unlimited power *vis-à-vis* all the opposition parties. The leaders in the party in power would have to be more than saints not to use these powers in their party and personal interests of survival, even if the result is a guided or controlled democracy or a near Emergency regime.

Under the present Section 29A of the Representation of the People Act, every party in order to get registered has to specifically declare its adherence to principles of socialism, secularism, and democracy. In whatever manner we define "socialism" – to take only one example – can the Congress party itself honestly affirm its faith in socialism? Would it pass the test of 29A and the proposed 29B, and would it not deserve to be deregistered forthwith? The fact is that such declarations, oaths, and affirmations are never taken seriously and there is always a wide gulf between the precepts and practices of politicians.

The constitution guarantees religious freedom to all. Misuse of religion in elections, etc., is already punishable under the Indian Penal

Code and the Representation of the People Act, and for it a person can be sent to jail for as long as three years besides losing his seat in the legislature. Unfortunately, such laws remain only in the statute book. The political will to implement them is lacking and litigation takes too long to conclude.

Finally, it would be necessary to make a distinction between religion and communalism. Commmunalism is misuse of religion that has to be prevented. Religion should neither interfere in political affairs nor should politics meddle in the religious business of citizens. Politicians should keep their religion to themselves and not bandy it about. We have to stop the communalization of religion as much as of secular politics. Also, the politicization of religious communities or the conversion of religious minorities into political minorities has already done tremendous damage to our polity and to the nation. There is no alternative to giving up hypocrisy and to really resolving not to use religion, caste, community, etc., for cultivating vote banks at the country's cost.

No one – not even those who have brought forward the Bill – seriously believes that it can achieve the purpose of delinking religion and politics. This can never be done by legislation. It is an issue that must be faced politically and it is for the electorate to decide to whom they would like to yield power over their lives. Ultimately, communalism has to be fought by honest political will, in the minds of men and women and by the honest conduct of our public functionaries. It cannot be fought by laws. Law as proposed is an alibi for inaction, a symbol of defeatism and political escapism. Matters of sentiment have to be understood. Thoughts and opinions have to be answered. Ideologies have to be faced politically. Thoughts, opinions, sentiments, and ideologies cannot be banished by being banned.

A new generation would have to arise with a new vision of love for the nation above party, power, and self-interests, with faith in the constitutional values of the equality of all citizens before the law, in nondiscrimination of any form on grounds of religion, caste, community, etc.; and in full freedom of religion for all.

Notes

1   For a fuller study of the theme, see Subhash C. Kashyap, *Delinking Religion and Politics* (Delhi: Shipra, 1993).
2   D.A. Desai, J., "Relevance of Secularism Today," *Indian Bar Review*, 14(3), 1987, p. 339.

3   M.H. Beg, J., *Impact of Secularism on Life and Law* (New Delhi: People's Publishing House, 1985), p. 61.
4   Ibid.
5   *Kesavananda Bharti* v. *the State of Kerala*, 1973 Suppl. SCR, pp. 1 and 871.
6   Cf. "an alliance between religion and politics has been evident during several periods of US history, when the church and the state have promoted various causes. For example, in the 1800s, northern liberal Ministers were the major inspiration behind the attempt to abolish slavery in the United States and many of them actually became leaders of the abolitionist movement. In the early 1900s, conservative rural Protestants mobilized to bring about the 'noble experiment' called Prohibition, culminating in the passage of the Eighteenth Amendment to the Constitution (forbidding sale and distribution of alcoholic beverages). More recently, the effectiveness of a religious and political alliance was demonstrated during the civil rights movement in the 1960s, when fundamentalist preacher and Reverend Martin Luther King, Jr., successfully challenged many of the discriminatory laws that maintained the *status quo* of US race relations. In the 1980s, a new religious/political movement known as the New Christian Right has been started. It has been organized and directed mainly by conservative fundamentalist preachers of generally large churches. The preachers appear regularly on religious television. Probably the best known among them, Rev. Jerry Falwell, founded in the latter 1970s the Moral Majority – the most widely publicized of the Christian Right religious/political action groups. Through television direct mail campaigns and political lobbying, Falwell and other representatives of the Christian Right are attempting to influence judges, legislators, and government executives to institute decisions that will bring back more conservative Christian values and practices among all US citizens. During the 1984 Presidential election campaign in particular, Ronald Reagan and the Christian Right had a well-publicized alliance. In fact, Falwell described Reagan and Vice-President George Bush as 'God's instruments in rebuilding America.' In turn, Reagan accused opponents of school prayer (an important Christian Right issue) of being 'intolerant of religion.' But later events showed that the movement 'seems to have not had too much impact on politics and will probably be withdrawing shortly.'" (Stephen D. Johnson and Joseph B. Tamney (eds.), *The Political Role of Religion in the United States* (Boulder, Colo.: Westview Press, 1986), pp. 99–100, 338.)
7   Balraj Puri, "Religion and Secularism," *Indian Express*, April 14, 1992.
8   Shyam Nandan Mishra, "Secularism: a Moment of Truth," *Hindustan Times*, Feb. 14, 1993.
9   *CA (Legis) Deb.*, 1948, vol. IV, pp. 3116–20.
10   Ibid., pp. 3120–3.
11   Ibid.
12   Ibid., pp. 3145–7.
13   Ibid., pp. 3148–9.
14   *CA Deb.*, vol. IV, pp. 737–41, 745–6, 748–9.
15   *Jawaharlal Nehru's Speeches*, vol. IV, p. 11; Subhash C. Kashyap, *History of Parliamentary Democracy* (Delhi: Shipra Publications, 1992), p. 353.
16   G.S. Sharma (ed.), *Secularism – Its Implications for Law and Life in India* (New Delhi: Indian Law Institute, 1985), p. 4.

17   P.B. Gajendragadkar, *Secularism and the Constitution of India* (Bombay: University of Bombay, 1971), p. 52.
18   *Secularism*, Patel Memorial Lectures, 1965, p. 484, cited by P.P. Rao, *Perspectives on the Constitution* (Delhi: Shipra, 1993), pp. 44–5.
19   A.I.R. 1974 SC 1389, AIR 1973 SC 1461, and AIR 1980 SC 1787.
20   P.P. Rao, op. cit., p. 46.
21   Ibid.
22   Mishra, op. cit.
23   *Ahmed Khan* v. *Shah Banu*, AIR 1985 SC 945.
24   C.P. Bhambhri, "All in the Name of God," *Hindustan Times*, Oct. 4, 1992.
25   Ashgar Ali Engineer, "The Muslim Dilemma," *Indian Express*, Oct. 19, 1992.
26   Subhash C. Kashyap (ed.), *Reforming the Constitution* (New Delhi: UBSD, 1992), p. 17.
27   Chand Joshi in *Hindustan Times*, Nov. 8, 1992.
28   Cited in B. Krishna, "Defining Secularism," *Hindu*, June 28, 1992; Subhash C. Kashyap, *History of Parliamentary Democracy* (Delhi: USBD, 1991), p. 102.
29   Iqbal Khan, "Concept of Secularism," *Times of India*, April 6, 1993.
30   Ibid.
31   *The Week*, July 25, 1993.

6
Historical Narrative and Nation-state in India

Steven A. Hoffmann

Introduction

For many years a number of India's leading historians have been trying to influence the content of Indian education by means of a series of high-school textbooks. These history books, which openly espouse secularism and combat "religious fanaticism," have been written for an organization called the National Council of Educational Research and Training.[1] Among its varied activities, the NCERT produces model textbooks for adoption by the school systems of India's many states.

The NCERT has been depicted as an autonomous organization, at least in principle. But the extent of its autonomy may be limited, since it is government funded, and its Director is a government appointee.[2] The historical worldview of the NCERT has been consistent with (although not always identical to) the ideological positions and nation-building policies adopted by the successive incarnations of the Congress Party. Although the NCERT history textbooks have been written by historians who are independent-minded academic professionals mostly employed elsewhere, these books can be viewed as the policy instruments of a semi-governmental agency.

How these textbooks, and particularly *Modern India* by Bipan Chandra, construct Indian history, by means of certain conventions or discursive devices specific to narratives, is one of the two main issues critically examined in this study. It is an important issue even though most of federal India's state governments, and therefore most of India's secondary schools, have not adopted these books.[3] The textbooks are important because they are used in schools associated in various ways with the central government, and are used in at least some private schools. Until 1976, and most probably thereafter, the books constituted a method whereby the central government illustrated "concretely to the State Departments of Education the general approach to be taken in writing about India's past and present." People preparing for national examinations use them as study books. NCERT history textbooks are also known outside of academia, as they have been involved in well-publicized political controversies.[4]

The NCERT books also constitute an abridged presentation of a kind of history with which many academic historians in India probably have a general familiarity. Such familiarity most likely exists because most of the authors of these books have published extensively, and some have held positions in the history departments of major universities. Moreover, certain NCERT historians have been prominent figures in one or more organizations that are important for the Indian history profession: namely the Indian Council of Historical Research, the Indian History Congress, and the University Grants Commission. The NCERT books themselves represent an effort to provide material on which there is some consensus among "secular" historians, especially historians not in the Hindu nationalist camps.[5]

What ultimately guarantees their importance, however, is that they contain a version of Indian history which has been given a semi-official status.[6] If the Congress Party regularly or permanently loses power at the national level to its powerful Hindu nationalist competitor, the Bharatiya Janata Party (BJP), the privileged position of this kind of history is likely to erode or even end. The BJP's approach to the teaching of Indian history is quite different. At least some of the points made in a curricular and/or textbook version of history favored by the Uttar Pradesh state government, when it was led by the BJP, bore "a closer relation to Hindu mythology than to more generally accepted historical accounts."[7]

Disagreement with the NCERT's brand of history comes not only from the ideological and historical outlook of the BJP. NCERT history is challenged by many Indian intellectuals holding diverse points of view. As of 1993, its legitimacy was being at least implicitly questioned by an internationally recognized group of mostly younger historians, most of them having ethnic Indian backgrounds. At least some of them are more strongly influenced by postmodernist ideas than are their NCERT colleagues. These are the "Subaltern" historians. The nature of the Subaltern critique of certain forms of Indian history is the second major issue to be discussed here, so that the antithetical relationship between this approach and NCERT history can be explored.

The NCERT books and postnationalist history

The NCERT historians aim to produce history that is free of certain notions adopted by some of the Indian nationalist historians during the pre-independence period, notions which simultaneously or subsequently became part of "communalist" (religiously and/or regionally chauvinist) historiography. At least some of these notions can be traced back, in one fashion or another, to Western historians writing during the British imperialist era. NCERT history is therefore not just anti-communalist, but postcolonial, postorientalist, and partly postnationalist too.[8]

NCERT history opposes the nationalist idea that the "ancient" era in India's past was an idyllic "golden age." One internationally renowned NCERT author, Romila Thapar, has written (in a separate essay) that certain earlier Indian historians glorified "the ancient past . . . as a kind of consolation for the humiliation of the present." They were reluctant to admit that conflicts and tensions existed in early India, "particularly conflicts of a socioeconomic and religious nature."[9] Another NCERT scholar, Arjun Dev, differentiates between nationalist historians and "obscurantists." The former glorified ancient India in order to blur Hindu–Muslim differences, while the latter still glorifies ancient India in order to denigrate the medieval "Muslim" period.[10]

NCERT history also rejects the tendency of certain nationalist historians (and of communalists generally) to treat medieval Muslim rulers (like the members of the Moghal dynasty) as foreigners, and blame them (along with the "alien West") for a steady Indian "decay" of many centuries. Another alleged nationalist error was to follow the British practice of labeling empires and states in India's medieval period as being either Hindu or Muslim. Those political units were thereby assigned religious identities that, upon close nonbiased examination, cannot explain many of their policies and actions. Medieval India was Muslim only in the sense that some rulers and some parts of India were Muslim. The NCERT textbook author Bipan Chandra, elsewhere in his writings, argues that communalist history (building on some earlier nationalist history) similarly extends present-day Hindu–Muslim communal politics back into the past where such tensions did not exist.[11]

Perhaps the most fundamental nationalist shortcoming, in the view of certain NCERT authors, was acceptance of the British argument that Indian history is best divided into a Hindu period, a Muslim period, and a British period. This periodization is allegedly invalid, partly because

Hinduism did not exist as a unified entity in ancient times, even though "shared myths and shared ritual patterns can account for some unity in the varieties of religious belief that we find in India over a long time." Nor was there one essential Hindu community, identity, race, or society, although multiple communities did exist, "identified by locality, languages, caste, occupation and sect."[12] Moreover, none of these historians described British rule as Christian rule, says Bipan Chandra, "even though the higher bureaucracy was Christian to a far greater extent than the higher nobility of the Mughals was Muslim."[13]

Still another fundamental problem with at least some nationalist historians (and with communalist history), according to Bipan Chandra, is their use of "myths" to foster and reflect the belief that the Indian historical process was exceptional. Partly because of India's mythical Hindu "golden age," and partly because of India's mythically superior "spiritualism" over time, Indian history was supposedly not "a part and parcel of universal history."[14] Nationalist historians failed to place Indian history within a "scientific" universalist context.[15] Chandra is doubtlessly using the term "scientific" to mean history that is objective, balanced, and empirically based, but he may be using it in the Marxist historiographical sense as well.

NCERT historians and Marxist theory

Most NCERT authors who use Marxism in their professional careers, have been too personally individualistic to be bound or even limited by it. Nor have they lost sight of many nationalist themes. Therefore, these particular historians can be called "left-nationalists."[16] They differ from those secular-minded Indian historians ("Liberals") who either disavow Marxism, or borrow from it rarely.[17]

Marxism can both universalize and secularize Indian history, by portraying it as a progression of economic systems rather than religions. Marxism also requires historians to focus upon economic and social history (history from the "ground up"), rather than just political/religious history. If competing histories of India have dwelt too much on such topics as the religious orientation of rulers, and the factional politics of the Indian nationalist movement, the NCERT historians think that the focus should be elsewhere.

With their "modes of production" approach to periodization, the NCERT books seemingly argue that the economic system of ancient India (approx. 2500 BC to approx. 750 AD) was based on production by artisans, peasants, agricultural laborers, and some slaves, on collection and distribution by merchants, and on the use of much of the economic surplus by the warrior, administrator, big-merchant, and priestly classes. The lower classes of ancient India were not composed of slaves (for the most part), and were therefore different from the laboring classes of Greece and Rome.

> What was done by slaves and other producing sections in Greece and Rome under the threat of [the] whip was done by the vaisyas and sudras out of conviction formed through brahminical indoctrination and the varna [caste/class] system.[18]

The kingdoms and empires of ancient India eventually began to decentralize their administrative structures by making land grants to priests, monks, officials, military leaders, and others. This process of infeudation brought India into its medieval period (approx. 750 AD to the early eighteenth Century). "Medieval" meant "feudal," but not in the European sense, since no equivalents of serfdom or manors appeared in India. India's medieval period began well before Islam became an important element in the superstructure of Indian society, and well before the appearance of the major Muslim ruling dynasties in the subcontinent. Transformation in the mode of production therefore made for epochal change in India, and not religious or dynastic change.[19]

The NCERT textbooks on modern India (eighteenth century to approx. 1950) take the view that British penetration and domination brought about another epochal change in the Indian socioeconomic substructure. Now India was drawn into the international capitalist economy. As Bipan Chandra points out elsewhere, capitalism had its progressive features in other centuries, where it served to develop the forces of production, but colonialism obstructed such development in India. Colonialism deliberately "repressed and prevented the growth of capitalism in India." Moreover, the Indian economic surplus was misappropriated in various ways by the colonial state, society, and economy, and part of that surplus was exported abroad. The colonial state-structure in India, believes Chandra, did not embody a relationship of power between the various Indian classes, nor did it perform an autonomous social function in the society. Instead, it was "the organized power of the entire metropolitan capitalist class for oppressing the entire colonial society."[20]

The Gramscian concept of ideological "hegemony" influences the NCERT perception of British rule. The British imperial system was what Bipan Chandra has elsewhere called "semi-hegemonic," because it did not base itself entirely on force. Instead it also relied upon such devices as the "rule of law," civil institutions, and "a degree of civil liberties [extended] in normal times," to help convince Indians that the colonizers held the moral, ideological, and political high ground.[21]

The Indian independence movement and the British empire fought a nonviolent war over hegemony, in the Chandra view. In one of his theoretical writings Chandra sees the Indian freedom struggle containing perhaps the only historical "actualization" of Antonio Gramsci's strategy of revolution. Phases of extralegal mass struggle (Gramsci's "war of maneuver") were separated by long phases of truce, in which political struggle (Gramsci's "war of position") took place within the available legal space. During each legal phase, political concessions (if any) from the colonial state were "worked and shown to be inadequate," while political contact between the movement and the masses was developed further. Subsequent extralegal struggle, "at a higher level," was thereby made possible, "till finally a call for 'quit India' was given and the ultimate concession of independence was extracted."[22]

NCERT history portrays the Indian nationalist movement as a genuine people's movement, rather than an elite affair of the Indian bourgeoisie. What Bipan Chandra elsewhere calls the "primary contradiction" was the contradiction between colonialism and the Indian people as a whole.[23] Certain "Subaltern" and other historians may explicitly or implicitly criticize the movement for failing to foster a class revolution of the underprivileged. But Chandra's theoretical writings on modern India argue that elite and mass were truly aligned in the nationalist cause, both tactically and in their understanding of objective interests.

Accordingly to Chandra, the class contradictions of Indian society were appropriately treated by the nationalist movement as being "secondary" to the cause of national liberation, and were never pressed to the ultimate extremes. Elite and mass within the movement engaged in the kind of dialectical relationship that is necessary for the success of any mass effort. India's nascent bourgeoisie did not dominate the Indian nationalist movement, which was multiclass in character and therefore lacked any fixed class "essence." The political outlook of the movement progressed constantly to the left, given the influence of socialist ideas, groups, and leaders, although socialism never achieved ideological hegemony within the movement as a whole.[24]

The India–Pakistan divide, which eventually climaxed the years of the independence struggle, is partly attributed by the Chandra textbook to British efforts to divide and politicize the religious communities. This is an old nationalist theme. But communal forces on both sides are blamed for spreading what Chandra elsewhere calls "false consciousness." This is false consciousness in the Gramscian sense, i.e., a fundamental misperception of group interests.[25]

Chandra's narrative on "modern India"

Central axis and main subject

As a story or narrative, the Chandra textbook on modern India follows certain rules of discourse. These are conventions common to tales of building the nation-state. One of them is that the formation of the Indian nation-state is the ordained goal of the narrative, i.e., its *telos*, even though the making of the nation-state is shown to be incomplete at the time of independence. Another convention is to include and emphasize those events, trends, and other elements which produced effects judged to be favorable to the creation of the nation-state. Those elements, and the causative connections between them, help to constitute the narrative's central axis.

Yet another convention is to construct or identify a central object or actor that either becomes the nation-state or is deemed primarily responsible for building it. The Chandra book constructs an object called the Indian "people," which possesses an evolving socioeconomic and political structure. The book starts its depiction of the "people" by employing the narrative convention of distinguishing the self from the other. Eighteenth-century India is portrayed as a "country" in which the declining Mughal dynasty (as a political symbol) still had a "powerful hold" on the "minds" of the "people." At this time India (as a country and a people) also has a "broad cultural unity developed over the centuries."[26]

A strong impression of what constitutes *otherness* at this moment is conveyed via references to the enormous tragedy about to occur. Europeans, "knocking at the gates of India," possess a "superior" economic system and an advantage in technology and science. A "foreign power" shall assume the "mantle" of the Mughal empire, and shall dissolve "in its own interests" the Indian "socioeconomic and political structure." This alienating process becomes possible because the Indian states or "powers" of the eighteenth century, which had possessed the strength to destroy the Mughal empire, lacked the strength to reunify it, or replace it with something unifying and new. Representing as they did the "same moribund social system as headed by the Mughals," these states were unable to forge "a new social order which could stand up to the new enemy from the West" (Chandra, 7).

The Chandra book employs another convention as it follows the evolution of the Indian "people" to the moment where it *recognizes itself*. Indeed, perhaps the most crucial convention of a nation-state narrative is to locate the moment at which the cohesive *object* becomes a *subject* in terms of self-recognition, self-consciousness, and self-directedness.[27] That moment, as depicted by Chandra, does not come until a modernizing process has gotten underway.

Certain modernizing trends encouraged the blurring of caste and class differences in British India. India's economy was being made into "a single whole" and the "economic fate of people living in different parts of the country" was becoming interlinked. Mutual contact among "the people" (and among its leaders especially) was being promoted as the railways, postal system, and telegraph were introduced (155). Education, plus the many other trends set in motion by British rule and by the nationalist movement, undermined the entire caste system (185–6).

But the key unifying element was the oppression of "all the Indian people" by foreign rule. People all over India perceived correctly that suffering was being inflicted upon them (whatever their class, caste, region, or religion) by a "common enemy" (155). For the peasant class, recognition of the objective contradiction between its interests and those of the ruling power came as the machinery of the British-Indian state took much of the produce as land revenue and supported the exploitative practices of zamindars, landlords, merchants, and moneylenders. The prototypical artisan or handicraftsman "saw" that foreign rule had ruined him by aiding foreign competition and had done nothing "to rehabilitate him." India's capitalists were (as a class) "slow in developing a national political consciousness." But they eventually realized that a contradiction existed between imperialism and their own interests. Only an independent Indian government would foster conditions favorable to the rapid development of India's own industries and trade. Later, in the early twentieth century, when conflict arose between the Indian capitalist class and "the worker in modern factories, mines, and plantations," the British–Indian government alienated the worker by siding with the capitalists, "especially the foreign capitalists." But even the worker allegedly came to understand that "growing unemployment could be checked" solely "by rapid industrialization which only an independent government could bring about" (153–4).

As for the "rising intelligentsia" of India, their modern knowledge led to their detailed understanding of the economic and political condition of the country (153–6). Their major contribution was to promote consciousness of Indian peoplehood through helping to develop a nationalist movement.

During the earliest phase of the movement (1858 to 1905) a generation of moderate but progressive leaders produced what would become the major organizational instrument of the movement, the Indian National Congress. Within this same phase, the movement exposed British imperialism's "true character" in India, "trained people in the art of political work," and evolved a common program upon which mass struggle could be based.[28] But during this phase the nationalist movement's social base was narrowly confined to the educated elite. The movement had not penetrated down to the masses, and "the leaders lacked political faith in the masses." These leaders erred in believing that a "militant mass struggle" was possible only after "Indian society had been welded into a nation." To the contrary, says Chandra, the formation of that nation could occur "mainly in the course of such a struggle" (167–9).

The next phase (1905–18) of the nationalist movement was one in which militant leaders believed in "direct political action by the masses," and in "the strength of the masses." They made national independence their main policy goal rather than reform of the colonial system, and tried to lead the popular (mainly urban) protest activities they had aroused or helped to arouse. Yet still the militants failed to provide positive or effective leadership to "the people," and did not make the Congress an effective guiding organization. Despite the use of some nonviolent mass tactics, such as Swadeshi (boycott of British goods), "passive resistance and non-cooperation remained mere ideas." The class base of the movement was "confined to the urban lower and middle classes and zamindars," and failed to include "the real masses of the country, the peasants" (Chandra, 192–3, 199).

These particular problems were solved, in large part, during the third (and most important) phase of the nationalist struggle (1919–47). Because Mohandas K. Gandhi basically understood and sympathized with the "problems and psychology of the Indian peasantry," he could appeal to that class, and bring it into "the mainstream" of the movement, while employing his new "satyagraha" tactic (222). He could also appeal to other oppressed classes, such as the urban educated, the artisans, and the workers. Therefore he was able to "arouse and unite all sections of the Indian people in a militant mass national movement" (219–23). Even as early as the 1920s, the activization and politicization of "millions of men and women" by the "Non-Cooperation and Civil Disobedience movement" had "imparted a revolutionary character to the Indian national movement" (234–5).

Gandhi was not the only source of mass participation in the nationalist movement. During this phase, mass activities appeared either autonomously or independently, including peasant agitation, strikes, and the Khalifat movement. These efforts could be harnessed to the nationalist cause by providing them with national-level leadership, and engaging them in the new nationalist tactics. But the mainstream activity was, according to the Chandra interpretation, whatever involved the Congress rather than activity that took place apart from it.

Thus the nationalist movement is presented in the Chandra book as helping to create more than a coalition of classes and interests. Phase by phase the movement became based upon "a politically awakened and politically active people" (272). Although the class nature of the movement is made clear at various points, the primary focus is placed upon "the people" as an independent political actor and the source of all political legitimacy.

"Sacralization" of the Indian state

Narratives depicting the creation of nation-states can follow the convention of making the state sacred (i.e., "sacralizing" it – to use a neologism) by linking it to certain values. Underpinning the central nationalist axis of the Chandra narrative are some fundamental assertions made about Indian states and values. One of them is that the presence of many states in a given historical period (i.e., political disunity) can coexist with uniform underlying political realities. The eighteenth-century states that succeeded the Mughal empire, or existed entirely apart from it, are described as demonstrating a form of politics that was "invariably non-communal or secular," because "the motivations" of their rulers were "similar in economic and political terms."

Such rulers did not practice religious discrimination "in public appointments, civil or military," nor did those rebels who fought against their authority "pay much attention to the religion of the rulers" (Chandra, 8). Both rulers and rebels employed religious appeals only "as an outer coloring to disguise the play of material interests and ambitions" (206). Although they fought among themselves and faced domestic resistance to their authority, Indian states each maintained law and order in their own lands well enough. It was British intervention that produced any administrative and economic anarchy whenever it appeared in eighteenth-century India, rather than Indian rulers.

Another Chandra assertion is that religious intolerance, exploitation of the peasantry by elites, and unwillingness to modernize the commercial and industrial base, are among the factors that led to the kind of state-centered weakness that rendered India vulnerable to external interference. The ultimate result was the imposition or perpetuation of "foreign" domination, and an impoverishment of Indians that was more widespread and severe than Indian rulers and ruling classes characteristically imposed.

The values guiding state structures are shown to be related to the demands of their economically dominant classes. As the Mughal empire had sometimes done, India's eighteenth-century states reflected the greed of a nobility steeped in comfort and luxury. Such "feudal" states sought to extract "the maximum amount" from the peasantry, through their "state, the zamindars, the jagirdars, and the revenue farmers" (26–7).

The class interests underpinning the eighteenth- and nineteenth-century British state in India are shown to be rather complex. Under the East India Company, English merchants and officials, who profited hugely from the sale of India's exports, found themselves challenged and eventually joined by other merchants, Britain's rising class of industrial capitalists, other advocates of free enterprise, and those who favored reduced taxes or less public debt. One major aim of the Company's administration in India eventually was "to exploit India economically to the maximum advantage of various British interests, ranging from the Company to the Lancashire manufacturers," or "all sections of the ruling classes of Britain" (66, 65). The policy of "law and order" was meant to maximize the market for British goods, while "India was to be made to bear the full cost of its own conquest as well as of the foreign rule" (80, 66).

Eventually, the class whose interests came to predominate was the British industrial capitalist class. After 1813 the absence of any governmental structure able to protect India from British capitalist demands was keenly felt as India's handicraft industries were all but destroyed. England's discriminatory trade laws, and competition from British machine-made goods, reduced India from a major center "of world trade and industry" (27) in the eighteenth century to an agricultural colony and vast market in the nineteenth century. India should have been protected by "high tariff walls" and given time to "import the new techniques of the West," just as the government of a "free India is doing ... today" (71). Trade discrimination against India should have been answerable by Indian governmental retaliation.

The economic "drain" was a peculiarity of the British period in India, since previous Indian governments (even the "worst" of them) had extracted revenue "from the people" but had spent it inside India itself. Whether they spent it on "personal luxury," or on public works, or on "palaces, temples, and mosques," or on "wars and conquests . . . it ultimately encouraged Indian trade and industry or gave employment to Indians." This was because earlier "foreign conquerors" such as the Mughals had adopted India as their home. But "the British remained perpetual foreigners," and much of their expenditure of taxes and income from India took place in "their home country" (72).

The Gandhian and socialist values found in the Indian nationalist movement helped to sacralize it, and give it a multiclass character (thereby further sacralizing it). By 1927 many young Indian nationalists were turning to Marxism "and other socialist ideas." Worker and peasant parties and groups were appearing, which propagated "Marxist and communist ideas," but "remained integral parts of the national movement and the National Congress" (239–40). The new Congress left wing, led by Jawaharlal Nehru and Subhas Chandra Bose, did not limit its attention to the anti-imperialist struggle, but "simultaneously raised the question of internal class oppression by the capitalists and landlords" (239).

Certain democratic and socialist values of the Indian nationalist movement are associated in the Chandra book with Jawaharlal Nehru, India's future prime minister, although not just with Nehru alone. Among them are: civil rights, "equality before the law," universal franchise elections, "free and compulsory primary education" (253), rent reduction and exemption, "control of money lending," improved conditions for industrial workers, union rights, and "state ownership or control of key industries, mines, and means of transport."[29] The implication here is that such values would give the future Indian state a multiclass, "people"-based, character as well, rather than one of domination by a capitalist elite.

Another linkage (besides Nehru) between the nationalist movement's values and the state-structure of postcolonial India is shown to be the 1950 Indian Constitution. If certain values of the movement helped to constitute a "vision of what free India would be like," the "first effort to give expression to this vision" was "the framing of the Constitution . . . by the Constituent Assembly," guided by Nehru and B.R. Ambedkar (272). The Constitution's guarantees of rights and equalities, its "Directive Principles of State Policy," and the form of government it outlines, are presented as if they commit the Indian state to the pursuit of the nationalist vision for the indefinite future. But the creation of a truly "just and good society" and a "secular, democratic and egalitarian India," is ultimately the task of the "people of India" (272–3).

Nationalism versus communalism

The Chandra textbook differentiates between the main nationalist axis of modern Indian history and the competing axis of communalism partly by describing communalism as an ideology of recent origin which claims that,

> because a group of people follow a particular religion they have, as a result, common secular, that is, social, political, and economic interests. [Thus, there can be] . . . no such thing as an Indian nation, but only [a] Hindu nation, Muslim nation and so on . . . India can therefore, only be a mere confederation of religious communities.
>
> (203)

An advanced "stage" in communalist development is reached when the

> interests . . . [of] different religious "communities," are seen to be mutually incompatible, antagonistic and hostile. Thus, at this stage, the communalists assert that Hindus and Muslims cannot have common secular interests, and that their secular interests are bound to be opposed to each other.
>
> (203)

In opposition to communalist claims, the Chandra book argues that eighteenth-century India, prior to the establishment of British rule, possessed a culture that had become "composite," i.e., jointly created and shared by Hindus and Muslims and others. Relations between the followers of the two major religions were "friendly," with little "communal bitterness or religious intolerance in the country," and with cooperation in the social and cultural spheres (33, 207). Societal divisions followed class lines, so that there was much more convergence of lifestyles among upper-class Hindus and Muslims, than among upper and lower classes within each religious sector. Similarly, region defined Indian social groups more than religion did, in that people within "one region had far greater cultural synthesis, irrespective of religion, than people following the same religion, spread over different regions" (33–4).

Communalism, both Muslim and Hindu, is said to have emerged as

the new and "modern" politics of "popular participation and mobilization" developed in India. The process required the forging of "wider
links and loyalties among the people" and the formation of "new identities" (203). Since these identities were unfamiliar, people quite often

> used the old, familiar, pre-modern identity of caste, locality, sect, and
> religion to grasp the new reality and to make wider connections . . .
> This has happened all over the world.
>
> (204)

Nevertheless, the identities that have gradually and eventually prevailed, worldwide, are the "historically necessary identities of nation,
nationality and class." These identities do not fully prevail in India basically because "India has been for the last 150 years or more a nation in
the making" (204).

Certain circumstances are cited in the Chandra book to explain the
growth of communalism as a virulent political force. Among them
was the "relative backwardness" of Muslims during the late nineteenth
and early twentieth centuries, in terms of education, trade, and industry, when compared with the Hindus, Christians, or Parsis. This situation meant that leadership roles among Muslims remained largely
in the hands of the landlord class. Reactionary Muslim leaders, who
(like their Hindu counterparts) had supported British rule in their
own self-interest, now turned to inflammatory religious appeals. While
political leadership within India as a whole was being assumed by
"independent and nationalist lawyers, journalists, students, merchants
and industrialists," Muslim political opinion was still being influenced
by "loyalist landlords and retired government servants" (Chandra,
205–6).

The British, for their part, are described as having helped to foster
the lag in modernization among Muslims by being especially venge-
ful toward them after the 1857 rebellion. But, from the 1870s onward,
when Indian nationalist activism gradually became an overriding British
concern, British officials were all too willing to accept and promote communal activists (such as those in the Muslim League) as genuine
spokespersons for Muslims and other religious groups. The British also
incited western-educated Muslims against educated Hindus, as did loyalist Muslim leaders. The opportunity for such an effort was provided
by the fact that educated Muslims, finding their opportunities in the
private sector to be limited (especially in a backward colonial economy),
sought government employment. Muslim leaders like Sayyid Ahmad

Khan demanded special treatment for Muslims "in the matter of government service" and urged loyalty to the British as a way to gain jobs and favors (206).

Both Muslim and Hindu communalist groups, "which talked so actively of Hindu and Muslim nationalism," allegedly took no active part in the Indian independence struggle (259). The activities of the Muslim League are described as being "directed not against the foreign rulers but against the Hindus and the National Congress." Hindu communalists, for their part, fully accepted the British colonial version of Indian history, speaking of "'tyrannical' Muslim rule in the medieval period and the 'liberating' role of the British in 'saving' Hindus from 'Muslim oppression'" (210, 212).

Like Muslim communalism, Hindu communalism began developing in the 1870s, and was propagated by "zamindars, money lenders and middle class professionals" (212). By the 1930s, landlords and moneylenders were opposing both the Congress's "radical" agrarian program, and growing peasant movements, and therefore "began to shift their support" to the communalist parties. "They found that an open defence of their interests was no longer possible in the era of mass politics" (258). Hindu communalism, by its work against minorities, abetted the Muslim minority's feelings of insecurity, and strengthened the appeal of Muslim communal leadership. Both Hindu and Muslim communalists came to champion the "unscientific" and "unhistorical" theory that India's Hindus and Muslims constituted two separate nations (203, 212, 258–9).

The Indian nationalist movement is criticized by Chandra for relying too heavily on negotiating with communal leaders (such as Muhammad Ali Jinnah), and for failing to engage in "an all-out ideological political struggle against communalism" (261). What was required was a campaign of the same weight and intensity as that conducted against imperialism. Not only did communalism "make deep inroads" into Indian society, the Chandra book concedes, it even made an impact upon the "ranks of the nationalists." Yet, "secular nationalism" always remained the predominant political force (260–1).

The subaltern antithesis

The Chandra textbook defines the object (and eventual subject) it calls the Indian "people" in at least six ways that specify cohesion. The Indian "people" is: (1) a collectivity possessing a common indigenous culture, and a common socioeconomic and political structure of some antiquity; (2) a collectivity that shares a common past, as well as a common present and future condition, even if not all of its members are yet aware of these commonalities; (3) a moral community created by a holy struggle, and dedicated to further struggle in order to realize its values fully; (4) an alliance of groups having economic interests that are perceived accurately by those groups, (5) a political collectivity able to act as one unit, and (6) an alliance of groups bound together by emotions and loyalties to leaders and causes.

To create a concept or a construct based on some sort of coherent, undifferentiated wholeness is a dangerous enterprise. "Totalization" is presently considered a sin by certain contemporary literary, intellectual, and political theorists influenced by such intellectual trends as post-modernism. They claim that the wholeness of the construct in question is too often elusive or demonstrably non-existent.

The "Subaltern" school of Indian historians emphasizes differentiation among Indian historical actors rather than coherence, although certain members universalize (and essentialize) when they discuss the workings of capitalism and colonialism, and the allegedly bourgeois nature of the elite level of the Indian nationalist movement. The Subaltern historian Gyanendra Pandey differentiates when he argues that:

> A united front of the whole Indian people – landlords and peasants, mill owners and manual laborers, feudal princes and the tribal poor – in the anti-colonial campaign was scarcely feasible: no major struggle for change anywhere has ever achieved such unity.[30]

The subaltern historical school seeks to portray both the nationalist movement and the independent state it produced as possessing "dominance without hegemony." To the extent that neither the movement nor the state ever absorbed the many consciousnesses of subordinate and oppressed (or formerly oppressed) groups of Indians, consciousnesses that legitimately seek expression, hegemony is either absent or woefully incomplete.

This supposed failure of the postcolonial Indian state to become more fully legitimate is emphasized by two of the Subaltern historians (Pandey and Partha Chatterjee), as they deconstruct the version of nationalist history most associated with Nehru. To them, Nehruvian-nationalist history creates an "ideology of which the central organizing principle is the autonomy of the state," and the major legitimizing principles are certain conceptions "of social justice," of economically-grounded rationality, and of political correctness. This is not the colonial state, but the national state that embraces "the whole people" and is based "on a consciousness of national solidarity which includes, in an active political process, the vast mass of the peasantry."[31] While the great state structures of the Indian past, including those of Ashoka and Akbar, were not national states in precisely this same sense, Nehruvian-nationalist history allegedly portrays them as trying to realize an ideal and dream found in India since ancient times. This was what Nehru himself, writing about Akbar, called "the old Indian ideal of a synthesis of differing elements and their fusion into a common nationality."[32] The idea of the essential nationhood of India, supposedly established at the beginning of Indian history, "was actualized, in this particular reading, by the exertions of India's – one should say, north India's – great rulers . . . and apparently by their exertions alone."

Such placement of Indian states at the center of a historical narrative, a practice borrowed from colonialist histories, was allegedly part of a larger effort by nationalist thinkers of the 1920s and later. Their objective was to oppose communalism (as well as colonialism). By reconstructing India's history in a certain fashion, nationalism and communalism were shown to be binary opposites of each other. That fashion was to show that India's synthesizing capacities, which had helped to create (and periodically recreate) Indian civilization, had promoted more than just the establishment of a civilization which was fundamentally tolerant and cohesive. India had long ago become a proto-nation, with a dream of unity actualized by the major states or empires, and an "almost automatic commitment of India's inhabitants – older and newer, 'Aryan' and Scythian and Afghan – to the soil of this land, to the Indian state and indeed to the Indian 'nation' in centuries past . . ." The nation, viewed by the Nehruvian-nationalists as an almost metaphysical being, had been essentially secular, since loyalty to it supposedly overrode "any loyalty to religion, caste, or race."

The NCERT historians, by rejecting the proto-nation conception of India and replacing it with a mode of production and "nation-in-the-making" interpretation of Indian historical development, escape one of the criticisms that the proto-nation idea is bound to attract, e.g., that it claims the existence of some metaphysical, unprovable Indian "essence." But, the NCERT conception of an Indian nation being "made" is itself critiqued, indirectly, by at least one of the Subalterns. According to Gyan Pandey, it is essentialist to argue that supposedly "communalist" – groups of people act fundamentally because of economic "class" grievances, which may find expression in the guise of communalism. Such an approach assumes a "universal bourgeois rationality – the pursuit of the economic self-interest of the individual above all else – as the explanation of all strife in Indian society." By extension, he would not subscribe to a theory of nation-building in which only groups of people who accurately perceive their economic class interests become unified by a common struggle against the colonial negation of those interests.

Moreover, from the Subaltern vantage point, both the proto-nation and "nation-in-the-making" constructions of the Indian past can be criticized for promoting a "statist perspective" in which the state of the future, as was done by the states of the past, supposedly establishes "order out of chaos," and reduces "the religious and other passions of Indians to 'civilized' proportions." The state does so, as an autonomous entity, outside and above the society it leads and regulates, as it carries India into "modernity." Like many historians, the NCERT group could be accused by Pandey of betraying "a deep-rooted faith in the primacy of the elite in determining the character of all political articulation and the course of all political change."[33]

Criticism of yet another kind is registered by the Subaltern historian Ranajit Guha (although he too does not specifically mention the NCERT texts), when (in an important article) he decries the acceptance by Indian nationalists of the "rationalist, evolutionist and progressivist ideas which had helped to assimilate colonialist historiography to the post-Enlightenment view of world and time."[34] Such acceptance ushered these ideas into Indian historical thinking and placed Indian historiography within the same post-Enlightenment metanarrative framework occupied by the colonialists. Even nationalist objections to British colonialism in India produced no break from that framework, a framework which (in Guha's view) attempts to justify the takeover of India by an indigenous bourgeoisie and its postcolonial state-structure.

Similarly, Gyan Pandey criticized history, whether devised by Indian nationalists or others, which represents "liberal (developmentalist?) opinion" or searches for the bourgeois rationality of the elite and the irrationality of the masses. He recognizes that the discourse of nationalism generally (whether in India or elsewhere) is "part of the post-Enlightenment discourse of modernity, of progress, of human capability" and that "nationalism must speak in the language of rationality, of the equality of all individuals and of 'construction.'" But he considers defective those histories which privilege those universalistic forms of nationalist discourse over other forms that might be called communalist.

One of the defects Pandey sees is that such discourses consign other nationalist language to the realm of all that is backward, irrational, and pre- or antimodern, rather than recognize it as the language of legitimately alternative forms of communitarian consciousness. Another is that the modernist nationalist discourses justify the presence of a post-colonial state-structure that (like the colonial state before it) claims neutrality amidst sectarian strife, and encourages the "naively optimistic" view that the unaligned autonomous state "could not, in its own interests, tolerate the more serious outrages that [have] accompanied sectarian strife." Such a view of the state, he indicates, has come to be challenged "in the wake of the . . . massacre of Sikhs in Delhi in 1984 [and] the Hindu–Muslim riots in Bhiwandi and Bombay, Meerut and Moradabad . . . in all of which the coercive arm of the state played an infamous role."[35]

But Pandey is not sympathetic either to the kind of history favored by Hindu nationalist organizations, such as the BJP. It too totalizes, by claiming the "natural unity of Hindus, of the Hindu community ('race', 'people,' 'nation,' are other terms that have sometimes been used), of Hindu tradition . . ." The militant Hindu construction of Indian history argues for an immanent Indian proto-nation, present from antiquity onward. The ancient Indian kings were inspired by the goal of uniting all Hindus, and Hindus incessantly battled for liberation from alien (Muslim and then British) rule "for a thousand years before 1947." Underlying such history is the proposition that "the Hindu nation" based on a mystical Hindu unity has always existed, as has a "fundamental, automatic, unquestioned (and unquestionable?) commitment to its preservation."

It is clear from Pandey's writing that militant Hindu history has its conventions or devices, as does any history employed to establish and legitimate a group identity (including Nehruvian or NCERT history). If positing a mystical, proto-nationhood is one of them, appropriation of competing streams or axes of nationalist thought and activity is another. Sometimes a proposition is offered, notes Pandey, that

> *all* social and political activities of the 19th and 20th centuries in which Hindus took part were geared to the task of re-establishing the Hindu nation in its superior and glorious splendour. Any political leader and reformer . . . who happens to have been a Hindu may be appropriated to the history of Hindu nationalism, including at times (albeit with some bitterness) Mahatma Gandhi and Jawaharlal Nehru.

Appropriated too, are Indian thinkers and publicists of the nineteenth century who are presented as modern founders of the Hindu national-ist movement "before the idea had gained the fixity of a popular prejudice that nations and nation-states are the only appropriate – the 'natural' – form of the political existence of peoples." Another device to which Pandey alludes is "suppression of history, even as history is paraded" as a "witness."[36]

In sum, Pandey and other Subalterns present a critique of forms of history that commit certain alleged sins. Their main target has been any mainstream Indian nationalist history centered on the Congress Party, Mahatma Gandhi, Jawaharlal Nehru, and the Indian "bourgeoisie." But militant Hindu historians are shown to commit many (if not all) of the same sins and can be critically deconstructed too.

Unlike the more extreme postmodernists, the Subalterns are not nec-essarily claiming that no historical convention can convey anything approaching historical "truth." The papers in the earlier volumes of the *Subaltern Studies* series were concerned with the "truth knowledge of the subaltern," although later papers became more concerned with analyz-ing ways in which the past has been represented.[37] But the major claim of the Subaltern group is that mainstream Indian history, with its many sins, does not represent historical truth, and that history is being misused when it attempts to legitimate a state possessing dominance but not hegemony.

Judgments on the "truth" of mainstream history versus Subaltern history, and on the quality of the representations of the past that each school provides, lie beyond the scope of this present and necessarily brief discussion. But a key question can be addressed, a question arising out of "Subaltern" studies and out of viewing the NCERT textbooks within the critical context that the Subalterns create. It is the philo-sophically pragmatic question of whether the uses to which the Indian mainstream conventions are put are as sinful as the Subalterns claim, or are merely conventions deserving of a less negative and more com-plex evaluation.

Conventions and conclusions

The conventions that structure efforts to accomplish what the political scientist Sudipta Kaviraj calls "narrativizing the nation" are not con-fined to histories and history textbooks. They are found wherever nationalism takes the form of story-telling, for example within jour-nalism, the writing of novels, or the making of films. In the preceding pages a number of these conventions have already been mentioned or made the subject of allusions, while discussing the Chandra book and the Subaltern disagreement with the Nehruvian, NCERT, and Hindu nationalist forms of history. To list them is to be made mindful of their general pervasiveness and tenacity.[38]

Some of them are: using the nation-state as the telos of a narrative; focusing upon those events and other historical elements having effects that promote the creation of the nation-state; differentiating "self" from "other"; constructing a cohesive "object" that becomes the nation-state or is primarily responsible for building it; and identifying the historical "moment" when the object becomes a "subject" capable of self-recognition and self-direction. One overarching convention is combining the foregoing elements, their causative relationships, and any fortuitous or accidental events or factors, into a central storyline or "axis," that is kept separate from any competing axis.

Two other practices have been described as a pair of alternative conventions. They are: arguing for the existence of a synthesizing immanent proto-nation, extant since ancient times, eternally striving for liberation and self-expression; or describing the path of a "nation-in-the-making" that is still not "made" at the moment of independence, but which comes into possession of a state around which further nation-building shall take place.

Closely associated with the "immanent proto-nation" convention and religious-nationalist forms of history, but likely to be used in connection with the nation-in-the-making convention, is still another practice. It is the claiming of historical, cultural, and even philosophical authenticity for the nation-state by linking it with past periods, activities, and systems of thought, rather than admitting that the nation-state is in most ways new, artificial, and experimental. Furthermore, historical narratives conventionally claim that the nation-state constitutes an emotionally constructed community, entitled to the same intensity of personal loyalty that older primordial communities received.

There are also conventions or rules for the ways in which subnational groups are to be treated and judged when they stand outside the main axis of the narrative. They can be "appropriated," despite the violence this does to their historical characteristics and despite the repression of historical evidence that is required. Their consciousnesses and interests can be considered secondary to other national priorities, but likely to be addressed by the nation-state after sovereignty is achieved. Their consciousnesses and interests can even be delegitimized by being described as regressive, premodern, or antimodern, or expressions of some immature form of nationalism. Another delegitimizing device is to consign the outlook of a group to the realm of "false consciousness" by claiming that its outlook is contrary to its members' true economic and other interests.

Certain conventions treat the creation of the nation-state as inevitable. One portrays the nation as the outcome of a linear historical process like "modernization," or the rise of capitalism. Another claims that the "modern" independent state is the only type of political organization capable of protecting the economic and other interests of a "modern" capitalist or socialist nation against foreign threats.

Finally, some conventions help impart an aura of sacredness to the nation-state. One does so by associating nation and/or state with values such as secularism, popular sovereignty, social justice, and scientific progress. Another sacralizes the national history itself by linking it to worldwide, eighteenth- and post-eighteenth-century, grand historical narratives of universal change. These are what postmodernists call metanarratives of (among other things) rationality, science, capitalism, technology, mass politics, and modernization, as well as enlightenment, rationality, development, progress, and liberation.

Whether or not the use that is made of each of these conventions by NCERT and other histories constitutes a historiographical sin depends largely upon the observer's evaluation of both the future nation-state and its legitimizing historical narratives. Much that is contained in the NCERT type of national narrative is likely to be assessed negatively if one accepts a certain Subaltern historian's vision of the nation-state as "a purely practical arrangement unadorned by passions or sentiments of nobility."[39] Such a view reflects another claim made at least implicitly by postmodernists – that the nation-state is a dangerous concentration of technologically and administratively directed power. As such, the nation-state is something worth limiting and containing by appropriate measures, including a process of desanctification by critical intellectuals. A more variegated approach leads to other conclusions about nation-states and legitimating narratives. For the sake of argument and exploration, let us assume that the most dangerous type of nation-state is one that glorifies and mythologizes its cultural authenticity, demands the highest levels of emotional commitment from its citizens, refuses to tolerate forms of consciousness that constitute alternatives to nationalism, exploits science, social science, and technology for the purposes of enhancing state power, and promotes an ideology based on metanarrative and pseudo-science. This kind of nation-state uses history to help constitute a "civil religion." That "civil religion" may be something separate from a conventional religion, or may be inclusive of it.

According to the definition given by the Israeli social scientists Charles Liebman and Eliezer Don-Yehiya, a "civil religion" contains the most "holy and sacred" elements in a political culture. Like a religion it projects a system of meanings denoted with symbols and rituals, but the core object of veneration in a civil religion is a "corporate entity" such as a nation and/or state. Although a civil religion may not necessarily transform its followers into a sect or cult, it does give its adherents the sense that they are a moral community. A civil religion favors the existing distribution of power among classes and other groups, since its ultimate objective "is the sanctification of the society in which it functions." It legitimates the social and political order by imparting a sense of the justness and rightness of things, but a civil religion also mobilizes "the efforts and energies" of individuals and groups "on behalf of socially approved tasks and responsibilities."[40]

A civil religion may perhaps be distinguished from a societal myth, the latter being less inclusive and less sacred. Human societies, including nation-states, do need to use history as a form of mythology. In the view of the American historian William McNeill, myths are tales told in such a way as to make "general statements about the world" and its human groups; statements which "are believed to be true." Such statements are often acted upon whenever circumstances suggest a common societal response. With its historical mythology, a people possesses a repertoire of "agreed upon statements," relevant to particular situations, and made acceptable "in advance through education" and other forms of socialization and acculturation.[41] Liebman and Don-Yehiya add that a civil and historical myth "is a story that evokes strong sentiments, and transmits and reinforces basic societal values."[42]

Which of the narrative conventions of nation-state histories can be confined by intellectual oversight to the service of the nation-state's mythology, without necessarily fostering a civil religion? Certainly, the convention of the teleological narrative is needed for both a civil religion and a national myth, as is the convention or practice of writing "effective" history, i.e., history biased by knowledge of one or more later effects, one such effect being the ultimate appearance or production of a nation-state.[43] Both mythology and civil religion also require differentiation of the national "self" from the "other," identifying the historical object which becomes or builds the nation and state, and singling out the historical moment when that object becomes a self-directed "subject." All told, a historical myth, like a civil religion, does need to have all of these practices combined so as to help formulate a central narrative axis.

Yet, the central axis of a myth can, more easily than that of a civil religion, accommodate the idea (which this writer has drawn obliquely from the philosopher Richard Rorty) that the nation-state will probably always remain an incomplete and therefore imperfect "telos."[44] The perfect nation-state can be treated as an ideal and dream, while the nation-state of the present remains a non-utopian entity and condition that civic effort by many social groups can (at least) construct and reconstruct, sustain and improve.

A civil religion is more likely to rely upon the practice of arguing for the existence of the mystical proto-nation, rather than rely on the "nation-in-the-making" convention. A civil religion is sure to claim historical, cultural, and even philosophical authenticity for the nation-state dating back to ancient times, rather than acknowledge the new, artificial, and experimental character that the nation-state may have. Both myth and civil religion can claim that the nation-state constitutes an emotionally constructed community, although it is the civil religion that is more prone to demand that the nation-state be entitled to the same intensity of personal loyalty once granted to older primordial communities.

Where the national myth and civil religion may diverge sharply is in their use of historical conventions that deal with subnational troupes and their consciousnesses. A myth can acknowledge that there are competing narratives, with their own axes, without attempting to appropriate those narratives in some crude fashion. A national mythology which places less emphasis on sacredness than does a civil religion may well treat the consciousnesses and interests of inconvenient subnational groups as being secondary to other national priorities, but it will more readily (than a civil religion) allow the nation-state to address their concerns after national sovereignty is achieved. A myth kept separate from any post-eighteenth-century metanarrative need not delegitimize subnational consciousnesses and interests by calling them regressive, unmodern, or expressions of immaturity. Nor need it equate the outlook of a group with "false consciousness."

Especially if a national myth does not rely on such metanarratives for legitimation, it need not regard the emergence of the nation-state as being inevitable because of modernization or the development of capitalism. It can place greater emphasis on accident and chance in history and less emphasis on causation. But on purely functional grounds, a national myth can properly draw on the historical practice of claiming that only the "modern" state can protect the interests of a nation against foreign and domestic adversaries.

In the end, it is difficult to conceive of a national myth that does not impart some degree of sacredness to the nation-state. But it can do so by associating nation and/or state with values, while not linking those values, or the national history, to metanarratives. Those values for which a nationalist movement fought, and about which the movement achieved some degree of genuine (rather than elite-imposed) consensus among its component classes and groups, themselves constitute a sufficient source of legitimation.

Even postmodernist thinking allows for the idea that "first-order narratives", i.e., those which are not universalized, do constitute legitimate forms of knowledge in themselves.[45] If so, they can properly be used for sociopolitical purposes like the legitimation of the nation-state. Without abandoning reasonable standards of historical truth, "first-order" national narratives can legitimately serve as myths. These are myths not in the sense of fiction but in the sense of structures of explanation and meaning. It is the scholarly content of those myths, and their use of certain narrative conventions but not others, that should ultimately determine whether intellectuals and others condemn, accept, or praise their use by agencies of the nation-state.

Notes

1   The quotation is from P.L. Malhotra, "Foreword" to Arjun and Indira Dev, *Modern India* (New Delhi: NCERT, 1989).
2   Autonomy in principle, and government appointment of the Director, were mentioned during an interview with Prof. Arjun Dev, NCERT official and historian, New Delhi, Dec. 26, 1989. The eminent historian Sarvepalli Gopal, who headed one of the editorial committees for the NCERT history books, has argued that the government cannot dictate the research done by the NCERT; see Parvathi Menon, "Credibility Crisis," *Frontline* 9:3 (Feb. 1–14, 1992): 93. One source that describes the NCERT as having been (at least between 1961 and 1976) "the academic wing of the Ministry of Education" is John Kurrien, *Development and Decolonization of the Social Studies in India: a Historical Delineation and Analysis of Textbooks with Special Reference to the Bombay Presidency and Maharastra* (Doctoral dissertation, University of Wisconsin-Madison, 1976), 103.
3   Sarvepalli Gopal, "History and Politicians, BJP Attack on the History Congress," *Frontline* 8:26 (Dec. 21, 1991–Jan. 3, 1992): 91; and telephone conversation with Prof. Arjun Dev, New York to Delhi, Dec. 16, 1992.
4   Information on the use of the NCERT books in private schools and as examination review books is from an interview with the then NCERT Director, P.L. Malhotra, New Delhi, Dec. 26, 1989. The quotation is from Kurrien,

Development and Decolonization, 299. For information on the public contro-versies involving NCERT history books, see Lloyd and Suzanne Hoeber Rudolph, "Rethinking Secularism: Genesis and Implications of the Textbook Controversy, 1977–79," in Lloyd Rudolph, ed., *Cultural Policy in India* (Delhi: Chankya Publications, 1984), 13–36, and *Frontline* (Feb. 1–14, 1992): 93–5.

5   The consensual nature of the NCERT books is from an interview with an NCERT official and historian, Prof. D.N. Panigrahi, New Delhi, Feb. 2, 1990; an interview with Prof. Romila Thapar, New Delhi, Feb. 21, 1990, and partly confirmed by Prof. Bipan Chandra, interview, New Delhi, Feb. 15, 1990.

6   One leading expert on the Indian educational scene, Prof. Krishna Kumar of Delhi University, views NCERT history as state-sponsored history in his article, "Secularism: its Politics and Ideology," *Economic and Political Weekly* (Nov. 4–11, 1989): 2475. But, "semi-official" seems the more accurate des-ignation, since the NCERT is not unambiguously an arm of the Indian gov-ernment, and since interviews with four of the authors of its high-school textbooks (Romila Thapar, R.S. Sharma, Arjun Dev, and Bipan Chandra) strongly suggest that they wrote what they believed, subject to some edito-rial review, rather than anything forced on them by government action.

7   *New York Times*, Jan. 24, 1993, and see N.K. Singh, "Madhya Pradesh, Inject-ing Propaganda," *India Today* (Aug. 15, 1992): 76–7.

8   Malhotra and Dev interviews, New Delhi, Dec. 26, 1989 and interview with Arjun Dev, New Delhi, Jan. 23, 1990. I have taken the term "postnational-ist" history from Gyan Prakash, "Writing Post-Orientalist Histories of the Third World: Perspectives from Indian Historiography," *Comparative Studies in Society and History* 32:2 (April 1990): 394–8, and some of my conception of it from Ann Norton, "Ruling Memory" (Paper presented at Annual Meeting, American Political Science Association, Washington DC, Aug. 28, 1991). Her paper equates what Prakash and I are calling postnationalist his-tories with the "Subaltern" histories, of the kind found in Ranajit Guha and Gayatri Spivak, eds., *Selected Subaltern Studies* (New York: Oxford University Press, 1988). But the NCERT version of Indian history is postcolonial and postnationalist without being "subaltern."

9   Romila Thapar, "Communalism and the Writing of Ancient Indian History," in R. Thapar, H. Mukhia, and B. Chandra, *Communalism and the Writing of Indian History* (New Delhi: Peoples Publishing House, Second Edition, 1977), 5–6.

10   Arjun Dev interview, New Delhi, Jan. 23, 1990.

11   Quotations and material from Bipan Chandra, "Historians of Modern India and Communalism," in Thapar et al., *Communalism*, 45, 47–51.

12   See Romila Thapar, "Communalism," 4–10.

13   Bipan Chandra, "Historians," 50.

14   Ibid., 47.

15   Bipan Chandra interview, New Delhi, Feb. 15, 1990.

16   The "left nationalist" characterization is borrowed from the historian Partha Chatterjee, interview, New York, May 28, 1990, although he seems to have used the term in a broader sense than is given here. Apparently, he would include an older generation of Marxists (e.g., A.R. Desai) in the "left-nationalist" camp also.

17   The "liberal" label comes from interviews with the historians D.N. Panigrahi

(New Delhi, Feb. 2, 1990), and Sumit Sarkar (New Delhi, Feb. 26, 1990). The characterizations of Prof. Romila Thapar and R.S. Sharma is based on interviews with them (Tharpar – New Delhi, Feb. 21, 28, 1990) and (Sharma – Patna, March 5, 1990).

18 R.S. Sharma, *Ancient India* (New Delhi: NCERT, 1990), 202.

19 These points are drawn from the NCERT books other than Bipan Chandra's.

20 Bipan Chandra, "Karl Marx, His Theories of Asian Societies, and Colonial Rule," *Review* 5:1 (Summer 1981): 80. A longer version of this article appears in *Sociological Theories: Race and Colonialism* (UNESCO, 1980).

21 Bipan Chandra, *Indian National Movement, the Long Term Dynamics* (New Delhi: Vikas Publishing House, 1988), 3, and Bipan Chandra interview, New Delhi, Feb. 15, 1990.

22 Chandra, *National Movement*, 3, 22–3, 29.

23 Ibid., 73, and see 68–73, 54–7.

24 Ibid., 4–5, 73, 69, and see 68–90.

25 The term "false consciousness," used in this context, is from Chandra interview, Feb. 15, 1990 and from Bipan Chandra, *Communalism in Modern India* (New Delhi: Vikas, 1987) (2nd edn), pp. 18–33.

26 Bipan Chandra, *Modern India* (New Delhi: NCERT, 1990), 7, 28.

27 The conception of "the narrative" used here is based on J. Hillis Miller's chapter on "Narrative" in F. Lentricchia and T. McLaughlin, eds., *Critical Terms of Literary Study* (Chicago: University of Chicago Press, 1990), 66–79.

28 Chandra, *Modern India*, 168–9. See also Arjun and Indira Dev, *Modern India* (New Delhi: NCERT, 1969), 162–4, 170, 172–5, 179–80.

29 Resolution of Karachi Congress session of the 1930s; see Chandra, 254.

30 Gyanendra Pandey, "Peasant Revolt and Indian Nationalism," in Guha and Spivak, *Selected Subaltern Studies*, 277.

31 Partha Chatterjee, *Nationalist Thought and the Colonial World: a Derivative Discourse?* (London: Zed Books for the United Nations University, 1986), 132, 146.

32 *Discovery of India* (1961 edn.), see 63, 147; quotation from Gyanendra Pandey, *The Construction of Communalism in Colonial North India* (Delhi: Oxford University Press, 1992), 249.

33 Pandey, *Communalism*, 250, 247, 20–1, 253, 20.

34 Ranajit Guha, "Dominance Without Hegemony and Its Historiography," *Subaltern Studies VI, Writings on South Asian Society and History* (Delhi: Oxford University Press, 1989), 308.

35 Pandey, *Communalism*, 16–20, 209.

36 Gyanendra Pandey, "Hindus and Others: the Militant Hindu Construction," *Economic and Political Weekly* (Dec. 28, 1991): 2997–3000.

37 Jim Masselos, "The Dis/appearance of Subalterns: a Reading of A Decade of Subaltern Studies," *South Asia* 15:1 (1992), 113.

38 The claim that the practices listed above are conventions of national narratives generally, and not just artifacts of the Chandra book, comes partly from comparing Chandra's *Modern India* with the appropriate portion of a textbook on American history – L.P. Todd and M. Curti, *Triumph of the American Nation* (Orlando, Fla.: Harcourt, Brace, Jovanovich, 1986), 2–302. I am indebted to another source for identifying some of the conventions on my list, particularly the one concerning the focusing of a historical narrative on

nation-creating effects, the one concerning the combining of elements into a central national-narrative axis, and the one emphasizing the newness of the nation-state and attempts to authenticate it by reference to past periods of history. See Sudipta Kaviraj, "The Imaginary Institution of India," in P. Chatterjee and G. Pandey, eds., *Subaltern Studies VII* (Delhi: Oxford University Press, 1992), 1–39. The phrase "narrativizing the nation" was used by Dr. Kaviraj as the title for an earlier unpublished draft of this article.

39   Dipesh Chakrabarty, "History as Critique and Critique(s) of History," *Economic and Political Weekly* (Sept. 14, 1992): 2166.

40   Charles Liebman and Eliezar Don-Yehiya, *Civil Religion in Israel* (Berkeley: University of California Press, 1983), ix, 4–12.

41   William H. McNeill, *Mythistory and Other Essays* (Chicago: University of Chicago Press, 1986), 23.

42   Liebman and Don-Yehiya, *Civil Religion*, 7.

43   The term "effective" history is from Kaviraj, "Imaginary Institution," 17–19, based on Hans-Georg Gadamer, *Truth and Method* (London: Sheed and Ward, 1975), 267–74.

44   See Rorty's *Heidegger and Others, Philosophical Papers* 2 (Cambridge: Cambridge University Press, 1991), 171–4.

45   The idea that "first-order" narratives may be legitimate in themselves is mentioned by Rorty, who takes the point from Jean-François Lyotard's, *Postmodern Condition*. See Rorty, *Heidegger and Others*, 166–8.

7
Hindutva – the Indian Secularists' Metaphor for Illness and Perversion

Shrinivas Tilak

Introduction

The purpose of this paper is to analyze the cognitive mechanism of metaphor as it is used by modern Indian advocates of secularism to denounce the religious/cultural/political ideal of *Hindutva* (Hinduness or Hindudom). In contemporary India the Vishwa Hindu Parishad (VHP), the Rashtriya Svayamsevak Sangha (RSS), and the Bharatiya Janata Party (BJP) are the major organizations that actively seek to promote and implement, respectively, the religious, cultural, and political programs enshrined in the ideal of *Hindutva*. The present inquiry will be restricted to the study of secular polemics controverting the espousal of *Hindutva* by the VHP and its sympathizers against the backdrop of the controversy over the birthplace of the Hindu God Rama at Ayodhya.

The concept of *Hindutva*, as it has come to mean today, cannot be found in the traditional Hindu scriptures. Essentially, it is a political and cultural concept based on certain key Hindu values and is of relatively recent origin. It began to be actively promoted in reaction to the tendentious reinterpretation of secularism by Indian intellectuals in post-independence India. The ideology of *Hindutva* promotes a plan of social analysis and a prescription for sustained action for revitalizing Hindu society and the nation along traditional lines. But, above all, it is a slashing attack on the alleged Hindu feebleness and timidity, and on the modern Hindus' deeply ingrained habit of seeking the sources of their ills within Hinduism, but their cures outside of it – more particularly in secularism.

The emergence of Muslim communalism at the beginning of the century contributed, in part, to its rise. The VHP was formally set up at the holy city of Prayaga (Allahabad) in North India in 1966 "to explain, protect, and to expand the eternal law (*sanatana dharma*)". It sought to bring about "unity by coordinating the various sects (*sampradayas*) and seeking to promote a common code of conduct for all Hindus." The VHP sought to provide a foundation on which the "whole edifice of Hindu cultural and social renaissance and religious awakening would stand" (Singh, 1993).

Illness as metaphor

In contemporary India, "Illness as metaphor" is a legitimate subject for reflection since it has become a favorite weapon in the armor of secular intellectuals' battles with the ideology of *Hindutva* in the post-Ayodhya context. As a basic figure of speech, metaphor works on an analogy, a similarity, or some other relation between two things. Metaphor consists in the transference to an object of an attribute or name that literally is not applicable to it, but which can be applied to it figuratively or by analogy (Kockelmans, 1987: xi). The human mind has a striking ability to advance its mental grasp on an interesting problem by the use of the metaphoric reasoning process. Meanings couched in metaphor can often be grasped faster than when only nonfigurative speech is used. In addition to being an inherently linguistic phenomenon, many social scientists today agree that metaphor is really the manifestation of a very fundamental *cognition* operation. In contemporary discussions of metaphor, therefore, concern has legitimately shifted from rhetoric to semantics; and from semantics to hermeneutics (Haskell, 1987: xii).

Metaphoric reasoning has been and continues to be an exciting and important overall strategy in traditional and modern Indian thought as well. Contemporary metaphorizing of a political ideal or disorder to an illness or a pathological condition is rooted in the classical metaphysical (Samkhya) and medical (Ayurveda) notions of balance. Illness and pathology originate in imbalance and refer not only to the sick body and soul, but also to the malaise of society. The *Carakasamhita*, the fundamental text of Ayurveda, commonly posits a close relationship between medicine and society and religion and philosophy. In the dominant concept of culpable insight (*prajnaparadha*), for instance, abnormal behavior patterns are understood as "illness" (Sarirasthana 2:40).

In the metaphor of illness the ill person acts as a social text through which moral corruption is made visible, rendering it an exemplum, an emblem of decay. Nothing is more punitive than giving a disease a meaning – that meaning being invariably a moralistic one. The disease itself, then, becomes a metaphor. Then, in the name of the disease (that is, using it as a metaphor) the horror of the disease is imposed on other things. The disease becomes adjectival. Something is said to be disease-like, meaning it is disgusting or ugly. Feelings about evil are projected onto a disease. The disease so enriched with meaning is projected onto the world (Sontag, 1978: 58).

Secularism in post-independence India

The *saeculum*, as Panikkar (1973) points out, is not simply the world and, certainly not the cosmos, but rather its temporal aspect: the *aion*, meaning life-span. The Sanskrit term *ayus* and its many compounds, including the Ayurveda, have the same meaning. Philosophically, *aion* expresses the specific manner of existence of beings – the great contro-versy being whether this "temporal manner of existence is proper being (Vedanta) or is only the sign of becoming (Buddhism). Secularization corresponds to the discovery of the positive, and at the same time real, character of time and temporal reality" (Panikkar, 1973: 10–11). The process of secularization is constitutively ambivalent, i.e. it has a double edge. For secularization ultimately implies a change, perceived in positive or negative terms, in fundamental human – that is religious – symbols.

In the current understanding of Indian secularists, religious symbols and traditions are true, good, or "healthy" only if they point beyond themselves to the secular ideal. Furthermore, they must contain, at least implicitly, the truth of secularism. In order to make the secular message in Indian religions explicit, they must be reconceived in terms of the fundamental principles of secularism. To understand religious traditions correctly, Indian intellectuals argue, they have to be seen as "secular" either explicitly or implicitly. This serves to make adherents of various traditions into either conscious or anonymous secularists. Whether we wish it or not, we are all herded in the direction of secularism.

The modern Indian secularist refuses to see religions in terms of their own self-characterization. Rather, religious traditions are accepted and reconceived from the vantage point of a "higher wisdom or experience of secularism." This makes Indians and their traditions into something they may not want themselves or their traditions to be. Secularists only grudgingly accept diversity of religious beliefs and practices. Diversity and pluralism are accepted not on their own terms, but only in terms of a reinterpretation favorable to secularism. Those who reject or resist this line of thinking (e.g. the VHP, RSS, and the BJP) are summarily branded as sick and perverted. A two-way process is discernible in the construction of the secular identity. The process involves idealizing on the one hand, and scapegoating and persecuting on the other. Tolerance, compassion, and social concern are idealized as the unique secular values. Those who oppose the secular ideal are the "arch" tyrants, Nazis, and Fascists.

This view of secularism by intellectuals in India may be traced to the fact that it was introduced there in the reverse order from the way in which the secular ideal developed in the West: in India, the implementation came first and then, gradually, the rationalization. Lawyers trained in the British and American legal traditions grafted the secular ideal onto the Indian constitution first. They did not define it formally, but simply appended to the preamble of the Constitution the basic outlines and principles of the secular ideal. They visualized in the newly written Constitution of India the source of the sacred, and hoped that the emerging secular religion would invoke commitment from the Indian nation. Theorization and apologetics by intellectuals on its behalf began in earnest much later. While they enthusiastically upheld the idea of freedom *from* religion, modern Indian secularists conveniently forgot the positive implication of secularism – the freedom to *be* religious, and in each person's own unique way, and that its concrete application can only come within the situation of religious pluralism (Arapura, 1987).

Hindutva as illness and perversion

"Hindutva as illness and perversion" was still a rather abstract notion during the pre-independence days, but by 1960 it had acquired a concrete form. In the secularist polemics, *Hindutva* became a defect, a deformity, and an illness – an affliction which cannot be escaped. In post-Ayodhya India, *Hindutva* has not only become a negative phenomenon but now it also implies that there are processes of degeneration inherent in the Hindu religion itself. The longstanding tactic of using "illness" to denote certain features of Hinduism as irregular and dangerous became even more fashionable when India was formally declared a secular state in 1977. In post-Ayodhya India the metaphorization of the ideology of *Hindutva* as an illness and perversion has made it possible to impute guilt on, and to prescribe severe punishment of, the advocates of *Hindutva*. There is an element of truth in some of this, but secularists assert more than they analyze and are often more jarring than convincing.

Instead of analyzing *Hindutva* in terms of an overall ideology and a concept, Indian secularists have transformed it into an elaborate metaphor of illness and alienation. Pseudo-secularism has become the criterion and basis of social criticism that increasingly uses *Hindutva* as a metaphor of perversion. The irrational fear of *Hindutva* is a major motif in modern Indian secularist idiom and ideology. Secularist dia-tribes usually conjure up secret *Hindutva* forces and the alleged Hindu attempts to control the destiny of India. For the secularists, however, it does not seem contradictory to claim the *Hindutva's* alleged superior strength and secret power over secular India emanates from a diseased and depraved religion of the Hindus. Then, from considering them depraved, it is not too difficult to reach the conclusion that the forces of *Hindutva* are the enemies of secular India (see Yelchuri, 1993).

From the beginning of the Ayodhya problem, English national news-papers and secularists in India have made it their habit to turn against Hindus and *Hindutva*. These days, scarcely a week passes without a new article appearing on the editorial pages of prestigious English-language dailies such as the *Times of India* denouncing "the virus" of *Hindutva* in a fit of medical and political metaphorizing. The analogy between disease, civil disorder, and Hindu ideology is promoted to coerce bureaucrats and rulers in New Delhi to pursue a more rational and, therefore, secular policy.

Recently, one intellectual produced a list of seven ills and curses of Hinduism, thereby giving the impression to the reader that this is a "rotten to the core" religion (Rao, 1993). Furthermore, being pro-Hindu becomes synonymous with being anti-Muslim. The fundamental tenet of the ideology of *Hindutva* becomes its alleged anti-Muslim thrust. The only explanation of this kind of instinctive assessment is the deep-rooted suspicion, bordering on allergy, on the part of these writers and other "secularists," of an ideology and movement seeking Hindu consolidation.

Hindutva and Hindu–Muslim relations

The alleged negative impact of the *Hindutva* movement on the Hindu–Muslim relationship is yet another occasion for metaphorizing *Hindutva* as illness. Indian intellectuals of the secular breed do not make any attempt to study and to understand the quite legitimate aspirations of the *Hindutva* forces – the urge to unite, strengthen, and reform Hindu society (the stated goal of the VHP, for instance). The typical secularist assessment of the Ayodhya episode is along the following lines: India is going through a second partition, this time around it is the partition of the mind. The blame is usually laid squarely at the door of Hindus advocating *Hindutva* (Chopra, 1993). But the same secularist intellectuals suddenly turn "diplomatic" in apportioning responsibility for the partition of India (whether the first or the alleged second) to Muslim Indians. Russell (1983) has denounced such a tendency as only a polite way of being "less than completely honest."

> Many writers of South Asian Islam know – and, because it is very important, should therefore *say* – that the viewpoint of nearly all Muslim thinkers about the position of Muslims in the subcontinent over the past three centuries has been that of Islamic chauvinism, which assumes that Muslims once occupied a privileged position among the inhabitants of the subcontinent, that they ought not to have lost it, and that they should do whatever historical circumstances allow them to do to regain it. That is a fact, and a very important fact, and whether you approve, disapprove, or are indifferent to it, it is impermissible not to state it as a fact.
>
> True, no responsible intellectual would advocate giving offence unnecessarily or stating honest conclusions in deliberately offensive language, but neither should one forget that if an offence comes out of the truth, better is it that the offence come than that the truth be concealed.

Unfortunately, modern Indian secularists (Hindu and Muslim) have ignored Russell's admonition to be honest. Sen (1993), for instance, brazenly declares that the BJP wants to rewrite the Constitution. The leading lights of the BJP, according to him, have framed a new statute which bears an uncanny resemblance to concepts of the German National Socialism which enabled Adolph Hitler to be voted to power in 1933.

Sen's analogy is patently fallacious. The fact is that the BJP has not called for the abrogation of the extant constitution and a return to the ancient Hindu code. Furthermore, the BJP has Muslims in higher party posts. Sikandar Bakht, for instance, is a Vice-president, and Arif M. Khan, a former high-profile minister in the Congress Party, is reportedly considering joining the BJP (*The Tribune*, Feb. 3, 1993). The Nazis did not have even token Jews in party posts. The Marxists, who often disguise themselves as secularists in India, hardly carry conviction as

proponents of religious pluralism and democracy. One need not, therefore, single out the BJP. It did not invent the Hindu upsurge. *Hindutva*
is, to use the secularists' own favorite metaphor, a symptom of the delib-
erate imposition and false interpretation of secularism, not the sickness
itself.

The rise of Hindu militancy and the *Hindutva* forces in modern India,
if not properly guided, can become troublesome indeed. But modern
Indian secularists wrongly posit the problem in India in terms of
Hindu–Muslim antagonism, pure and simple. In fact, it is an argument
between secularists and devout Hindus over the meaning and interpretation of secularism. The Muslims are far too few to prevent India
becoming a Hindu theocracy, if it so chooses. The main critics of Hindu
militancy and *Hindutva* are secular Hindus, not Muslims (*The Economist*,
1993).

Hindutva is not a form of fundamentalism aiming to take India back
to the Middle Ages as is ceaselessly argued by the secularists. Historically, a fundamentally Hindu India would have to be a pretty tolerant
one (*The Economist*, 1993). The long-term history of India shows considerable resistance to communal abuse. The main aim of the BJP seems
to be to transform Hinduism from an amorphous collection of quarrel-
some groups into an organized society fit for the twenty-first century –
a unified Hinduism as such has not before existed. The BJP, therefore,
cannot be promoting *Hindutva* to usher in a Hindu theocracy, which
makes no sense for a decentralized faith such as Hinduism which lacks
a centralized authority and hierarchy. The goal of the influential ideologues of *Hindutva* – Savarkar and Golvalkar – has always been cultural
unity rather than religious purity. They argue that Muslim Indians,
like their counterparts in Indonesia, should embrace the dominant
culture of India. In Indonesia, for instance, Rama is still embraced as an
intrinsic part of the culture (*The Economist*, 1993).

The courts in India seem to interpret the ideal of secularism and the
rationale of *Hindutva* in a novel and nonpathological manner. In 1993
the Allahabad High Court, for instance, delivered a detailed judgment
on allowing prayers and *darshan* at the makeshift temple of Lord Rama
in Ayodhya. In the process it also gave a novel method for the interpretation of secularism in India. The High Court (Lucknow bench)
judges, Mr. N.H. Tilhari and Mr. A.N. Gupta, opined that an image or
an illustration is as valid a source of meaning and interpretation as a
text. They drew strength from the fact that the original Constitution
also includes the sketches of such Hindu gods as Rama, Shiva, and
Krishna drawn by the well-known artist Nandalal Bose. They noted that

portraits of Akbar, Shivaji, Govind Singh, and Gandhi are also to be found in the original Constitution adopted by the Constituent Assembly on November 26, 1949 (Bhatnagar, 1993; Irani, 1993).

By virtue of the sketch of Lord Rama in the original Constitution, adopted over 43 years previously, the learned judges argued that Rama became a "constitutional entity and admittedly, a reality of our national culture and fabric and not a myth."

Interpreting the Constituent Assembly's decision to include the sketches and illustrations depicting different periods of the national history in the Constitution, the high court said the founding fathers of the Constitution themselves chose to give a secular Constitution on the basis of such sketches and illustrations. The judges thus rejected the western concept of secularism and upheld the genuinely Indian understanding of secularism (*panthanirpeksha*).

Concluding remarks

One positive and salutary outcome of the Ayodhya controversy has been that it has exposed the fundamental flaw and weakness of the secular ideal in India.

If *Hindutva* is something with a universal value and is not merely tied to a particular form of Hinduism, then it must be made relevant to the secular ideal in India. Conversely, the meaning and the relevance of secularism in India has to be re-forged periodically. If secularization, for better or for worse, must exist as a living reality in India, it has to come to grips with *Hindutva*. A meaningful dialogue and dialectic between these two ideologies is today necessary if "positive secularism" – i.e. equal respect for all religions (*sarvadharmasamabhava*) – is to become a reality in India. Such an exchange of ideas can also potentially prevent secularism in India from becoming anti-Hindu, and *Hindutva* from being misunderstood as anti-Muslim and/or fundamentalist.

Muslim Indians, on their part, too, must play an active role in the above dialectic between secularism and the forces of *Hindutva*. Javed Akhtar, a noted Urdu writer, made a similar point metaphorically at a national convention organized by the Aligarh Muslim University on "The Present Crisis: Challenges to Constitutional Ethos and Psyche." Said Akhtar (1993):

> The life-breath of the ogre of Hindu communalism lies in the heart of the parrot of Muslim communalism. Kill the parrot and the ogre will die.

Traditional Quranic scholars in India have not yet responded to the theological challenge presented by and to the Muslim minority. Islam in India does not provide adequate sociopolitical guidance regarding Muslim behavior as a minority community toward the larger Hindu community (see Prithipaul, 1992). According to Abid Husain, a noted Muslim Indian intellectual, Muslims in India must strive to come to an understanding with the Hindu majority. One concrete step that the Muslims must take to ease the undercurrent of misunderstanding, mistrust, and antipathy is to make the Indian past – including the cultural life of the Hindus – their own, thereby "bringing themselves in harmony with the soul of India" (Millar, 1987). They must understand the acute feelings of a shared social and cultural loss felt by Hindus. Of course, Hindus must also do the same. All Indians must develop a rational attitude and response to history. Neither the Muslim nor the Hindu communities as a whole can be held responsible for the irrational and oppressive acts of their rulers in the past.

If understood properly and positively, secularism in India need not represent a danger to religion nor an impossible contradiction. Then, Indians would not have to sneer at the term "secularism." Since the general value orientation of Indian secularism is essentially religious, it also has to be a Hindu secularism informed by typical Muslim and Christian concerns. Only then can specific religious truths that are uniquely Hindu, Muslim, or Sikh be pursued separately within the confines of Indian secularism. The secret of religious pluralism and secularism in India lies in the overlapping and sharing of common basic values. What is needed is not so much the promotion of either secularism or *Hindutva* alone, but rather, an active dialogue between the two.

If the great majority of Indians think of themselves as Hindus as well as Indians, India must pursue Hindu ideals as well as Indian ones – if it is to pursue any ideals wholeheartedly, including secularism. To pursue its ideal of secularism constructively and without inner conflict, India will have to develop unique mechanisms compatible and consistent with its own culture and identity. A specific dilemma for post-Ayodhya India is how to insulate the secular process from communal tampering without offending Hindu sentiments by the very insulating mechanisms. Marking its boundary is not enough to protect and maintain the positive secular identity. For identity cannot be an achievement but is, rather, a process constantly threatened with rupture by forces from within and without. The proper way to ensure that the *Hindutva* movement does not tamper with the secular ideal or get into the hands of reckless desperadoes is to undertake serious and more scholarly and historically grounded studies. It would be suicidal for the Indian secularists to dismiss the evocation of the Hindu past on the yardstick of the currently fashionable and "in" postmodernist perspective which considers every past a social construction that is shaped by the concerns of the present. Many Indian social scientists, too, love to engage in the cultural devaluation of the past. They trivialize it by equating it with outmoded social and/or religious practices. Endeavors to draw on the past in looking for solutions to current problems are often ridiculed and resented. Any reference to the past itself is regarded as an expression of romantic nostalgia or reaction.

In the ideology of secularism, progress is linked up with modernity, education with verbal literacy, fashion with culture, and success with worldly wisdom. Everything from the past is reduced to an infantile attitude, people of the past become illiterate and uneducated, and their faith and devotion to their religion becomes their weakness. So arose the justification for the secular ideal and a change and reform to catch up with new values, new virtues, and new lifestyles based on modern science and technology. The past became a veritable obstacle for progress. Centuries of colonialism and foreign rule uprooted all links with the Hindu past.

Consequently, contemporary secular education has no connection with the values of Hindu life. Achievement today is linked with success. Consumption of sulphuric acid industrially and electricity domestically, for instance, have become indices for civilization. Not surprisingly, intellectuals, leaders, and writers are honored for promoting secularism.

Modernity, which today has become synonymous with progress, has virtually come to the conclusion that the present-day achievements are of a nature not achievable in the past. This vanity dubs all oral, religious, and ritual tradition of India as unrealistic, unreliable, irrational and illogical. This leads to denying all credibility to this ancient civilization. The Hindu tradition, religion, culture, and literature today are victims of the modern ego.

Yet, even radical movements habitually draw strength and sustenance from the myth or memory of a golden age in the distant past. At a more individual level, this observation is reinforced by the psychoanalytical insight that loving memories originating in the past constitute a valuable psychological resource and strength in one's mature years. The belief or the hypothesis that in some ways the past may have something meaningful to contribute to the resolution of current problems by no means rests on a sentimental illusion (Hill, 1961). Lasch (1978) too has observed that a denial of the past superficially couched in "progressive" rhetoric may, on closer analysis, turn out to embody the despair of a generation that cannot face the future.

If the test of the hardiness and vitality of any cultural and religious tradition is its capacity to draw on the resources of its own symbol system to meet the challenge of new circumstances, then one way to examine the usefulness of the composite Indian religious tradition as a basis for the proper evaluation of secularism is to explore how that very tradition drew upon its resources in similar circumstances in the past in order to understand religious pluralism and secularism. The *Hindutva* movement, therefore, need not be construed as a nostalgic dip into a vanished past but rather as a tryst with the past that will realign it with India's present and future concerns vividly and imaginatively.

We must endeavor to understand how human creativity and potential was expressed through religion, philosophy, and social sciences in the past. We have to get rid of our arrogance that secularism alone knows the transmission of knowledge, creativity, and art. Hindu tradition, which transmitted knowledge with patience, gentility, dignity, and precision – be it education, dance, music, or spirituality – from generation to generation, must have a say in defining and formulating secularism as a policy for modern India.

Teams of independent scholars should, accordingly, focus on the recovery and reinterpretation of the relevant material from those Buddhist, Jain, Hindu, Sikh, and Muslim texts which may help enhance our understanding of the meaning and significance of secularism. In India's religious and spiritual heritage there is a wide range of attitudes and images that would be conducive to the promotion of a true and positive secularism.

References

Akhtar, Javed, 1993, "Muslims Grapple with Enemy Within," *Times of India*, Feb. 10, 1993.

Almog Shmuel, 1991, "Judaism as Illness: Antisemitism Stereotype and Self-image," *History of European Ideas*," 13, no. 6, 793–804.

Arapura, J.G., 1987, "India's Philosophical Response to Religious Pluralism," in *Modern Indian Responses to Religious Pluralism*, ed. Harold G. Coward, Albany, NY: SUNY Press.

Baig, M.A., 1974, *The Muslim Dilemma in India*, Delhi: Vikas.

Bhatnagar Rakesh, 1993, "HC's Unique Interpretation of Secularism," *Times of India*, Jan. 11, 1993.

Chopra, G.M., 1993, "Wrong Emphasis," Letter to the *Times of India*, Jan. 13, 1993.

Das, Arvind, 1992, "Hindutva and Hinduism: Pseudo-Religion Debases Spirituality," *Times of India*, Dec. 28, 1992.

The Economist, 1993, "The Hindu Upsurge: The Road to Ayodhya," Feb. 6, 1993, 21–3.

Haberman, David, 1988, *Acting as a Way of Salvation*, New York: Oxford University Press.

Haskell, Robert E., ed., 1987, *Cognition and Symbolic Structures: the Psychology of Metaphoric Transformation*, foreword by Joseph Kockelmans, Norwood, NJ: Alex Publishing Corporation.

Hill, Christopher, 1961, *The Century of Revolution 1603–1704*, Edinburgh: Thomas Nelson & Sons.

Irani, C.R., 1993, "A Matter of Faith and Fortune," *The Statesman Weekly*, Jan. 16, 1993.

Kockelmans, Joseph, 1987, "Foreword," in *Cognitive and Symbolic Structures: the Psychology of Metaphoric Transformation*, ed. Robert E. Haskell, New Jersey: Alex Publishing.

Lasch, Christopher, 1978, *The Culture of Narcissism: American Life in the Age of Diminishing Expectations*, New York: W. W. Norton & Co.

Millar, R.E., 1987, "Modern Indian Muslim Responses," in *Modern Indian Responses to Religious Pluralism*, ed. Harold G. Coward, Albany, NY: SUNY Press.

Neufeldt, R.W., 1987, "The Response of the Ramakrishna Mission," in *Modern Indian Responses to Religious Pluralism*, ed. Harold G. Coward, Albany, NY: SUNY Press.

Panikkar, Raimundo, 1973, *Worship and Secular Man*, London: Orbis Books.

Prithipaul, K.D., 1992, "Reason, Law, and the Limits of Indian Secularism," *International Journal of Indian Studies*, 2, 2 (1992), 1–38.

Rao, P. Bhujanga, 1993, Letter to the *Times of India*, Jan. 12, 1993.

Russell, Ralph, 1983, "Aziz Ahmad, South Asia, Islam, and Urdu," in *Islamic Society and Culture: Essays in Honour of Professor Aziz Ahmad*, eds. Milton Israel and N.K. Wagle, Delhi: Manohar.

Sen, Anikendra Nath, 1993, "Periphery to the Force: Challenge to Hindutva Heartland," *Times of India*, Jan. 11, 1993.

Singh, Prem, 1993, "VHP: Origin and Metamorphosis," *Link*, Jan. 3, 1993, 10–13.

Sontag, Susan, 1978, *Illness as Metaphor*, New York: Farrar, Strauss and Giroux.

Yelchuri, Sitaram, 1993, "The Indian SS: Democracy under Siege," *The Statesman Weekly*, Jan. 16, 1993.

8

India's Only Communalist: an Introduction to the Work of Sita Ram Goel

Koenraad Elst

Is there a communalist on board?

A lot of people in India and abroad talk about *communalism*, often in grave tones, describing it as a threat to democracy, to India's unity and integrity, to regional and world peace. There is a whole industry of communalism-watching, with an output of hundreds of books and many thousands of articles per year. But can anyone show us a communalist? If we look more closely into the case of any so-called communalist, we find that he turns out to be something else.

Could Syed Shahabuddin be a communalist? After all, he played a key role in the three main "Muslim communalist" issues of recent years: the Babri Masjid campaign, the Shah Bano case, and the Rushdie affair. (It is he who got *The Satanic Verses* banned in September 1988.) Surely, he must be India's communalist *par excellence*? Wrong: if you read any page of any issue of Shahabuddin's monthly *Muslim India*, you will find that he brandishes the notion of "secularism" as the alpha and omega of his politics, and that he directs all his attacks against Hindu "communalism". (The same propensity is evident in the "fundamentalist" Jamaat-i Islami weekly *Radiance*.) Moreover, on *Muslim India's* editorial board, you find articulate secularists like Inder Kumar Gujral and Khushwant Singh.

For the same reason, any attempt to label the All-India Muslim League as communalist would be wrong. True, it is the continuation of the party which achieved the Partition of India along communal lines. Yet, emphatically secularist parties like the Congress Party and the Communist Party of India (Marxist) have never hesitated to include the Muslim League in coalitions governing the state of Kerala. No true communalist would get such a chance.

On the Hindu side then, at least the Rashtriya Swayamsevak Sangh (RSS, "National Volunteer Corps") could qualify as "communalist"? Certainly, it is called just that by all its numerous enemies. But then, when you look through any issue of its weekly *Organiser*, you will find it brandishing the notion of "positive" or "genuine secularism," and denouncing "pseudo-secularism," i.e. minority communalism. Moreover, in order to prove its noncommunal character, it even calls itself and its affiliated organizations (trade union, student organization, political party, etc.) "National" or "Indian" rather than "Hindu." The allied political party, the Bharatiya Janata Party (BJP, "Indian People's Party"), shows off the large number of Muslims among its cadres to prove how secular and noncommunal it is. No, for full-blooded communalists, we have to look elsewhere.

There is only one man in India whom I have ever known to say: "I am a (Hindu) communalist." To an extent, this is in jest, as a rhetorical device to avoid the tangle in which RSS people always get trapped: being called "communalist!" and then spending the rest of your time trying to prove to your hecklers what a good secularist you are. But to an extent, it is because he accepts at least one definition of "communalism" as applying to himself, especially to his view of India's history since the seventh century. Many historians try to prove their "secularism" by minimizing religious adherence as a factor of conflict in Indian history, and explaining so-called religious conflicts as merely a camouflage for socioeconomic conflicts. By contrast, the historian under consideration accepts, and claims to have thoroughly documented, the allegedly "communalist" view that the major developments in medieval and modern Indian history can only be understood as resulting from an intrinsic hostility between religions.

Then again, his positions are incompatible with the description "communalist" at a more fundamental level, particularly his plea that the Hindus do not constitute a "community" on a par with the Muslim and Christian communities: Hindus, defined in the broad sense (which is also the original usage of the term *Hindu*, viz. all Indian "Pagans" including Buddhists, Sikhs, "animists," Jains), constitute the Indian nation. Though denying the presupposition of the whole notion of "Hindu communalism," this position is of course also labeled "communalist."

Unlike the Hindutva politicians, he does not seek the cover of "genuine secularism." While accepting the notion that Hindu India has always been "secular" in the adapted Indian sense of "religiously pluralistic," he does not care for slogans like the Vishva Hindu Parishad's advertisement "Hindu India, secular India." After all, in Nehruvian

India the term "secular" has by now acquired a specific meaning far removed from the original European usage, and even from the above-mentioned Indian adaptation. This is exemplified by the fact that Christian missionaries now brandish the slogan of "secularism" as a weapon against "communalist" Hindu resistance to their conversion efforts, even while in Christian Europe, secularism was started as a movement for expelling *Christian* institutions and controls from state affairs and for rationally questioning *Christian* dogmas. If Voltaire, the secularist *par excellence*, were to live in India today and repeat his attacks on the Church, echoing the Hindutva activists in denouncing the Churches' grip on public life in Christianized pockets like Mizoram and Nagaland, he would most certainly be denounced as "antiminority" and hence "antisecular." In India, the term has shed its anti-Christian bias and acquired an anti-Hindu bias instead, a phenomenon described by the author under consideration as an example of the current "perversion of India's political parlance." Therefore, he attacks the whole Nehruvian notion of "secularism" head-on, e.g. in the self-explanatory title of his Hindi booklet *Saikyularizm: rāshtradroha kā dūsra nām* ("Secularism: the Alternative Name for Treason").

The name (seldom mentioned and mostly only pronounced in whispering or hissing tones) of India's only self-avowed communalist is Sita Ram Goel. Our position is that he is one of the bravest and most important intellectuals in modern India.

Brief biography

Sita Ram Goel was born in 1921 in a poor Hindu family (belonging to the merchant Agrawāl caste) in Haryana. As a schoolboy, he got acquainted with the traditional Vaishnavism practiced by his family, with the *Mahābhārata* and the lore of the *Bhakti* saints, and with the major trends in contemporary Hinduism, especially the *Arya Samāj* and Gandhism. He took an MA in History in Delhi University, winning prizes and scholarships along the way. In his school and early university days he was a Gandhian activist, organizing intercaste dinners and participating in the Freedom Movement.

In the thirties and forties, the Gandhians themselves came in the shadow of the new ideological vogue: socialism. When they started drifting to the Left and adopting socialist rhetoric, S.R. Goel decided to opt for the original rather than the imitation. In 1941 he accepted Marxism as his framework for political analysis. At first, he did not join the Communist Party of India, and had differences with it over such issues as the creation of the religion-based state of Pakistan, which was actively supported by the CPI but could hardly provoke the enthusiasm of a progressive and atheist intellectual. He and his wife and first son narrowly escaped with their lives in the Great Calcutta Killing of August 16, 1946, organized by the Muslim League to give more force to the Pakistan demand.

In 1948, just when he had made up his mind to formally join the Communist Party of India, in fact on the very day when he had an appointment at the party office in Calcutta to be registered as a candidate-member, the government banned the CPI because of its hand in an ongoing armed rebellion. A few months later, a friend from Delhi came to stay in Goel's house for awhile, someone he had known since 1944 as easily the most impressive mind among the proliferating progressives: Ram Swarup. Born in 1920 in Haryana, this economics graduate proved to be a powerful and highly independent thinker. On this occasion, it turned out, he had moved away sharply from the ideological fashion of the day, to become one of India's leading anticommunists. His most important books on communism were *Russian Imperialism: How to Stop It* (1949), and *Communism and Peasantry* (1950, but published only in 1954).

In his intellectual autobiography *How I Became a Hindu* Goel describes several instances where Ram Swarup's influence shook him out of deadend ideological loyalties and unhealthy personal attitudes. In fact, Goel's career as a combative and prolific writer on controversial matters of historical fact can only be understood in conjunction with Ram Swarup's sparser, more reflective writings on fundamental doctrinal issues. The crucial moment in their friendship came when Ram Swarup made him see the appalling record and the true nature of communism, and invited him to join him in starting an Indian center of fact-finding and consciousness-raising about the communist menace: the *Society for the Defense of Freedom in Asia*. They published some important studies, which were acclaimed by leading anticommunists in the West and Taiwan, and were on one occasion vehemently denounced in the *Pravda* and the *Izvestia*. Until its closing in 1956, the center was the main independent focus of ideological opposition to communism in the Third World.

In those years, Goel was not active on the "communal" battlefield: not Islam or Christianity but communism was his priority target. Yet, under Ram Swarup's influence, his struggle against communism became increasingly rooted in Hindu spirituality (the way Aleksandr Solzhenitsyn's anticommunism became rooted in Orthodox Christianity). He also cooperated with (but was never a member of) the Bharatiya Jan Sangh, the then political affiliate of the RSS, and contributed articles on communism to the RSS paper *Organiser*. In 1957 he contested the Lok Sabha election for Khajuraho constituency as an independent candidate on a Jan Sangh ticket. At that time, he had a job with a state-affiliated company, the Indian Cooperative Union, for which he did research concerning cottage industries. The company also loaned him for awhile to the leading Gandhian activist Jayaprakash Narayan, who shared Goel's anticommunism at least at the superficial level (what used to be called "anti-Stalinism"): rejecting the means but not the ends of communism.

During the Chinese invasion in 1962, some government officials (including I.K. Gujral) demanded his arrest. But at the same time, the Home Ministry invited him to take a leadership role in the plans for a guerrilla war against the then widely-expected Chinese occupation of eastern India. He made his cooperation conditional on Nehru's abdication as Prime Minister, and nothing ever came of it.

In 1963, he had a book published under his own name which he had published in 1961–2 as a series in *Organiser* under the pen name *Ekaki*: a critique of Nehru's consistent pro-communist policies, titled *In Defense of Comrade Krishna Menon*. While refuting the common explanation that the pro-communist bias in Nehru's foreign policy was merely the handiwork of Minister Krishna Menon, he also drew attention to the harmfulness of this policy in India's national interests. Even though this criticism was eloquently vindicated by the Chinese invasion, the book cost him his job. He withdrew from the political debate, went into business himself, and set up a company of book imports and exports.

His only subsequent involvement in politics was when he was asked by the BJS leadership to mediate with the dissenting party leader Balraj Madhok in a last attempt at conciliation (which failed: Madhok stood as an independent candidate in subsequent elections and has remained a sharp critic of the BJS–BJP); and when he drafted a statement for the Janata alliance after it defeated Indira's Emergency regime in the 1977 elections. As a commercial publisher, he did not seek out the typical "communal" topics, but nonetheless kept an eye on Hindu interests. That is why he published books like Dharampal's *The Beautiful Tree* (on indigenous education, as admiring British observers found it in the nineteenth century), Ram Swarup's *Word as Revelation* (on the value of polytheism), K.R. Malkani's *The RSS Story*, K.D. Sethna's *Karpāsa in Prehistoric India* (1981; on the chronology of Vedic civilization, implying decisive objections against the Aryan Invasion Theory).

In 1981 he started the nonprofit publishing house Voice of India in the margin of his company, which he handed over to his son and nephew. Voice of India's declared aim is to defend Hinduism by placing before the public correct information about the situation of Hindu culture and society, and about the nature, motives, and strategies of its enemies. Its publications are practically boycotted in the media, both by reviewers and by journalists collecting background information on the communal problem. Though most Hindutva stalwarts have some Voice of India publications on their not-so-full bookshelves, the RSS *Parivar* refuses to offer its organizational omnipresence as a channel of publicity and distribution, for reasons we will discuss below. That S.R. Goel is simply not mentioned in numerous recent books and papers on the Hindu movement is a case of deliberately partisan scholarship in India, and of poor (mostly second-hand) scholarship among Western India-watchers.

Under Muslim pressure, several Voice of India books have been banned: Colin Maine's *The Dead Hand of Islam*, a survey of hate-mongering passages in the Scriptures of Islam; and Ram Swarup's *Understanding Islam through Hadis*, a faithful summary of the Muslim traditions concerning the words and deeds of the Prophet. Others have at least been the object of banning petitions, especially Ram Swarup's *Hindu View of Christianity and Islam*, a ground-breaking essay processing the doctrines of Christianity and Islam in terms of Hindu spirituality. A ban on Goel's *Hindu Temples, What Happened to Them, vol. 1*, which includes a list of 2,000 mosques built over Hindu temples, was proposed in the Uttar Pradesh state assembly in 1990 but not pursued, apparently to avoid drawing attention to the book.

The "Society for the Defense of Freedom in Asia"

S.R. Goel's first important publications were written as part of the work of the Society for the Defense of Freedom in Asia, based in Calcutta, then as now the center of Indian communism. Though routinely accused of being lavishly financed by the CIA, this organization started with just Rs. 30,000, half of which was brought in by Goel, and continued its work with the help of donations by friends from Bombay, Madras, and Calcutta, its budget seldom exceeding Rs. 10,000. These are the titles which Goel wrote as part of the SDFA's work: *World Conquest in Instalments* (1952); *The China Debate: Whom Shall We Believe?* (1953); *Mind Murder in Mao-land* (1953); *China is Red with Peasants' Blood* (1953); *Red Brother or Yellow Slave?* (1953); *Communist Party of China: a Study in*

Treason (1953); *Conquest of China by Mao Tse-tung* (1954); *Netaji and the CPI* (1955); *CPI Conspire for Civil War* (1955).

During the fifties, apart from these topical books in English, he wrote and published 18 titles in Hindi: 8 titles of fiction and 1 of poetry written by himself; 3 compilations from the *Mahabharata* and the *Tripitaka*; and translations of 6 books, mostly of obvious ideological relevance: the three *Dialogues* of Plato centered around Socrates' last days (*Apology, Crito*, and *Phaedo*); a history of the seventeenth-century Hindu freedom fighter Shivaji; *The God that Failed*, a testimony by prominent ex-communists; Ram Swarup's *Communism and Peasantry*; Viktor Kravchenko's *I Chose Freedom*; George Orwell's *Nineteen Eighty-Four*.

The aim of the SDFA's publications was to expose the lies that formed the backbone of communist propaganda, many of which had entered popular belief. Thus, in *Conquest of China* Goel demonstrated that Mao Zedong's victory against Jiang Jieshi (Chiang Kai-shek) was not determined by the level of popular support, but rather by the hard supplies which Mao received from the Soviets (including lots of American weapons given to the Soviet Union for a war against Japan which it only declared when Japan was already defeated). Jiang received no supplies at that time from the US, first due to the American prioritary concern for Europe at the expense of the Asian front, later due to an American arms embargo against "both parties in the Chinese Civil War." He documents the poor military value of what aid Jiang received at all, and what unfriendly price the Americans asked for it.

His thesis was based in large measure on primary (including communist and "fellow-traveler") sources; it also finds independent support in data revealed in the contemporaneous McArthur Hearings. Though till today, journalists and China-watchers keep on repeating that "Mao, with the peasants as his only support, easily defeated Jiang who was heavily supported by the US," Goel's documentary evidence shows that actually it was Mao and not Jiang who enjoyed the benefits of massive superpower aid. To quite an extent, Goel's critique, solitary and therefore looking like a querulous oddity next to the flood of pro-Mao literature, has recently been vindicated in Steven Mosher's study of China reporting, *China Misperceived: American Illusions and Chinese Reality* (New Republic/Harper Collins 1990).

In his book Goel developed his perception of intellectual understanding, or the lack of it, as a crucial factor in political struggles. The startling fact that the US imposed an arms embargo against an allied government threatened by a communist takeover, in order to force it into a coalition with its mortal enemy, was largely the consequence of the reporting in the American media, who depicted Mao as a harmless "agricultural reformer" and refused to see his unconcealed commitment to a communist action program. Even after Mao's victory, Western commentators have claimed that Mao had only been forced to ally himself with Stalin by the American aid to Jiang, and that by himself, Mao was a good democrat who would have been a loyal partner in the coalition into which the US should have forced Jiang.

Against this self-deception (foreseen by Lenin as an incurable trait of the bourgeoisie in the face of the Revolution: "The bourgeois will sell us the rope with which we will hang him"), Goel lets Mao's political writings speak for themselves: his book is indeed conceived as an introduction to Mao's works: *Strategic Problems of China's Revolutionary War* and *China's New Democracy*, in which the "alliance with the national bourgeoisie" is explicitly described as merely a stage in the communist takeover, after the model of the parliamentary regime in Russia in February–October 1917. Similarly, in his book *The China Debate: Whom Shall We Believe?*, he confronted the propaganda put out by the Communist Party of India and its camp-followers about communist performance with the rather more sobering accounts and figures given in official Soviet and Chinese publications.

Then, and all through his career as a polemicist, the most remarkable feature of Sita Ram Goel's position in the Indian intellectual arena was that nobody even tried to give a serious rebuttal to this theses: the only counterstrategy has always been, and still is, "strangling by silence" – simply refusing to ever mention his name, publications, or arguments. But as the cover of his book *Hindu Temples, vol. 2*, proudly proclaims, "The numerous studies published by the [SDFA] in the fifties exist in cold print in many libraries and can be consulted for finding out how the movement anticipated by many years the recent revelations about communist regimes."

An aspect of history yet to be studied is how such anticommunist movements in the Third World were not at all helped (in fact, often opposed) by Western interest groups whose understanding of communist ideology and strategy was just too superficial. Most US representatives starkly ignored the SDFA's work, and preferred to cultivate the company of more prestigious (implying: fashionably antianticommunist) opinion-makers.

The critique of communism formulated by these Indian thinkers was often intellectually superior to Western analyses of communism. Ram Swarup and Sita Ram Goel have of course addressed the economic policies and failures of communism, but their central concern was not the free market: rather, it was human freedom and dignity, and an understanding of the spiritual roots of the self-righteous communist attempt to devise "the new mankind" at the expense of really existing human beings. This critique emphasized the common materialist roots of capitalism and communism (here again, the similarity with Solzhenitsyn's position is noteworthy).

One of the most lucid and original pieces in Goel's publications on communism was an article written in 1956, sent untitled to the British anticommunist activist Freda Utley for publication, turned down by several American conservative papers, but finally included by Susanne Labin in a paper submitted to NATO and to the *Bulletin* published by Soviet émigrés in West Berlin (now included in Goel, *Genesis and Growth of Nehruism*, pp. 207ff). It explains how "dialectical materialism" is oddly the presupposition of American anticommunist strategy, while its official adherents, the communists, are careful not to trust it in practice.

Indeed, American policymakers often declared that poverty was the root cause of people being attracted by communism, and that a rise in living standards thanks to American economic aid would make people immune to it (the same argument is currently heard concerning the spread of fundamentalism in Muslim countries). In Marxist fashion, they assumed at least implicitly that one's ideological commitment is mechanically caused by one's material situation. By contrast, the communists never believed their own dogma, and put into practice the "idealist" assumption that a certain orientation of consciousness is not caused by certain material conditions, but by contact with other consciousnesses already thus oriented: the candle's wick will only alight by the touch of another flame.

For the SDFA, seduction by or opposition to communism has nothing to do with material wealth or class position: "Every class, every social status, every nation, every creed and every interest will become an opponent of communism the moment it becomes conscious of certain moral and spiritual values which ought not to be sacrificed in exchange for any amount of material good or political benefit" (Goel, 1993: 211). The communists have realized this primacy of mind over matter and class very well, and the result during the Cold War period was that first, Western aid to the Third World would help to build schools and equip them with nice library shelves, and then Communist activists would fill these shelves with their own literature: the West would take care of the bodies, the communists would work on the minds.

In the communal debate of the 1980s and 1990s, the most formidable obstacle for Hindu spokesmen turned out to be precisely the intense grip of the communists on the mind of the public through their methodically acquired positions of power in the media and the academic world. The achievements of India's strong communist movement cannot be called spectacular at the material level, with their stronghold, Calcutta, still counting as the epitome of Third World poverty; but in the intellectual sector, their activity has been intense and highly successful. Even most noncommunists look at political issues through the colored glasses which communists have put on their noses. This was true until recently of economic policy, on which most parties would adopt communist categories and prejudices and it is still true of the "communal" issue.

In the communal debate, communist sympathy has been solidly with all the anti-Hindu forces in the field, from the Christian mission lobby to the Kashmiri separatists (even while their Chinese counterparts, the Christian underground Church and Muslim separatism in the northwestern provinces, are mercilessly suppressed by the communists). Mostly of upper-caste Hindu extraction, the Indian communists are the fiercest enemies of every kind of Hindu self-assertion. In this respect, Sita Ram Goel's pro-Hindu position in the communal debate is a continuation of his anticommunist position in the Cold War context.

Hindu Society Under Siege

The nonprofit publishing-house Voice of India was started as an instrument for informing Hindu society and alerting it to the machinations of its enemies, i.e. those ideologies committed to the annihilation of Hinduism. For, as the title of the opening publication *Hindu Society Under Siege* (1981) indicates, Hindu society has been suffering a sustained attack from Islam since the seventh century, from Christianity since the fifteenth century, and this century also from Marxism. The avowed objective of each of these three world-conquering movements, with their massive resources, is the replacement of other ideologies, cultures, or social systems with their own.

The Hindu concern about the designs of these hostile ideologies is not as paranoid as their own spokesmen are sure to allege in reply. The facts from the recent past are a solid testimony to their two-pronged strategy against Hinduism as a culture (through conversion) and against India as a state with which Hindus can identify (through support for separatism). Research may fill in the details about their strength and the consequent magnitude of the menace, but there can be no honest doubt about their intentions.

If the Christian and Islamic conversion squads are remarkably unsuccessful in modern India, it is certainly not for lack of trying, much less for lack of money spent on the effort. For all their talk about ecumenism and religious pluralism, the missionaries of these religions have never felt inhibited wherever they had a chance to advance at the expense of religions which could not muster the same kind of means. Consider the situation in Africa: in 1900, 50 percent of all Africans practiced Pagan religions; today, Christian and Islamic missionaries have reduced this number to less than 10 percent, and Paganism is on the defensive even in those pockets where it is still in the majority. In communities on the geographical or sociological periphery of Hindu society, the missionaries have achieved similar mass conversions, small in comparison to India's demographical size but locally quite consequential.

In the mainstream of Hindu society, the missionaries' hopes have been frustrated (at least in the modern period; in the Muslim period, large numbers went over to the dominant religion, mostly from the middle castes). But even there, a kind of advance has been achieved, viz. at the level of thought: many Hindus have interiorized the depreciation of Hindu culture and society which their enemies have been feeding them from the relative power positions they have had in the past or are enjoying today. Even the revivalist movement Arya Samaj borrowed anti-Brahmin and anti-idolatry planks from Christian propaganda. The fact that after independence this psychology has become generalized among urban Hindus, is mostly the handiwork of the communists and the Christian churches: both have a very strong presence in the publishing, media, and education sectors, largely maintained with foreign funding. But Islam has by now also learned the right language to instill a negative image of Hinduism in Hindus – witness especially the stereotypes in Bombay films.

It is remarkable that Christian, Islamic, and communist pressure groups have stood together in controversial issues, from the Niyogi Committee Report in the 1950s (calling for curbs on Christian missionary activities in central India) to the Ayodhya affair, an occasion to blacken Hindus worldwide and to support the Muslim claim to the controversial Hindu sacred site.

Though India is a secular state, it is still perceived as a homeland for the Hindus, so anti-Hindu movements are usually also anti-India movements. Tribal separatisms are supported openly by the World

Council of Churches and certain Catholic mission centers (Jharkhand, Nagaland, Mizoram, worldwide propaganda for treating the Indian tribals on a par with the Native Americans), and by communism (Chinese military support in the northeast, propaganda for the notion that India is an artificial colonial creation not deserving its unity and integrity). In 1947, Christian schemes for creating a chain of alternately Christian and Muslim states from Kanyakumari through Malabar-Hyderabad and Jharkhand to Pakistani Bengal and the northeast were thwarted by Sardar Patel, but even as daydreams they were sufficiently revealing of expansionist designs which have not been given up but merely adapted to new circumstances.

The most formidable proven enemy of Hinduism and often also of India's unity and integrity is no doubt Islam. In the past, Afghanistan, the Maledives, and most Hindu parts of Malay and Indonesian society were already islamized and completely lost to Hinduism. In Baluchistan, the Northwest Frontier Province, and much of Kashmir, the Hindu presence had also been annihilated even before the British period. In 1947, the same process was initiated in Sindh, West Punjab, and East Bengal by the creation of Pakistan, a state bound to squeeze out all remnants of Hinduism. The 1970s saw decisive moves towards full Islamization of the polity in Pakistan and in newly independent (and initially secular) Bangladesh. The Hindu presence in these states has been reduced to less than 1 percent and less than 10 percent, respectively, and the trickle of refugees continues. Today, Hindutva and government of India sources are in agreement that Pakistan organizes armed separatism in Kashmir and various terrorist activities elsewhere in India, while Bangladesh allows various armed guerrillas to use the border region as a strategic base. Bangladesh is also flooding India with millions of illegal immigrants and turning large parts of the northeast into Muslim-majority areas (tomorrow's Kashmir), but leftist and Islamic media in India have joined hands in criminalizing beforehand any attempt to send them back.

Such is the alliance of forces Hinduism is up against: "the Muslim and British invasions of India, though defeated and dispersed, have yet managed to crystallize certain residues – psychological and intellectual – which a battered Hindu society is finding very difficult to digest. These residues are now in active alliance with powerful international forces, and are being aided and abetted on a scale which an impoverished Hindu society cannot match. And lastly, though at loggerheads amongst themselves, these residues have forged a united front which is holding Hindu society under siege" (Goel, *Hindu Society Under Siege*, pp. 5–6).

Standing up to the challenge of those mortal enemies, Voice of India works for the intellectual mobilization of Hindu society.

These are the titles of S.R. Goel's books published by Voice of India: *Hindu Society Under Siege* (1981, revised 1992); *Story of Islamic Imperialism in India* (1982); *How I Became a Hindu* (1982, enlarged 1993); *Defence of Hindu Society* (1983, revised 1987); *The Emerging National Vision* (1983); *History of Heroic Hindu Resistance to Muslim Invaders* (1984); *Perversion of India's Political Parlance* (1984); *Saikyularizm, Rāshtradroha kā Dūsrā Nām* (1985); *Papacy, Its Doctrine and History* (1986); *The Calcutta Quran Petition by Chandmal Chopra* (1986, enlarged 1987, enlarged again 1994); *Muslim Separatism, Causes and Consequences* (1987); *Catholic Ashrams, Adapting and Adopting Hindu Dharma* (1988); *History of Hindu–Christian Encounters* (1989); *Hindu Temples, What Happened to Them* (1990, vol. 1; 1991, vol. 2, enlarged 1993); *Genesis and Growth of Nehruism* (1993).

In this brief introduction, I cannot hope to do more than to bring a few salient points of S.R. Goel's analysis of the "communal" equation to the reader's attention.

View of the Hindu movement

Since most India-watchers have been brought up on the belief that Hindu activism can be identified with the RSS Parivar, they are bound to label Sita Ram Goel (the day they condescend to mentioning him at all, that is) as "an RSS man." It will therefore surprise them that the established Hindu organizations have so far shown very little interest in Voice of India's work.

It is not that they would spurn its services; in its Ayodhya campaign, the Vishva Hindu Parishad ("World Hindu Forum," VHP) has routinely referred to a "list of 3,000 temples converted into or replaced by mosques," meaning the list of 2,000 such cases in *Hindu Temples, vol. 1*; and the VHP argumentation in the government-sponsored scholars' debate of 1990–1 was published by Voice of India (titled *History vs. Casuistry*). But organizationally, the Parivar is not using its networks to spread Ram Swarup's and Sita Ram Goel's books and ideas. Twice (1962 and 1987) the RSS intervened with the editor of *Organiser* to have ongoing serials of articles (on Nehru and on Islam) by Goel halted. And ideologically, it is simply turning a deaf ear to their analysis of the problems facing Hindu society. Apparently the RSS is mentally too slack to see the importance of fostering a developed Hindu viewpoint among its own activists, who invest their energy in lots of physical locomotion rather than in studying and thinking. The consequence of this anti-intellectual bias is that the RSS Parivar has had to function in an ideological atmosphere created by its enemies, that it has tried to live up to the standards set by them (secularism, socialism), and that it is pushed around by them. What the movement should do if ever it is to be successful, is to change the conceptual framework of Indian politics by processing the hostile ideologies in Hindu terms rather than subjecting Hinduism to the standards imposed by its enemies.

Insofar as the RSS Parivar has developed an ideology at all, it diverges on essential points from Sita Ram Goel's position, e.g. on the central doctrine of *nationalism*. To be sure, Goel agrees with the RSS on the importance of loyalty to the Indian state for the sake of Hindu interests in the present conditions; after all, anti-India political movements (creation of Pakistan, separatism in Kashmir, Punjab, the Northeast, Tamil Nadu) always turn out to be instruments of anti-Hindu ideologies. But in Goel's view, it is a mistake of most political Hindus to cast their political program in terms of Western secular nationalism, and to redefine a conflict between Hindu and anti-Hindu as one between "nationalist" and "anti-national." The RSS position on Christianity, Islam, and Marxism is limited to alleging foreign roots and extraterritorial loyalties. The RSS solution for the simmering conflict with Islam is that "Islam should Indianize itself," and that Muslims should consider themselves as – *abracadabra* – "Mohammedi Hindus." Instead of an ideological critique of the foundations of these hostile ideologies, there is only an emotional patriotism dividing the world into home-made goodies and foreign baddies.

Thus, the RSS people often plead that on Ayodhya, the Indian state should support the Rama party against the Babar party because Rama was an "Indian" hero while Babar was a "foreign" invader. In fact, if Babar did demolish Hindu temples, it was not because of his foreign birth (many foreign invaders preserved Hindu temples, lastly the British) but because of the Islamic doctrine of iconoclasm: Indian-born Muslims, like the convert Malik Kafur, destroyed temples in the name of Islam. So, formulating this conflict in terms of foreign vs. Indian is a thinly veiled attempt to express in terms of secular nationalism what is really a religious conflict. And this is not only done in order to comply with the dominant secularist standards of discourse, but rather because RSS people really think in these terms.

Against this, Goel quotes what Ram Swarup told him in the fifties, when "nationalism" seemed to him the only alternative to foreign-based communism: "But foreign should not be defined in geographical

terms. Then it would have no meaning except territorial or tribal patriotism. To me that alone is foreign which is foreign to truth, foreign to
Atman" (*How I Became a Hindu*, 2nd edn., p. 45). The RSS variety of
Hindu nationalism puts things upside-down: it starts with the Indian
territory as the center of its ideology, and then deduces that the society
and the culture and religion born on this soil are worth defending. Goel,
by contrast, starts from the civilization of *Sanatana Dharma* (the "eternal
value system," commonly known as Hinduism) as a value worth defending, then deduces the value of Hindu society from its upholding this
Sanatana Dharma, and concludes that the Indian territory and state are
worth defending because and only because they house Hindu society
and its civilization.

Therefore, the problem with Islam (as with other hostile ideologies)
is not that it is *foreign*. This is amply proven by the doomsday history
of another culture, as pluralist and polytheist as Hinduism, but for
which Islam was not a foreign but a geographically internal enemy: the
Pagan culture of Arabia which was annihilated by Mohammed and his
immediate successors Abu Bakr and Omar. One of the most original contributions of S.R. Goel to the study and evaluation of Islam is his
drawing of attention to the impact of Mohammed on Arab Pagan
society *from the Pagan viewpoint* (*Hindu Temples*, vol. 2, section IV). For
the Arabs, Islam did not come from abroad, yet it had the same deadly
effect on their traditions as it had on Hindu–Buddhist traditions in
Turkestan, Afghanistan, the Maledives, Sindh, and parts of Southeast
Asia. The Pagan Arabs fought Islam tooth and nail, until they had
to acquiesce in its superior military strength. Their problem with
Islam was not its geographical provenance but its intrinsic hostility
to religious pluralism and idol-worship, coupled with a ruthless self-
righteousness stemming from the belief in its God-given right to subdue
the nations.

Sita Ram Goel's struggle is an ideological struggle, not directed against
any foreign nation, like the medieval Turks or present-day Pakistan, nor
against a community of people, like the Indian Muslims, but against a
system of ideas.

View of Christianity and Islam

The first thing a Hindu ought to know about Christianity and Islam, if
at all he wants to evaluate them, is what they have done to his own
and other Pagan cultures. Therefore, Sita Ram Goel has worked, both as
a writer and as a publisher, to inform the public about some significant

aspects of the encounters of Hinduism with these two Abrahamic religions. Thus, for this purpose he has republished A.K. Priolkar's *The Goa Inquisition* (1991, original 1961), a description of the anti-Hindu policies of the Portuguese missionaries and colonial administrators in India, including an annotated edition of two testimonies from 1684 and 1808. In *History of Hindu–Christian Encounters*, he details both the episodes of Christian persecution and more subtle forms of aggression, and the cases of vivid Hindu counterargument. Though Mahatma Gandhi's slogan of "equal respect for all religions" is now interpreted as a prohibition on Hindu criticism of other religions, it turns out that the Mahatma himself was one in a series of Hindu spokesmen who were very candid and articulate in their rejection of Christian exclusivist claims to reveal truth.

In this brief survey, we will limit ourselves to his critique of the anti-Hindu campaign of Islam, which is parallel to that of Christianity but now of greater immediate political importance.

In *Story of Islamic Imperialism of India*, Goel takes issue with official guidelines to rewrite history textbooks, especially to minimize or deny the religious factor in Indian history, more particularly as an explanation of episodes of conflict and destruction. He documents, from readily available records mostly written by Muslim chroniclers, that the Muslim attacks on Hindus were a regular feature of medieval history, and that they often assumed staggering proportions in terms of people killed, deported, and enslaved. He goes on to demonstrate that the Muslim swordsmen concerned invariably justified the persecution of Hinduism, the suppression of its expressions, the slaughter of its spokesmen, and the enslavement of its followers, as the fulfillment of a pious duty taught by the Quran. Moreover, Muslim clerics exhorted Muslim rulers to intensify these anti-Hindu policies and reprimanded them when circumstances or personal temperament made them willing to compromise with the Hindus.

In *Hindu Temples, What Happened to Them*, Goel details Islam's systematic campaign of temple destruction. A wealth of quotations from original sources simply blows away all claims that temple destruction was a minor and occasional phenomenon unrelated to the fundamental message of Islam. Goel's conclusion is that, from the destruction of the idols in the Kaaba down to the destruction of more than twenty Hindu temples in Great Britain in December 1992 and the bomb attacks on ancient temples unearthed by archaeologists in Egypt in 1993, the physical destruction of idolatry has always been an intrinsic part of Islam's political program.

An important contribution of these books is the rebuttal of the well-known arguments of the "secularist" historians to explain away these well-documented facts. Thus, it is always pointed out that many Hindu rulers collaborated with Muslim suzerains; but obviously, the history of *every* occupation is also the history of a large-scale collaboration. British rule in India benefited from the cooperation of large segments of the Indian population, yet the secularists have not yet cleared British colonialism of the stigma of being a foreign, illegitimate, and oppressive regime. It is also claimed that Muslim rulers only destroyed temples as a symbol of conquest, but no case has ever been revealed of a Muslim ruler destroying prominent mosques in Muslim territory after defeating a fellow Muslim adversary. Similarly, the claim that temples were only looted for their wealth is not borne out by a similar behavior towards magnificent mosques, and is contradicted by the large-scale destruction of even poor and insignificant temples.

In judging a movement, it is necessary to keep an overall perspective of the context and of the record of similar movements. It is in the context of the general history of religions that Islam stands out more starkly as a perpetrator of violence on its rivals. This remains true when we compare it with even an avowedly missionary religion like Buddhism. However, secularist historians have been claiming again and again that even what fanaticism they are willing to admit in the case of Islam, is merely an application of a general rule that all religions foster some fanaticism. In particular, they claim that Hinduism itself has practiced the same persecution against Buddhism and tribal "animism." Goel has no difficulty in showing that this is a very cheap claim, consistently contradicted by first-hand sources.

As for animism, Hinduism itself is but a more cultured evolution of animism, continuing most animist practices including worship of trees and animals; no historically demonstrable case of an "animist shrine destroyed by Brahminical onslaught" has ever been pointed out. As for Buddhism, it is an easily verifiable fact that Buddhist institutions continued to flourish in India until the Muslim conquest, and that in Central Asia, where no Brahmins were around, Buddhism was annihilated by Islam. The cases of Brahminical, Buddhist, and Jain violence against rival sects are few and far between, mostly honestly traceable to nonreligious factors, and – most importantly – *not traceable to the doctrinal contents of the religion*. No Hindu sect teaches that it is a pious act to destroy other people's places of worship or wage war on them because of their beliefs. This, Goel argues, is the radical difference with Christianity in its prime, and with Islam.

The undeniable Islamic attempt, persistent over thirteen centuries, to destroy Hindu civilization root and branch, has an ideological cause which is easy to identify. In Ram Swarup's and Sita Ram Goel's opinion, the fact that Christianity and Islam have such a terrible record in the persecution of others, is ultimately due to their theology, especially to their doctrine of prophetic monotheism. In this doctrine, a jealous God tolerates no rival gods and reveals himself through a privileged spokesman, a prophet or messiah. In the Quran, the injunctions to wage war on the unbelievers are explicit and numerous; they are given and discussed in Goel's *The Calcutta Quran Petition*. Mohammed himself has shown the way: as detailed in Ram Swarup's *Understanding Islam through Hadis* and in Goel's *Hindu Temples, vol. 2*, the Prophet's overall achievement has been the replacement of a pluralistic "Pagan" society with a monolithic Islamic one within a mere two decades, by military means.

Most Hindu leaders expressly refuse to search Islamic doctrine for a reason for the observed fact of Muslim hostility. RSS leader Guru Golwalkar once said: "Islam is a great religion. Mohammed was a great prophet. But the Muslims are big fools." This is not logical, for the one thing that unites the (otherwise diverse) community of Muslims, is their common belief in Mohammed and the Quran: if any wrong is attributed to "the Muslims" as such, it must be situated in their common belief system. Therefore, Goel's position is just the opposite: not the Muslims are the problem, but Islam and Mohammed.

In the Ayodhya dispute, time and again the BJP leaders have appealed to the Muslims to relinquish all claims to the supposed birthplace of the Hindu god Rama, arguing that destroying temples is against the tenets of Islam, and that the Quran prohibits the use of a mosque built on disputed land. In fact, whatever Islam decrees against building mosques on disputed property, can only concern disputes within the Muslim community (or its temporary allies under the treaty). Goel has demonstrated in detail that it is perfectly in conformity with Islamic law, and established as legitimate by the Prophet through his own example, to destroy Pagan establishments and replace them with (or turn them into) mosques. For an excellent example, the Kaaba itself was turned into a mosque by Mohammed when he smashed the 360 Pagan idols that used to be worshipped in it.

Therefore, S.R. Goel is rather critical of the current Ayodhya movement. In the foreword to *Hindu Temples, vol. 2*, he writes: "The movement for the restoration of Hindu temples has got bogged down around the Rama Janmabhoomi at Ayodhya. The more important question, viz. *why* Hindu temples met the fate they did at the hands of Islamic invaders, has not been even whispered. Hindu leaders have endorsed the Muslim propagandists in proclaiming that Islam does not permit the construction of mosques at sites occupied earlier by other people's places of worship . . . The Islam of which Hindu leaders are talking exists neither in the Quran nor in the Sunnah of the Prophet. It is hoped that this volume will help in clearing the confusion. No movement which shuns or shies away from truth is likely to succeed. Strategies based on self-deception stand defeated at the very start."

Goel's alternative to the RSS variety of "Muslim appeasement" is to wage an ideological struggle against Islam and Christianity, on the lines of the rational criticism and secularist politics which have pushed back Christian self-righteousness in Europe. The Muslim community, of course, is not to be a scapegoat (as it is for those who refuse to criticize Islam and end up attacking Muslims instead), but has to be seen in the proper historical perspective: as a part of Hindu society estranged from its ancestral culture by Islamic indoctrination over generations. Their hearts and minds have to be won back by an effort of consciousness-raising, which includes education about the aims, methods, and historical record of religions.

View of Mahatma Gandhi

An excellent illustration of S.R. Goel's special position in India's ideological spectrum is provided by his evaluation of Mahatma Gandhi. The classical Hindutva view of the Mahatma is summed up in Prof. Balraj Madhok's assessment that Gandhi was a failure headed for the dustbin of history, whose reputation was saved only by his martyrdom at the hands of Hindu Mahasabha activist Nathuram Godse (*Rationale of the Hindu State*, Delhi, Indian Book Gallery, 1982, p. 68). There is some truth in this view, but only if we limit Gandhi's politics to his tragic quest of "Hindu–Muslim unity." Obviously, this reduction is questionable.

But in the Hindutva literature, it is hard to find a fair account of the Mahatma's achievements and failures. On the one hand, there is the A.B. Vajpeyi line which imitates Congress and therefore uncritically exalts Gandhi, e.g. by calling its own political program "Gandhian socialism"; on the other, there are the hardliners who merely despise Gandhi's "appeasement" policy and its failure to contain Muslim separatism. Voice of India is the only think-tank which has produced a straightforward, sincere, and balanced analysis of Mahatma Gandhi's life and death from the Hindu viewpoint, without reducing Gandhi's significance to his stand on a single issue.

As authentic veterans of Gandhism, Ram Swarup (author of *Gandhian Economics*, 1977) and Sita Ram Goel can address the issue with an undisturbed conscience. They emphasize Gandhi's unconditional commitment to the well-being of Hindu society, and they have put Gandhi's defeat in the struggle against Partition in a proper perspective. The chapter on Mahatma Gandhi in Goel's *Perversion of India's Political Parlance* is a sharp rebuttal both to Nathuram Godse's justification for the murder of the Mahatma, and to the numerous attempts to use the Mahatma as a "secularist" argument against the Hindu cause ("He who died with '*He Ram*' on his lips would have been the first to oppose the Ram Janmabhoomi movement"). Briefly, this is what it says.

First of all, the Islamic and communist lobbies who currently invoke the Mahatma's name as a stick with which to beat the Hindu movement, had no use for the Mahatma when he was alive. They thwarted his policies and opposed him tooth and nail, and their press attacked him in the crassest language. On the issue of Partition, of course, the Muslim political leadership (and also the Muslim electorate in the 1946 elections) and the Mahatma were poles apart. Less well-remembered today is that the communists too supported the Partition plan. Apart from politics, there were numerous personal attacks on Gandhi from those quarters as well. It was the Hindu who revered him, and if the anti-Hindu alliance considers the use of the Mahatma's name profitable today, it is because the public mainly consists of Hindus who still revere or at least respect him.

Secondly, the Mahatma's first and foremost loyalty was towards Hindu society. If he criticized it, it was for its own upliftment, to force it out of its inertia, to rejuvenate and reawaken it. He was a proud and combative Hindu. The Mahatma's defense of Hinduism against the claims and allegations leveled by Christianity and by colonialism was very clear and unwavering. So was his opposition to the seeds of separatism which hostile forces tried to sow within Hindu society, via the Tamils, the Harijans, the Sikhs.

Thirdly, in the Freedom struggle, it was his strategy that managed to involve the masses. Unlike the Hindu Mahasabha, which championed religion but thought and worked in strictly political terms borrowed from Western secular nationalism, the Mahatma understood that the Hindu masses could only be won over by a deeply religious appeal. The ethical dimension of politics which he emphasized regained for Hinduism a good name throughout the world, and is still highly relevant (for an example of how Gandhi's strategy of appeal to morality and "change of heart" is made relevant by a writer of Hindutva persuasion in the 1990s, see Arun Shourie, *Individuals, Institutions, Processes*, Delhi, Viking, 1990).

Therefore, it is nothing short of morbid to remember the Mahatma only as the leader who failed to stop Islamic separatism, as Nathuram Godse did, and as a minority within the Hindu movement still does.

On the other hand, writes Sita Ram Goel, "it must be admitted that the failure which the Mahatma met *vis-à-vis* the Muslims was truly of startling proportions ... his policy towards Muslims had been full of appeasement at the cost of Hindu society. But nothing had helped. Muslims had continued to grow more and more hostile ... there must be something very hard in the heart of Islam that even a man of an oceanic goodwill like Mahatma Gandhi failed to move it" (*Perversion of India's Political Parlance*, pp. 46–7).

But the failure to prevent Partition can only be attributed to the Mahatma for the period (and to the extent) that he dictated Congress policy. The political course which led to Partition, had been started before his arrival on the Indian scene. And when he was at the helm, most Congress leaders had equally approved of decisions which we can now recognize as steps on the road to Partition. For instance, the 1916 Lucknow Pact between Congress and the Muslim League, which legitimized the privileges (separate electorates, one-third representation in the Central Assembly) which the Muslim League had obtained from the British, was signed by Lokamanya Tilak, an unquestionably staunch Hindu. The involvement in the Khilafat movement, that giant boost for Muslim separatism, was accepted not only by the Nehrus ("whose support for Islamic causes was always a foregone conclusion"), but also by such Hindu stalwarts as Lala Lajpat Rai, Bipin Chandra Pal, and Pandit Madan Mohan Malaviya. Even Swami Shraddhananda spoke from the steps of the Jama Masjid in Delhi in support of the Khilafat agitation. For another example, less consequential but highly illustrative, it was when Mahatma Gandhi was in prison in 1922 that Dashbandhu C.R. Das led the Bengal Provincial Congress into signing a Hindu–Muslim pact which permitted Muslims to kill cows during their festivals but forbade Hindus to play music before mosques.

It is true that the Mahatma did not adapt his policies to the feedback he was getting from reality, viz. that concessions to the Muslim League were never reciprocated but were, instead, followed by new and higher demands. But this stubborn blindness before the grim facts was not Gandhi's invention. In Goel's opinion, a correct assessment of Muslim separatism would have implied a fundamental critique of Islam, something which the Mahatma rejected completely: he called Islam "a noble faith," and even when faced with Muslim misbehavior, he attributed it to non-essential circumstances such as Islam being "a very young religion." Whether right or wrong, Gandhi's positive prejudice towards Islam was not at all a personal idiosyncrasy, but was quite common among Hindu politicians and intellectuals of this century.

The failure of the Mahatma before Islamic separatism was the failure of Hindu society. Sita Ram Goel strongly rejected Nathuram Godse's allegation that the Mahatma by himself was the chief culprit for the Partition: "It is highly doubtful if Hindu society would have been able to prevent Partition even if there had been no Mahatma Gandhi. On the other hand, there is ample evidence that Hindu society would have failed in any case" (ibid., p. 47).

From a weapon in the hands of Hindutva's enemies, Goel turns Mahatma Gandhi into a pioneer of the Hindu revival. And it is true, the Mahatma has repeatedly propounded the following three views which are in stark contrast with those of the Nehruvian establishment:

1. India is one nation. It is not, as self-glorifying Britons and Nehruvians thought, "a nation in the making." It has a common culture called *Sanatana Dharma* ("eternal value system," Hinduism), and the adherence to this common heritage transcends the borders between language areas and other divisions which elsewhere would define a nation.

2. Hinduism is in no way inferior to other religions and ideologies. On the contrary: in Gandhi's own words, "whatever of substance is contained in any other religion is always to be found in Hinduism, and what is not contained in it is insubstantial or unnecessary."

3. Political achievements like independence, national unity, and social transformation can only be based on a religious and cultural awakening of Hindu society (it is for this reason that communists often allege that communalism started with Gandhi, because he introduced religious language and imagery into politics).

These are viewpoints which the political Hindu movement shares, so it could assert that secularism's claims on the Mahatma are entirely false. In the Indian political culture where sycophancy and hero-worship reigns supreme, it is tactically useful to have revered personalities on your side, and to quote their infallible statements. That is why in the struggle for the Mahatma's heritage, the Nehruvians have invested a lot in representing him as a "secularist." The organized Hindu movement has so far been too slack intellectually to try and claim the Mahatma back for Hinduism, but Ram Swarup and Sita Ram Goel have made a start.

Sita Ram Goel's conclusion puts the Mahatma in the center of the

Hindu revival: "The one lesson we learn from the freedom movement as a whole is that a religious and cultural awakening in Hindu society has to precede political awakening. The language of Indian nationalism has to be the language of Sanatana Dharma before it can challenge and defeat the various languages of imperialism. The more clearly Hindu society sees the universal truths of Hindu spirituality and culture, the more readily will it reject political ideologies masquerading as religion or promising a paradise on this earth. Mahatma Gandhi stands squarely with Maharshi Dayananda, Bankim Chandra, Swami Vivekananda, Lokamanya Tilak, and Sri Aurobindo in developing the language of Indian nationalism. His mistake about Islam does not diminish the luster of that language which he spoke with full faith and confidence. On the contrary, his mistake carries a message of its own" (ibid., p. 52).

Conclusion

One of the grossest misconceptions about the current "Hindu awakening," is that it is an artificial creation of political parties like the BJP and the Shiv Sena. In reality, there is a substratum of Hindu activist tendencies in many corners of Hindu society, often in unorganized form and almost invariably lacking in intellectual articulation. There is a widespread Hindu unrest about the uncertain future of Hindu culture, and to this vague awareness, Voice of India provides an intellectual focus.

The importance of Sita Ram Goel's work, along with Ram Swarup's, can hardly be overestimated. I for one have no doubt that future textbooks on comparative religion as well as those on Indian political and intellectual history will devote crucial chapters to their analysis. They are the first to give a first-hand "Pagan" reply to the versions of history and "science of religion" imposed by the monotheist world-conquerors, both at the level of historical fact and of fundamental doctrine, both in terms of the specific Hindu experience and of a more generalized theory of religion free from prophetic-monotheistic bias.

Their long-term intellectual importance is that they have contributed immensely to breaking the spell of all kinds of monotheist prejudices and misrepresentations of Paganism in general, Hinduism in particular. They have done so in an explicit manner, addressing the polemical positions taken by the world-conquerors squarely, not merely eulogizing the qualities of Upanishadic thought and other Hindu achievements, as too many Hindu revivalists tend to do.

Voice of India's shorter-term political importance consists in its breaking through the weak, apologetic position taken by the established Hindu movement. This movement wastes quite a bit of its energy on proving its "secular" credentials and its harmlessness for Muslims and other minorities, unsuccessfully trying to acquire a new "secular" identity, and meanwhile undermining its natural Hindu identity. This way, it is still playing by the rules imposed by the alliance of its declared enemies. Voice of India changes the values by questioning the premises and motives of Nehruvian secularist discourse. There is no doubt that in the near future, Voice of India will be the main point of reference in the development of Hindu ideology and politics.

9

The Strains of Hindu–Muslim Relations: Babri Masjid, Music, and Other Areas Where the Traditions Cleave

Vasudha Narayanan

Sheikh Chinna Moulana Saheb, a renowned musician from the state of Tamilnadu, is a noted player of the instrument called *nadaswaram*. His repertoire is traditional Karnatic music fare with devotional lyrics addressed to Hindu Gods and Goddesses. Sheikh Chinna Moulana Saheb teaches the *nadaswaram* to Hindu and Muslim students in a school called "Saradha Nagaswara Sangeetha Ashram," a school named after Saradha or Sarasvati, the Hindu patron goddess of Music; the musicians play traditional Karnatic ragas, including some called Husseini and Paraz, names clearly of Persian origin. In the intellectual arena, one notes that Justice M.M. Ismail is a famous scholar of the Tamil *Ramayanam*,[1] a work written by Kampan in the ninth century. He is just one, albeit the most renowned, in a long tradition of Muslim scholars whose mother tongue is Tamil and who have studied many Tamil texts, including the Ramayana, in great depth. One notes that in the ritual sphere, Hindus and Muslims regularly flock to the shrine of Muslim saints in the cities of Nagore and Madurai in Tamilnadu. In Visnu's temple at Srirangam there is also considerable latitude to participate in what is perceived to be shared heritage. Holy men who work miracles, devotees, vernacular texts (we shall focus on the Tamil epics in this paper), and some aspects of performing arts are seen to be part of the shared heritage, the shared worlds of the Hindu and Muslim traditions in south Asia in general, and south India in particular.

The tearing down of the Babri Masjid, the mosque that was built over what some Hindus believe to be the actual birthplace of Lord Rama in Ayodhya, gave notoriety to the tensions that exist between Hindus and Muslims in parts of northern India. The partition of India and Pakistan in 1947 and the insurgency in Kashmir in recent years have all contributed to the perception that an acrimonious relationship exists between the two communities in the subcontinent. The intellectual and cultural exchanges that have taken place between Muslims and Hindus in many areas and fields are not focused on by the media; encounters in the fields of ritual devotion, scholarship, and musical collaborations do not make sensational news. The enduring image that haunts the Indian is that of Sadhvi Rithambara's penetrating voice on December 6, 1992, urging the demolition of the Babri Masjid: *"Ek dhakka aur do, Babri Masjid to do."* "Give another shove and tear down the Babri mosque," she goads the Hindu "volunteers," while she herself seems to be in an ecstatic trance.

Is this scene the legacy of over a millennium of Hindus and Muslims inhabiting India? Or do we look for other enduring pictures that convey a different impression, a different motif than that of contested power or militant malice? Syed Ahmed Khan had whimsically said: "India is like a bride which has got two beautiful and lustruous eyes – Hindus and Mussulmans,"[2] but romantic images such as these have trailed far behind the reality and stereotypes of violence. In this paper, I shall focus on a different geographic area than the north, and portray the relationship of Hindus and Muslims in the state of Tamilnadu deep in the south. Here these Muslims trace their heritage not with the Islam of Iran/Persia or Central Asia, but directly with seventh-century Arabia. I will initially trace the catalyzing incidents leading to the demolition of the Babri Masjid with a discussion of the *political* and *judicial* highlights that immediately preceded the demolition of the Babri Masjid. In the second part of my paper, I will review why the reaction to this incident was considered to be "lukewarm" in the south. Our search for answers will lead us to examine the literary and aesthetic heritages of Muslim and Hindu communities that have shared the same geographic and cultural spaces for centuries. I will focus on those forums where there have been creative and fulfilling encounters between Hindus and Muslims in Tamilnadu. These are the fluid and pliant areas of textual scholarship, performing arts, and religious ritual. While the media focuses on the strains of the Hindu–Muslim relationships, we may briefly tune in to the strains of music and scholarship where the religious traditions cleave together. The cleaving – the splitting and the holding together – of the two traditions has been the leitmotif of Indian culture, cooking, politics, and society for several centuries.

The strains of religion and politics

On December 6, 1992, a group of Hindu militants broke through the lines of police, paramilitary personnel, and government administrators, and demolished the Babri Masjid in the city of Ayodhya. The Babri Masjid was a mosque allegedly built by the first Mughal emperor Babar in 1528 on the actual birth place of Rama, one of the ten incarnations of Lord Vishnu. Liberal newspapers and the media decried the demolition of the mosque. *India Today*, a magazine that self-consciously models itself on *Time* magazine, called the event "A Nation's Shame" and gave a detailed hour-by-hour commentary of this event. *The Indian Express* called this event an "outrage" in its editorial entitled "A Nation Betrayed," and in a rare gesture, published the editorial on the front page (*Indian Express*, Madras, Dec. 7, 1992). Like *India Today*, the *Indian Express* had a delineated a full commentary of the last few hours, entitled, "Five Hours to Ram" (*Indian Express Sunday Magazine*, Dec. 13, 1993, p. 1). "Outrage in Ayodhya" said *The Hindu*, a leading newspaper in the south, and added in the Sunday Magazine, "We have met the enemy, and he is us" (*The Hindu Magazine*, Dec. 13, 1993, p. 1).

The demolition of the mosque and the subsequent installation of the images of Rama and his wife Sita in the disputed site brought to a head several centuries of simmering tensions, and about seven years of active political involvement in the "liberation" of the *janmabhumi* or birth site. The battle cry to "Free Ram from incarceration" had been echoing in the streets since 1984. The agitation for this so-called liberation by the Hindu nationalists gathered momentum in the wake of two incidents. The *first* was a landmark court decision in 1985 in a case involving Muslim Personal law and the government's subsequent effort to abrogate the Supreme Court decision by introducing legislation demanded by a very conservative faction of the Muslim theologians. These Muslim leaders also controlled a sizable vote bank in the upcoming elections. The legislation passed by both houses of parliament negated the Supreme Court decision. This was considered by liberals as a sell-out of secularism and by the Hindu nationalists as the sell-out of Hindu interests, and as a "pampering" of the Muslim minority. The *second* incident was the release (and threat of implementation) of the Mandal commission report, a report which urged the government to adopt quotas or reservations of seats in educational institutions and in the public job market for the so-called backward classes which had been historically discriminated against in India.

The *Ramayana* or the story of Rama, a Sanskrit epic, was composed around 600 BCE and according to later texts, the hero Rama was really an incarnation of Lord Visnu. Valmiki, the author of one of the earliest and best-known versions of the *Ramayana*, says that Rama was born in Ayodhya, and later literature reiterates this point. In the eighth century

CE, Kulacekara Alvar, a Tamil-speaking poet from the deep south, sang thus:

> In the beautiful city of Ayodhya, encircled by towers,
> A flame that lit up all the worlds
> > appeared in the Solar race
> > and gave life to all the heavens.
> This warrior, with dazzling eyes,
> Rama, dark as a cloud, the First One, my only Lord,
> is in Citrakuta, city of Tillai.
> When is the day when my eyes will behold him
> > and rejoice?
> > > (*Perumal Tirumoli* 10.1)

In the ninth century, Kampan, a poet who rendered the *Ramayana* in the Tamil language, glorified the city of Ayodhya in several cantos. Ayodhya has also been a pilgrimage center through the centuries. While no one disputes that Ayodhya is the legendary birthplace of Rama, the actual birth site has been debated. It is alleged that in the nineteenth century, the British encouraged the rumor that the first Mughal emperor Babur built a mosque over the actual holy spot. This was done as part of the British policy of "divide and rule," and the bait from all available accounts seems to have been successful. While there were tensions, adequate compromises had been worked out between the Hindus and Muslims until soon after the partition of India and Pakistan. In 1949, images of Rama and Sita were installed within the mosque with the tacit approval of the district magistrate, Mr. Nayar, and the house of worship became disputed territory again.[3] Still this was hardly news for years. Tense encounters between the two religious traditions were and are still seen regularly in other parts of India, like Kashmir, but Ayodhya was in the freezer. However, in 1984, *India Today*, in an article entitled "Ramjanmbhumi: Conflicting Claims," ominously warned:

> Ayodhya, the birthplace of Lord Rama and the holiest of holies of the Hindu, has been the site of at least 76 holy wars over the past 500 years. Last week, it became the rallying point for the start of yet another battle threatening to pour fuel on communal fire.[4]

In the 1980s, the relationship between the Hindus and Muslims appears to have become strained for a new set of reasons. It has been alleged that Hindus became nervous with the oil boom and the money from the Gulf countries which started pouring into India. Indian Muslims began to build opulent mosques, in some cases close to temples and recreational places. Let us briefly look at south India, where the relationship between the two communities has traditionally been calm. Both tourism officials and conservative Hindus were agitated. Commenting on a mosque being built right next to Kerala's famous Kovalam beach, *India Today* said in 1984:

> the mosque does little to enhance the beauty of the picturesque beach. For another, loudspeakers rigged up on a coconut palm lustily broadcast namaz five times a day, disturbing the peace of the hotel's clients. Said a top official: "After the mosque comes, do you think the mullahs will allow nude sunbathing as it is done here today . . ."[5]

Two political parties which support Hindu nationalism, the RSS (Rashtriya Swayam Sevak) and the BJP (Bharatiya Janta Party), got embroiled in the controversy and placed an image of Shiva about 35 meters from the mosque. This scene was repeated in many states.

In addition to the building of mosques, it was alleged that many of the traditional homes belonging to Hindus around the temples of Thanjavur, a town in Tamilnadu, south India, were bought at very attractive prices by Muslims coming from the Gulf. The Hindus did sell their houses at high prices and made a lot of money, but in the process, the entire atmosphere of the streets around the temples changed. The houses around the temple were now predominantly occupied by Muslims. The reasons apparently were economic; according to *India Today*, the average Muslim family in Thanjavur earned substantially more than the average Hindu family. Almost every Muslim family had at least one member in West Asia, Singapore, or Malaysia; the implication was that this member was remitting lucrative foreign exchange to their families at home. Apparently the Brahmins who held the agricultural lands were not at liberty to sell them without permission from various labor unions; hence, they tried to make money by selling their households at exorbitant prices. The atmosphere around the temples had changed. *India Today* reported:

> But today, instead of the fragrance of jasmine and sacred ash around temples, one smells spicy Muslim food. And instead of sari-clad women genuflecting before shrines in the temple compound, the majority of the women in sight are burkha-clad ones peeping out from half-shut doors in the agraharams [a cluster of Brahmin

households around a temple]. Replacing the *kolams* [floral patterns in front of doorways made out of rice powder] is the crescent moon above the door. Says 35-year-old Mohammed Bhasha of Avoor: "The temple culture is slowly disappearing. We Muslims have come to occupy most of the agraharams."[6]

The houses were sold and now there was some nervousness about taking out processions of the deities through these streets which were occupied by Muslims. In the past, several temple processions were taken out through Muslim dominated areas without any hint of tension. In fact, as we shall see soon, such processions still take place in some areas, with participation by Muslims. In Thanjavur, however, there seems to have been a new self-consciousness about these rituals.

In 1981, there was an uproar when it was revealed that in Meenakshipuram, in the state of Tamilnadu, Hindus were converted to Islam. Some accounts said that Hindus were bribed by a cassette boom box in exchange for conversion, and other descriptions said they were outcaste Hindus ("scheduled caste") who had a raw deal from their own religion. Political parties alleged it was the money promised to the new converts that induced them to convert; Mr. Nanaji Deshmukh said that about 500 rupees had been offered to a man called Ayyappan, and he had refused to convert. While conversions to Christianity had largely been ignored by the massive Hindu majority, this incident in Meenakshipuram sparked some tension among politicians. In Meenakshipuram alone, 180 families converted on February 19, 1981, and later, another 27 families followed on May 23, 1981. The real reason for the nervousness was, of course, political. Mumtaz Ali Khan says that it was alleged that "mass conversion would lead to an increased Muslim population which would then give them a political advantage."[7] While all these incidents, especially the worry over the influx of Gulf money giving Muslims more financial power, aggravated many south Indian Hindu communities; in the North, one may say that the Supreme Court decision on the famous Shah Bano case triggered Hindu nationalism, in the form that is sported and supported by the Bharatiya Janata Party.

In 1978, Ahmed Khan of Indore, Madhya Pradesh, divorced his wife Shah Bano. He had been married to her for 44 years. He then returned the money, Rs. 3000, which had been the mehr or marriage settlement given by her family. Shah Bano did not accept this and sued him for maintenance under Section 125 of the Criminal Procedure code of India, and was eventually granted an alimony of about Rs. 175 by the high court. Her husband refused to pay. He claimed that under Muslim Personal Law he was not obligated to pay her anything more than the three-month *iddat* or maintenance. The case was appealed all the way up to the Supreme Court which upheld the lower court's ruling.

The Supreme Court held that under section 125 of the Criminal Code, a husband was required to pay maintenance to a wife if she had no means of support. In addition to upholding the initial verdict of the lower court, the Supreme Court also went beyond the parameters of the case and interpreted the Koran. The court said that the Koran decreed that impoverished wives should be taken care of by their husbands. The justices added on their own accord that if no one was able to take care of the Muslim woman, the *waqf* board (a charitable board which collected the religious contributions of Muslims) should do so. The justices also asserted that it was a matter of regret that Article 44 of the Constitution remained dormant. Section 44 of the Constitution of India provided that the State shall endeavor to secure for the citizens a uniform civil code throughout the territory of India. The conservative Muslim community was in an uproar at this decision, especially at the remark regretting the implementation of a civil code. The conservative Muslims had always opposed the implemetation of a uniform civil code. Muslim women protested outside the Parliament, urging the government to withdraw a bill which would exempt Muslim marriages from Section 125. Saifuddin Chowdhury, a Muslim and a Marxist MP, called the bill a "black bill" and said: "This bill will throw Muslim women to wolves." Prominent in its opposition was the Bharatiya Janata Party.[8]

The political strains between Muslims and Hindus that were precipitated by the Shah Bano case were enhanced with the Hindu perception that Muslims were being favored by a quota system (a form of "affirmative action" program) recommended by the Mandal report. The eighties had seen the emergence of this controvesial report. This government of India report on the Backward Classes Community urged the reservation of seats in educational institutions, professional colleges, and public-sector jobs to people belonging to "other backward classes." 22 percent of jobs were set apart for scheduled castes and tribes, and 27 percent of the "other backward" castes; in all 49.5 percent of all government jobs and seats in government schools were reserved. Indira Gandhi did not implement these controversial recommendations and on August 13, 1990 Prime Minister V.P. Singh issued a government order implementing one part of the recommendations. Upper-caste, educated Hindus who had held many of the plum jobs for centuries were outraged at this reverse discrimination. It is probable that caste issues were predominant in their support of the BJP and the eventual Ram-janmabhumi debacle.[9]

In this furor, the Muslim community's exasperation with the government's new decision on Ayodhya was ignored. Both Muslims and Hindus had not been allowed access to the disputed shrine, lest there be an outbreak of violence. In January 1986, Rajiv Gandhi had told the chief minister of the Uttar Pradesh state to ignore these restrictions. On February 1, 1986, the Faizabad sessions court decided to open the controversial Ayodhya shrine for worship, allowing unhindered access to Hindu devotees.[10] Twenty people died immediately in the communal riots that followed. On February 14, after the Friday prayers, the Shahi Imam of Delhi's Jama Masjid, Syed Abdullah Bukhari, addressed a large Muslim congregation and called for a jihad against the "government conspiracy."[11] The crowd turned violent, and showed its anger against the transport buses and policemen. Two Muslim men were killed in the police firing. In the Muslim backlash, two Hindu temples were set on fire in Kashmir.

It was evident that the government had agreed to the opening of the Babri Masjid shrine to reassure Hindus that despite the legislation abrogating the Supreme Court decision, it was not pandering to the Muslim electorate. But the opening of the shrine was more agitating than Pandora's box. In March 1987, 300,000 Muslims gathered at the Delhi Boat Club and demanded that the Babri Masjid be handed over to them. The following month, Hindus gathered at Ayodhya to pledge liberation of the shrine. By 1989, *India Today* warned that the "simmering cauldron of communal frenzy" was alarming.[12] The BJP was accused of setting the tone for the Hindu nationalism, and its state unit chief Sunderlal Patwa criticized the then prime minister Rajiv Gandhi's personal life. Rajiv Gandhi was married to Sonia, who was Italian. The concern and anger of the party is evident from Patwa's statement: "[the] prime minister . . . has kept in his house a *videshi* and a *vidharmi* [foreigner and nonbeliever] wife who has endangered the independence and sovereignty of the country by providing easy access to the Italian mafia, Christian missionaries and foreign intelligence agencies."[13] The Viswa Hindu Parisad ("World Hindu Society") started *ratha yatras*, that is, politicians traveling on cars converted into chariots making pilgrimages to Ayodhya. The most famous of them, led by L.K. Advani, the leader of the BJP, began in 1990. His chariot was an air-conditioned Toyota disguised as a vehicle from the epics. He was followed by hundreds of people chanting that after liberating Ayodhya, they would liberate the holy spots of Mathura and Kashi (Benares). Earlier slogans such as "We swear by Ram that we will build the temple in the same site" gave way to harsher ones like: "A Hindu whose blood does not boil in anger has water in his veins; if you do not serve the Ram Janmabhumi in your youth, you have lived in vain."

On December 6, 1992, after adequate warning to the government, the Hindu "kar sevaks" ("Hindu volunteers"), with active encouragement from the BJP leaders and a shouts of encouragement from a political activist, a woman called Sadhvi Rithambara – an ascetic – demolished the mosque. Most of northern India erupted in riots. The "Hindu card" had been played. The saga goes on, tossed by the Hindu nationalists, Muslim leaders, religious heads, and the various courts.

The aftermath of the demolition of the Babri Masjid led to considerable violence in many parts of northern India. The south, despite all the minor tensions we noted earlier in the paper, was relatively calm, and in a few months it was clear that the southern states were immune from the Ram hysteria. The south has always been suspicious about north Indian imperialism, and resented the imposition of Hindi, a north Indian language, on the southern states. Even during the partition, the south had remained relatively insulated from the rest of the country. After the Babri Masjid was demolished, Veerappa Moily, the chief minister of Karnataka, shrugged: "The Ayodhya issue has been viewed more as a battle between Aryan Muslims and Aryan Hindus."[14] The BJP saw the reaction from the south as tepid at best; the party's slogans of freeing India from centuries of Muslim domination – something that the media perceived as being very effective up north – left the south cold.

The south has been free of major foreign invasions, and more important, the religious minorities are generally better integrated there. Instead of Urdu, most of the southern Muslims (with the exception of course of the Hyderabadi Muslims) speak the local languages. The Tamil-speaking Muslims also hold themselves to be superior to those of the north. It is the understanding of many Tamil Muslims that they are descendants of seafaring people who encountered Islam[15] and converted after accepting it. It is important to note that the Marakkayars (a Muslim group from Tamilnadu) believe that their ancestors either came directly from Arabia, or were Tamil people who accepted Islam after direct contact with Muslims traders from the Middle East, within a few years of the prophet's death (and by some accounts in the lifetime of the prophet himself), and not after the conquest by Muslims from northern India. The marakkayars generally claim superiority over north Indian Muslims, claiming that their community has older connections with Islam and the middle East. It is interesting that British anthropologists seem to have thought that the Urdu-speaking Muslims were in some way more "authentic" than the vernacular-speaking ones.[16] Ironically enough, the Tamil-speaking Muslims had a self-perception of their antiquity and their deep ties to seventh-century Arabian Islam.

But the real reason why the Ram issue was not important in the south for the Hindus was this: Rama was not the primary deity being worshiped. In Andhra Pradesh, the Visnu temple at Tirupati is the most popular and certainly the richest temple by way of offerings in all of India. Here too, it is not a generic Visnu, but one with a specific name, Venkateswara, who is worshiped. Srisailam, with a large Siva temple, is also a major pilgrimage spot, with a long history of royal patronage.[17] In Tamilnadu, Visnu is known as Ranganatha in Srirangam, and the large temple complex (155 acres) has about 60 shrines in it, including one for the Muslim wife of Ranganatha. According to the local legend, a Muslim princess fell in love with this God and followed him here. She is offered what is perceived to be "Muslim fare" in the daily food offerings; i.e., milk and wheat bread, rather than the rice which is offered to the south Indian deities regularly. The dargahs[18] – Muslim shrines – are visited regularly by Hindus, and in some districts the ritual procession of Visnu on certain festival days stops at the dargah of a Muslim saint before winding its way out. The chief minister of Tamilnadu, Jayalalitha, was so nervous about the Muslim vote in her state after the Babri Masjid incident, that she traveled to many mosques, offering namaz. Hindus in the state of Kerala generally worship a god called Ayyappan or another incarnation of Visnu called Krishna, not Rama. Even when the epic *Ramayana* was telecast – an event which drew the largest viewership week after week – Kerala had the lowest number of viewers. During the annual pilgrimage to the Ayyappan shrine, the nearly 200,000 male pilgrims stop at a mosque which honors the Muslim friend of Lord Ayyappa, give their donations, and then embark on the uphill climb. The BJP realized that the south was lukewarm about the Babri Masjid disaster, and if anything, were angry with the north Indian "fundamentalists." This is, of course, the Hindu reaction.

The Muslims in south India were distressed and dismayed at the anti-Muslim slogans in the north and wondered when the gun would be pointed towards them. Their distress is seen in the popular songs sold in prerecorded cassettes which we will discuss later in this paper.

While the tragedy of the confrontations cannot be minimized, the cordial relations that have existed between the two communities have been ignored by the press and certainly suppressed by the politicians. There are many areas of encounter and integration, including as one may expect, entertainment. Entertainment includes sports, and popular and classical music. In these arenas, where both art and monetary considerations are supposed to be above politics and discrimination, one sees integration in more visible and audible ways. To some extent, one may even argue that it is more real, more deep in India, than in the United States in these fields. Hundreds of millions of Indians, whatever their native language, listen to and sing with the melodious strains of duets by Lata Mangeshkar and Mohammed Rafi, and one seldom associates the singers as being Hindu or Muslim.

The most remarkable Hindu–Muslim encounters in India are seen in the shared worlds of scholarship, art, and ritual. To illustrate these issues, I will primarily choose my examples from the south of India, especially the state of Tamilnadu. We have already noted that many Hindu participate in ritual pilgrimages to Muslim shrines in Tamilnadu and Kerala. While the Muslims do not reciprocate on this level by visiting Hindu temples or shrines, there is a long history of Muslim scholarship on Hindu literature. The intellectual and cultural exchanges that have taken place between Muslims and Hindus in the state of Tamilnadu in southern India, however, have hardly been studied by western scholars until recently.[19]

Intellectual encounters: the Muslim scholarship on the Tamil *Ramayanam*

There has been a long history of Muslims committed to the understanding of different aspects of the Hindu tradition. The Shattari order of Indian Sufis practiced Yogic austerities. 'Abd al- Qadir Bada'uni (1540 to *c.*1615) translated the Hindu epics the *Ramayana* and the *Mahabharata* into Persian, and Dara Shikoh (1615–59), a son of the Emperor Shah Jahan, translated the *Bhagavad Gita* and the Upanishads.[20] In southern India, there is a long tradition of Muslim scholarship on the ninth-century Tamil version of the *Ramayana*, written by Kampan.

Over the centuries, Muslims in Tamilnadu have studied both secular works and Hindu religious poetry in Tamil and utilized many of the traditional Tamil literary conventions with great skill in their religious writings. Some of the greatest scholars of the ninth-century Tamil *Ramayanam* composed by Kampan (known as *Iramavataram*, "the descent of Rama," or the *Kampa Ramayanam*) have been Muslims. M.M. Ismail, the former Chief Justice of the Madras High Court, and a noted scholar on the Tamil *Ramayanam* who has written several books on the subject, remarked with justifiable pride that in every generation there is at least one Muslim who is an authority on the Tamil *Ramayanam*.[21] There is strong participation by Muslims in the Kampan Vila or "Festival of Kampan," an annual celebration devoted to the scholarship on this poet.

Kampan, who lived in the ninth century CE, was born in Terezhundur on the banks of the Kaveri river. Kampan's *Ramayanam* is by all accounts a literary masterpiece, and sections of the text can be found in the reading list of many Tamil courses in college curricula. It can be shown that at least in the last 300 years this Tamil epic has been studied and enjoyed by generations of Muslim scholars in Tamilnadu. One of the earliest serious scholars of this text and one whose own writing owes a lot to the *Kampa Ramayanam* is Umaru Pulavar ("Omar the Poet," *c*.1665–1773).[22]

Umaru Pulavar is the author of the Tamil epic poem the *Cira Puranam* ("The Purana of the *Sirat* or the Life of the Prophet.") The Tamil title of Umaru Pulavar's *Cira Puranam* (The Life of the Prophet) is indicative of the style in language and content that emerges in the text. *Cira* is the Tamil form of the Arabic *sirah*, a word used for hagiographic tradition. In this context, when one has to place oneself as part of a literary or religious tradition, it is in fact the kiss of death to assert that one is completely original or that one's ideas have never been enunciated before. For example, in the political and religious correctness of the Vedic tradition, the "orthodox" schools of philosophy always dutifully said that what they were saying was only an explanation of what was already in the Vedas and other earlier literature. Musicians, dancers, artists usually credit their talent to the training received from their teachers. To borrow and to improve on it or to embellish the idea is not plagiarism, it is a mark of one's humility and deference to the weight of tradition.

Many of Kampan's ideas can be traced to other earlier poets; however, he leaves his own distinctive mark on his *Ramayanam*. Umaru too shows striking knowledge of other literature, and is also in turn strikingly original. Like Kampan, he begins his epic narration of the prophet's life with a chapter describing the country, followed by one where he describes the main city. Typical Tamil literary conventions are used by both poets to talk about the wealth and prosperity of the land. Let us consider just one simple example. Kampan talks of the heavy rolling clouds that drench the Kosala kingdom with rain; Umaru describes the torrential rain in Arabia which makes the fields of rice and sugarcane rich and fertile. Both poets, of course, are projecting the fertile Chola countryside onto northern India and Arabia. The rains fall from the mountains like waterfalls, and swiftly flows through the land, carrying with it aromatic wood and jewels (which float away from the rich women who bathe in the waters), and by bearing these riches, the torrents look like *vaniya* merchants carrying precious goods:

> Carrying the pearls, gold, peacock feathers
> beautiful white ivory from an elephant, aromatic *akil* wood
> sandalwood, matchless in fragrance,
> the floods looked like the *vaniya* merchants.
> (*Kampa Ramayanam Bala Kandam, Arruppatalam*, 7)

This simile is repeated by Umaru in describing the Arabian landscape:

> Carrying the fallen sandalwood,
> branches from the dark *akil* tree,
> pearls from the broken elephant's horn, white ivory,
> more precious than these, red rubies, radiant in three ways,
> carrying these all towards the sea,
> the stream laden rich bamboo, looked like a *vaniya* merchant.
> (*Cira Puranam, Vilattattu Kantam, Nattu Patalam* (the Chapter
> on the Countryside), 12)

The floods sweep away gems from the mountains just as a courtezan embraces a king and sweeps away his gold, gems, and priceless pearls (9). Kampan, in his *Ramayanam*, also uses the analogy of the courtesan embracing a king and taking away his jewelry:

> Like a courtezan embracing her lover
> his head, his body, his feet, as if in desire
> all for a minute [and fleeing with his ornaments]
> the floods embrace the peak, the slopes, the foothills
> and sweep away everything.
> (*Kampa Ramayanam Bala Kandam, Arruppatalam*, 6)

This analogy is also used by Umaru Pulavar:

> Like a courtezan embracing the king
>   majestic like the mountain,
>   giving him pleasure,
> and then sweeping away gold which gives us prosperity,
> precious gems, pearls and all splendid things,

and flees the frontiers,
the floods swiftly flow
carrying with them all riches.
(*Vilattattu Kantam, Nattu Patalam* (the Chapter on the
Countryside), 9)

Waterfalls carrying gems is also a traditional image in Tamil literature. Nammalvar, a ninth-century poet, speaks of the waterfalls of Tirupati hills sweeping down priceless gems:

Lord of Venkata hill
where clear waterfalls crash
spilling gems, gold and pearls . . .
(*Tiruvaymoli* 6.10.3)

Umaru continues his description of the countryside. The river flows through the Kurinci (mountainous) land, presumably of Arabia, springs through the desert (a recognized category in the landscapes of Tamil poems), and flows into the forests (12–13). Reaching *marutam* (cultivated land) it fills the lakes, ponds, and tanks (15). The streams break through the lakes and approach farming lands. They sweep through the sugarcane plantations, slush up the ponds where the lotus flowers, beautiful and fragrant, bloom (18). The water is then contained and used for irrigation (17). The single body of water held in many tanks, ponds, lakes, and areas where the lotus flower blossoms is compared by Umaru to life (Tamil: *uyir*) which appears in hundreds of millions. This idea reminds one of the Advaitin notion that a single soul (*atman*) appears in many forms and bodies and seems to be many. While Umaru does not elaborate on his analogy, it is striking that he seems at home with these Vedantic ideas.

Where did Umaru get these ideas from? The earliest Tamil literature composed in the earliest centuries of the Common Era recognizes five landscapes. The "*cankam*" poems (also known as the poems of the classical age or the "bardic corpus"), dealing with romantic or heroic themes, refer to five basic situations. These situations correspond in poetry to five landscape settings (*tinai*), birds, flowers, times, gods, etc. The five basic psychological situations for *akam* or "inner poems" are love-making, waiting anxiously for a beloved, separation, patient waiting of a wife, and anger at a lover's real or imagined infidelity. These correspond to the mountainous (*kurinci*), seaside (*neytal*), arid (*palai*), pastoral (*mullai*), and agricultural (*marutam*) landscapes.[23] More specifically, Umaru's descriptions closely resemble the descriptions of Kampan in the first two chapters of his version of the *Ramayanam*. However, even though the details are exquisitely similar in spirit and in concept, both poets have their own inimitable style in literature and their individuality also shines out. Reading both descriptions is similar to listening to the same *raga* played by two maestros.

Umaru Pulavar had availed himself of the riches of the Tamil language through the *Ramayanam* and he in turn enriched Tamil literature through his *Cira Puranam*. Umaru Pulavar was not an isolated example of a Muslim scholar at home with the Tamil *Ramayanam*. When we peruse the annual programs on the "Festival of Kampan" held every August in Madras, we regularly encounter names of Muslim scholars who have studied the Tamil *Ramayanam*. Perhaps the best-known among the Muslim scholars committed to the scholarship of the Tamil *Ramayanam* is Justice M.M. Ismail, former chief justice of the Madras Hight Court.

Dr. M.M. Ismail was born on February 8, 1921 in Nagapattinam, on the eastern coast of the state of Tamilnadu. This is an area with a high Muslim concentration. His parents were Muhammad Kasim Marakkayar and Rukaiya Bibi. After three years in a *madrasa*, and elementary education in the Nagore Municipal Muslim Boys school, he attended the Nagai (Nagapattinam) National High School. He majored in Mathematics for his undergraduate education in the Presidency College of the Madras University and later attended the Madras Law College. He received his degree in law in 1945 and then became an advocate attached to the Madras High court. In 1967 he was appointed a justice of the Delhi high court; later that year he moved to the Madras high court, where he eventually became the Chief Justice in 1979. He was the interim Governor of the Tamilnadu state in 1980. In 1981, the government transferred him to the Kerala high court. Justice Ismail resigned in protest because the order had been given on short notice without prior discussion or negotiation.

Throughout his life, Justice Ismail has been recognized and decorated for his scholarship. In south Asia, scholars are recognized for their erudition with titles, medals, symbolic shawls, and prizes. Justice Ismail has received dozens of prizes for his oratory talents, writings, and knowledge of Tamil literature. When he was nine, he stunned his village with his oratorial skills during the Milad un Nabi (the prophet's birthday) celebrations. His forte was – and continues to be – the *Kampa Ramayanam*. In 1978 the *Kampan Kalakam* (the Kampan Society) of Palaymkottah and Tirunelveli invited the well-known Tamil scholar

P. Sri to confer upon him the title of "The Beacon light of the *Kampa Ramayanam.*" In 1979, he was awarded an honorary doctorate by the Annamalai University. The Rotary Club of Madurai honored him with the Paul Harris Fellowship in 1989, citing his scholarhsip, especially in the *Kampa Ramayanam*, and his efforts in disseminating that scholarship and Indian culture. In 1991, Narada Gana Sabha, an elitist cultural organization in Madras, honored him with the title "Rama Ratnam" (the Gem of Rama). The honor that he cherishes immensely is the esteem shown by the "Sankaracarya"[24] of Kanchi Kamakoti Pitham. This Sankaracarya, known as Chandrasekhara Saraswati, was the former Hindu pontifical head of a *smarta* (a sectarian brahmin community) monastery and had a large following numbering in the hundreds of thousands all over India.

The Sankaracarya and Justice Ismail apparently have had several friendly and scholarly discussions and conversations over the last thirty years. Justice Ismail has written about some of these conversations. Apparently after Justice Ismail had published an article where he interpreted Rama's actions in one episode of the *Ramayanam*, the Sankaracarya was so pleased that he sent for the author. The article had focused on a particular incident in the *Ramayana* which some Hindus find hard to accept and justify. It involves Rama's killing of a monkey king called Vali, and giving the throne to Vali's brother, Sugriva. Justice Ismail's interpretation is based on the context of the episode, and Vali's final words entrusting his son to Rama. Remember, Rama had just shot Vali; but instead of ranting against his killer, Vali entrusts his son to Rama's care. Based on these lines and other issues, Justice Ismail had shown how Rama's character remains flawless in Kampan's version of the story. The Sankaracarya's words approving Justice Ismail's treatment of the episode were simple: "You are the Chief Justice. You have rendered justice to Rama."[25]

Perhaps the most interesting honors for Justice Ismail came in 1993 from the Hindu communities in the diaspora. Hindus from the Cleveland area and the Canadian Council of Hindus celebrated Justice Ismail's scholarship of the *Ramayanam*. The Hindus of the Greater Cleveland area annually celebrate the Festival of Tyagaraja. Tyagaraja, an eighteenth-century musician and composer, was an ardent devotee of Rama. His compositions are sung and his devotion is celebrated in almost every classical Carnatic music concert and in special music fests dedicated to him. These music fests are celebrated all over the world. Rama, the object of Tyagaraja's devotion and of Kampan's epic, has been the focus of Justice Ismail's scholarship and erudition for decades. The

Cleveland association and the Canadian Council of Hindus honored the decades of scholarship and achievements of Justice Ismail.

In Tamilnadu, Hindus have tended to take the scholarship of Justice Ismail and other Muslims on the *Ramayanam* for granted. After the Babri Masjid incident that Hindus in the diaspora at least have become self-conscious about the irony of the south Indian situation where the great scholars of the *Kampan Ramayanam* are Muslims. One may wonder why this text is so important in Tamilnadu and why it has been the focus of scholarship, especially for the Tamil-speaking Muslims. As we noted earlier, Justice Ismail had noted with justifiable pride that in every generation there is a great Muslim scholar of the Tamil *Ramayanam*; Umaru Pulavar in the seventeenth century is the first celebrated example that we know about. Tamil literature has a long history, going back at least to the first century of the Common Era (some say even earlier), and has both secular poems of love and war and, later on, moving devotional hymns to Visnu, Siva, Murukan et al. There is also considerable Tamil literature in the Jain tradition as well some Buddhist works. The *Civika Cintamani* and the *Cilappatikaram*, epics written by Jains, are extremely important in the study of Tamil literature and form part of any core curriculum in Tamil studies. It is in this context that we can see Kampan's *Ramayanam*. Kampan's age seems to have either coincided or come soon after the time of the Tamil Vaisnava poets known as the *alvars*. But, interestingly enough, while the *alvar* poems became part of domestic and Visnu temple liturgies, and the Saiva poems were used in Siva temples and Saivaite homes, the Tamil *Ramayanam* was never pressed into devotional use. It has never been part of domestic piety, nor did it attain the popularity of the seventeenth-century *Ramayan* of Tulsidas in Hindi. The Tamil *Ramayanam* was not considered to be "revealed" or inspired in a manner analagous to the poems of the *alvars*.

It would be interesting to speculate why this text never attained ritual status. While a discussion on this theme may be outside the scope of the focus of this paper, one may look for a complex cluster of reasons, which will again have to be explored with a "why." Rama seems to have been a relative newcomer to the south and his limited popularity was comparatively late; archeologists have noted that images of Rama and temples to him are not among the earlier remains of Tamilnadu.[26] Lack of high-caste and royal/political patronage, and lack of sponsorship by prominent Vaisnava leaders, may have been other possible reasons which would have to be explored to see why the Tamil *Ramayanam* was not enacted, sung, and used in devotional exercises like the poems of the *alvars*. Kampan's work has been counted as a literary if not devotional masterpiece, and it seems to be that it is the very lack of appropriation on the ritual level that made the work a "safe" text to be intimately studied by people of the other religions. Muslim scholars have studied Hindu devotional works as well, but their reliance on and intimate knowledge of those works was far less than that of the Tamil *Ramayanam*. The fact that the *Ramayanam* was not appropriated by any one community, except the scholarly one, certainly helped in its acceptance by other religions. Internally, within the Tamil *Ramayanam*, one may sense a lack of polemic against other sects and other religions. This certainly helps in being accepted by a wider audience. While Tamil-speaking Muslims were intensely knowledgable about Tamil literature, they have not extensively participated in the religious rituals and worship patterns of the Hindus. (We will notice some exceptions to this statement soon.) The Hindus, however, while not making much of an effort to read the Koran or any other Islamic literature, nevertheless incorporated Muslim holy men as part of their devotional exercises and made pilgrimages to many of their tombs.[27]

Ritual encounters: Hindus in Muslim dargahs

Hindus in many regions of India have incorporated some Muslim saints and teachers into their pantheon, made pilgrimages to their tombs, and woven stories of Muslim devotees into the legends of their gods. Thus the tombs of many Muslim saints in Nagore, Tamilnadu, or Badaun in Uttar Pradesh attract thousands of Hindu devotees. Devotion to holy men was an integral part of Tamil Muslims religious practice. It is estimated that there are between 500 and 600 active *pir* shrines in the Tamil country and southern Andhra Pradesh.[28] The local nature of Islam is stressed in many shrines which venerate Tamil Muslim saints, many of whom are not known outside the borders of Tamilnadu. This pattern is also seen in the state of Andhra Pradesh, which is culturally (though not linguistically) very similar to Tamilnadu. While a comprehensive description of even the important pilgrimage centers would not be possible in this paper, I shall discuss some sites in Tamilnadu and Andhra Pradesh where about half the devotees visiting the Muslim shrine are Hindus. The shrines discussed in this paper are those at Nagore (near Nagapattinam), Sri Mushnam, Madurai, and Nellore. It must be noted that Hindus visit these shrines usually for the same reasons that they visit Hindu temples: for the fulfillment of a wish such as getting a job, a spouse, or a child. One of the most important reasons is seeing a cure for a disease. When these wishes are fulfilled, they become "regulars" to the shrine.

The individual shrines are praised in songs and prayers, and the specific places in Tamilnadu are frequently glorified, as in this song:

> In the refined land of the Tamils
> Near Tirunelveli,
> In the town of Melappalaiyam
> lives Bashir Appa Wali.
> O Lord (*natha*) Bashir Wali (2)
> King of Grace and Wisdom
> O Lord (*yajamana*) who banishes
> the grief of the poor and the lowly,
> O Yajamana, give us grace . . .
> give immediately

In this and other songs, the Muslims and Hindus stress the local nature of the hierophany, sacralizing the Indian blessed by a holy man.

The shrine of Shahul Hamid at Nagore: The local wali of Nagore, well-known all over Tamilnadu, is hailed thus in a modern song:

> You are the lord (*yajamana*)
> who came to protect us
> in the city of Nagore.

Hindus frequent the darga in Nagore as they do many other Muslim shrines. This is the burial place of Shahul Hamid (Tamil: Shahul Hamitu Nayakar).[29] Shahul Hamid was apparently a thirteenth-generation descendant of Muhiyudin Abdul Khadir Jilani, a renowned Sufi saint. Shahul Hamid was born in 1490 in Manikkapur, in the modern state of Uttar Pradesh. The name given to him at birth was Sayid Abdul Khader. He left home when he was 18 and was to meet his parents only 18 years later. He went in search of spiritual truth and found a teacher in Sayid Muhammad Kavud of Gwalior. Shahul Hamid stayed with him for 10 years. He is credited with a charismatic personality and with several miracles. After extensive travels all over the Middle East, with a vast entourage of disciples, he reached the city of Nagore when he was 44. Apparently Acutappa Nayakar, the Hindu ruler of Thanjavur, received him with honor and donated 200 acres of land to his entourage. Local stories include several miracles both during his lifetime and after death.

Shahul Hamid died in 1558 when he was 68 years old. His dargah as it stands now is about 194,790 square feet.

During his lifetime he is said to have saved ships from sinking. A popular story relates how he saved a Dutch ship from drowning by miraculously floating a piece of glass in the sea. The glass apparently plugged the leak in the ship. After his death, his disciples – who numbered 404 by then – split into four groups and spread in different directions, with the idea of gathering once a year during the anniversary (*kanturi*) celebrations. The first *kanturi* celebrations took place in 1559. This is celebrated annually from the first day of the waxing moon in the month of Jamatul ahir, until the tenth day. Shahul Hamid's shrine is visited by Hindus and Muslims, and hundreds of stories narrating miracles and spiritual healing abound.

Almost all written narratives about Nagore miracles include the benefactions of the Hindu businessman, Palaniyanti Pillai (no date is given), Tirumalai Chetti, and the donations of the Thanjavur kings, Pratap Singh and Tulasi. Apparently Palaniyanti Pillai incurred considerable debt, and sought help from Shahul Hamid by meditating outside his shrine for three days. Palaniyanti Pillai was able to overcome his financial obligations, and to commemorate that Shahul Hamid had miraculously helped him with the payment of 19 lakh rupees (Rs. 190,000), he built the 19 gateways of the dargah.

Through the donations of Tirumalai Chetti, a Hindu devotee, major portions of the dargah were built. Raja Pratap Singh (1739–63), a Hindu king of Thanjavur, paid for the fifth minaret (131 feet tall) after he was blessed with a son through the grace of Shahul Hamid. Later on King Tulasi is said to have bestowed 15 villages to the dargah.

Gorappalayam: Madurai:[30] Going to dargahs in expectation of faith healing is a phenomenon seen in many parts of south Asia. Hindus and Muslims go regularly, with Hindus sometimes outnumbering the Muslims, as in Badaun in northern India. In Gorappalayam, a suburb of Madurai, Tamilnadu, Hindus and Muslims go to the shrines of the Sufi brothers Khaja Syed Sultham Alaudeen Aulia and Khaja Syed Sultham Shameudeen Aulia in search of miraculous cures for those who are mentally ill. About 60 percent of the incoming "patients" are said to be Hindu. People who desire a faith healing have to first show that they have consulted a western "allopathic" doctor before they come here. No information except the name and address of the patient is collected. Patients are diagnosed as either being possessed or as being victims of black magic. Through the prayers and intercession of the Auliars, the patient is eventually cured. The patient is taken inside the shrine, the fatiha or another prayer is recited, and a small lump of brown sugar (jaggery) is given to him. A *tayatu* (a protective amulet), that is, a black thread with a metal tube containing verses from the Koran, is tied to the patient's wrist. The real treatment consists of the interaction between the two babas (saints) and the patients. The *auliars* question the patients and aim to annoy the spirit possessing the patient. The patient is cured when the evil vacates him or her. Men and women live here in separate quarters and are segregated according to the degree of violent behavior that they exhibit. Patients wear chains on their wrists and ankles and are sometimes chained to a stone block. The chains are removed when the patients are cured; they may then leave the darga. The auliars tell the patients in their dreams that they are cured; this is narrated to the caretakers who then discharge them.

Nellore: In Kasamuru, between Nellore and Gudur in Andhra Pradesh, Hindus flock to the local dargah. Here Muslim caretakers of the shrine give blessed *roti* (bread) as marks of favor (*prasada*) to Hindu and Muslim devotees. There are specific *rotis* given to devotees, depending on their needs and supplications. Those who desire jobs or career satisfaction are given *udyoga* (from the Sanskrit word for "work") *roti*, those who pray for children (Sanskrit: *santana*) are given *santana roti*, and so on.[31] The ritual is said to have been started around 1932 or 1933 by a drummer (*naubathvale*) family of A.S. Peta/ Rahmatabad, a village in the Nellore district of Andhra Pradesh. The ritual is conducted now for specific reasons and vows. Two women stand face to face in a foot of water. They immerse two chappathies (*roti* or flat bread) in the water and distribute it with a leafy vegetable curry to their relatives. The ritual is made in the name of any saint that they pray to regularly, but the locals do it in the name of Hazrat Iliyas Raziullatala Anhu, protector of water. This was generally done on the 12th day of the Bakrid festival at A.S. Peta. Due to shortage of water in that place, the ritual is now conducted on the 12th day of Muharram at Nellore. This was performed at a local canal, and after objection from neighbors, the ritual was moved to the Nellore water tank adjacent to Bara Shaheed Dargah, near the Superintendent of Police's office. Initially only the Naubathvale families did the ritual. From 1940 to 1942 the ritual was suspended due to riots, and then resumed. There are more than 100,000 pilgrims who come now to perform the rituals in the name of the Muslim saints; more than half are said to be Hindus. After women ritually perform the vow and immerse the *rotis* with particular reasons in mind, they are distributed to those who want that favor most; for instance someone seeking a job may buy a "employment" *roti*. The ritual is not connected with the Bara Shaheed Dargah, though it is performed near it.

Sri Mushnam and Thaikal rituals: While the Nagore and Madurai dargahs and the *roti* rituals of Nellore articulate the devotion of Hindus to Muslim saints, some rituals that emanate from Sri Mushnam highlight Muslim donors whose philanthropy included gifts to Hindu temples. During a particular annual festival in the shrine of Visnu at Sri Mushnam (near Chidambaram), the procession of the deity stops in a dargah[32] on the way to the sea. Visnu, the main deity in this town, is called Bhu Varaha ("The Boar who lifts the Earth"), and it is interesting that devotion was shown to the *boar* form of the Lord by some Muslim devotees. Apparently, a local king called Hazarat Rahamatulla Walliulla Suthari had his capital in a village called Thaikal near Killai, and endowed large tracts of land to this temple. He also built a pavilion in Killai. The income from this land is used to celebrate the festival for Visnu in the month of Masi (Feb. 15 to March 14). At this time, the procession carrying Visnu goes through the Muslim village of Killai accompanied by band music and offerings are made in front of the dargah where the ruler is buried. A garland from Visnu is placed on the tomb (called *samadhi*, like the burial place of Hindus) and camphor is lit. The Kazi of the mosque recites from the Quran, food offerings are made to the deity and the *prasadam* is taken to the descendants of the nawab. That night, Visnu is taken in a flower-decked palanquin to the dargah and Hindus and Muslims participate in the fireworks show that follows.[33]

This ritual seems similar in some ways to an incident connected with the *rath yatra* (the chariot festival, more popularly known as the "juggernaut") in Puri, Orissa.[34] Here, the chariot of Visnu (known in Puri as "Jagannatha" or Lord of the World) stops outside the *samadhi*, the burial place of Salebeg (b. 1592). Salebeg was the son of Jehangir Quli Khan Lalbeg, who was sent to Orissa around 1590 by Emperor Akbar to assist Man Singh in putting down Afghan rebels. Akbar's son Jehangir made Lalbeg the governor of the areas in the modern state of Bihar, and later he was made governor of Bengal and Orissa. Salebeg's mother was a brahmin widow, and Salebeg was raised in Orissa. Lalbeg was killed on the battlefield and Salebeg wounded. His mother asked him to pray to Lord Krishna of Puri; Salebeg was healed and became a devotee of Lord Krishna/Jagannatha. However, because he was born as a Muslim, he was not allowed to enter Jagannatha's temple, and Salebeg's devotional songs express his ardent longing to see the Hindu God. To commemorate the devotion, Jagannatha's chariot is made to stop near Salebeg's burial place. Arguably, the parameters of this ritual are quite different from the Sri Mushnam ritual. In Sri Mushnam, the donor was an orthodox Muslim, and not a Muslim turned Vaishnavaite as was Salebeg. Again, in Sri Mushnam, the local Muslim population takes part in the hoopla. In Orissa, the situation is comparable to the adoption of the *tulukka nacciyar*, the Muslim consort into the pantheon of devotee-deities seen in states in south India. What we do perceive – and this point has to be emphasized – is the easy permeability and osmosis through which devotion takes place across Hindu–Muslim lines. These lines were obviously not as hardened then as they have been in the twentieth century, and this is a point that will be underscored over and over again.

The participation of Hindus in the ritual atmosphere of the Nagore, Sri Mushnam, and Madurai dargahs is not an unique incident in the map of Hindu–Muslim relations in Tamilnadu. Muslim personages were incorporated into the ever-flexible Hindu pantheon. Occasionally, as in the temples at Srirangam (mentioned earlier), Madurai, and Melkote, a Muslim princess was even portrayed as a consort of Visnu.[35]

One must also not forget the extensive participation of many Hindu communities and groups in the observance – or increasingly in India, the celebration – of Muharram. In the south Indian state of Andhra Pradesh which borders on Tamilnadu, many villages participate extensively in the Muslim rituals.[36] Muharram highlights the mourning of the Shia community for the death of Hussain, the grandson of the Prophet. During this festival, the *alams* or the replicas of the staffs carried by Imam Hussain and his followers at Karbala are taken out in procession. Hindus and Muslims pay respect to the *alams* which are housed in places called *ashurkhanas*. Faith healing is sought, and it is believed, attained. In a folk song on Muharram composed in the Telugu language (and apparently there is a whole body of them) in the Rangareddy district of Andhra Pradesh, there is a plea for cures and for progeny:

> Moharram brings joy and pleasure . . .
> The eager folks coming in groups
> Enjoy themselves in the moonlit night
> Those with stomach aches
> those with eye sores
> Each and everyone prays with devotion
> And is relieved of the affliction
> Hassan and Hussain and the happy Imam

> Qasim dulah's palanquin has started . . .
> The vows have been fulfilled
> And the boon of pregnancy granted to the sterile.[37]

While Muharram commemorates the death of Imam Hussain and the Shiite processions mark the intense grief of the participants, in many villages of Andhra Pradesh women participate in the Muharram functions to be blessed with the birth of a child. This does seem ironic, considering that it was during Muharram that Imam Hussain saw his infant son die and many members of his family perished without water.

In Vijayanagaram Hindus set up *alams* along the road side and call them *pirulu*. The *alams* are locally called *pirulu*; the Telugu language adds the suffix *lu* as an honorific to *pir*. A devotee who set up an *alam* is quoted as saying that if one worships the *pirulu*, "bad luck will stay away . . . just as we worship Rama, we pray to *pirulu*."[38]

Similar narratives of shared space between Hindus and Muslims in the areas of devotion and ritual can be seen in many parts of India. While much of the evidence in this paper comes from Tamilnadu, we find Hindus participating in Muslim rituals in almost every state. Talking of the Chishti shrine in Ajmer, Syed Liyqat Hussain Moin writes:

> The various customs and ceremonies that developed under the patronage and control of the Mughals, Rajputs and Marathas generated an atmosphere of mutual understanding among different sections of society and gave stimulus to the growth of cultural affinity and a spirit of cordiality between Hindus and Muslims of the subcontinent. . . .
>
> The appointment of non-Muslims to the important posts of *mutal-walli* (custodian) and *amin* (revenue officers) etc., their participation in the ceremonies at the shrine in an official capacity, the grant of stipends and daily allowances to Hindus – including *zunnardars* (Hindu priests), *bairagi* (Hindu *faqirs*) and the fixation of their shares in the daily *langar* (free food) reflected the increasing presence of non-Muslims in the internal management of the dargah. But this development did not cause any tension or discord, and the atmosphere has remained as serene as it was before this significant development.[39]

The Ajmer shrine is perhaps one of the best-known in northern India for participation by Hindus in shrines that are primarily Muslim. There are hundreds of such shrines all over south Asia. The figures of Satya Pir in Bengal and Baba Ramdeo in Rajasthan have thousands of devotees.

Ramdeo is considered to be Visnu's incarnation by Hindus, the rein-carnation of a Sufi-named Samas Pir by Muslims, and as an incarnation of Guru Gobind Singh by some Sikhs.[40] While the acceptance of rein-carnation by these Muslims may be considered as problematic by other Muslims, we must not forget that in Rajasthan alone there are groups such as the Meherat ("Rawat Rajputs") who follow Islam in many ways (males are circumcised, the marriage is a *nikah* ceremony, the dead are buried, and *halal* meat is eaten), but also pray to Hindu Gods and Goddesses.[41]

These communities are the clearest examples of those who cannot and will not be induced by politics or census pressures to identify themselves as Hindu or Muslim. Communities like the Meherats in Rajasathan and Memmons in Gujarat fall between the cracks of the census figures which insist that one declare one's faith as Islam or Hin-duism. In the last census, the Meherat of Rajasthan apparently simply declared themselves not as Muslims, not as Hindus, but as "Meherat."[42] Maule-e-Salaam Garasiyas of Gujarat, a community numbering in the hundreds of thousands, have a Muslim lifestyle but carry Hindu names.[43] It is only now, in the wake of Hindu fundamentalism, that these groups are being made to choose between calling themselves Hindu or Muslim.

While the participation of Hindus in the Muharram rituals of Hyder-abad and Andhra Pradesh continues even now, and while Hindus and Muslims continue to make pilgrimages to many Muslim shrines in south India, there have been considerable changes in the last few years in the area of ritual integration. For instance, in the north Indian town of Badaun, Hindus and Muslims regularly visited a Muslim shrine which was known to have miraculous power in healing the sick. In 1989, this town fell victim to Hindu–Muslim riots.

Badaun, in western Uttar Pradesh, is the place where Sayyed Hassan (Bare Sarkar), his brother Shah Vilayat Saheb (Chote Sarkar), and sister Banno Bi, all of the thirteenth century, are buried. Near these graves are those of other saints whom the worshipers referred to as Doctor Saheb or Compounder Saheb. This was home to ecstatic behavior on the part of Hindus and Muslims every Thursday. People who were physically and mentally ill came here in search of cures, by cajoling, pleading, and even abusing the saints. Reporting on the behavior of the devotees, Inderjit Badhwar, a journalist, wrote as late as 1986:

> Here are no gods of vengeance. The saints are all-forgiving, ever
> merciful to their enemies. They answer abuse with compassionate
> benediction. The pilgrims – Sikhs, Hindus, Chisitians and Muslims

from all over India – continue to circumambulate. They ask for settlement of land disputes, forgiveness for robberies committed, punishment for errant lovers, sanity for the insane, health for the sick, vindication for crimes. . . .

At any given time some 2,000 pilgrims camp, or live in rented tents in colonies near Bare Sarkar. There are no Hindu or Muslim or Sikh or low caste or high caste areas. Here they all live together, eat together, pray and curse together . . .

The miracle, ultimately, is that there are no distinctions here.[44]

On October 31, 1989, the same author reported simply: "Badaun died last fortnight . . . The *ziyarat* lies abandoned of the faithful."[45] Badaun was now caught up in the communal tensions that had been building up in other parts of northern India and the perception that the Muslims were being "pampered." Ironically, this town which had spoken Urdu laced with Hindustani for centuries had erupted in flames over a language issue. Apparently Urdu had been introduced into the local governing body, the Vidhan Sabha. Several groups in Badaun which had been stirred up by fiery speeches of Hindu politicians trying to cash in on communal sentiments, equated the introduction of the Urdu language with the government's pampering of Muslims. In the riots that followed 30 people were killed on September 28, 1989. Inderjit Badhwar, who had marveled at the integration he perceived in 1986, now lamented;

> What the future holds is anybody's guess. But Badaun used to be Indian. Today it is Muslim and Hindu.[46]

Hindu and Muslim pilgrims have started coming back to Badaun, but presumably some scars remain. While Hindus are not likely to stop making pilgrimages to Muslim tombs in the near future, especially because many of these are *pirs* and considered to be powerful to fulfill the wishes of the devotees, the politics of the dargahs is bound to change and will have to be remapped.

The strains of classical music

Sheikh Chinna Maulana Saheb, whom we encountered in the beginning of this essay, Sheikh Mahaboob Subhani, (Mrs.) Kaleeshabi Mahaboob (Begum), and a handful of other Muslims in south India participate in the performance and perpetuation of Karnatic music.

Although they play instrumental music, they know the (Hindu) devotional lyrics and their meaning only too well; the songs themselves are, in fact, named for the lyrics. On the northern end of the subcontinent, one may say that Hindusani classical music as we know it today is substantially derived from the work of musicians who experimented with Indic and Persian forms of music.

We must bear in mind that it is difficult to distinguish "Indian" from "Hindu" and "Persian" from "Islamic" as the initial contributors to the confluence that took place over the centuries. National and religious identifications melded together in the initial stages of the encounter in the subcontinent; thus the Tamil word for Muslim is "Tulukka," from "Turushka" or Turk. After the blending of the various styles takes place, we can no longer identify forms of expression as distinctively Muslim or Hindu. The cities of northern India are filled with elegant examples of architecture that have risen from adaptations of styles associated with many countries, with mutual borrowing and adaptation. Miniature painting from northern India shows the shared world of Persian and Indian styles.

The interaction between Persian and Indian forms of music has probably produced the richest and most splendid harvest in India. The coming together of the musical systems resulted in a new form of music called Hindustani music, new musical instruments – or as some would have it, startling new improvisations on existing systems, and new *raga* or melodic structures. It must be noted at the outset that this area of musical origins is much disputed by musicologists and is clouded by political predispositions. For example, it is a matter of controversy as to whether instruments such as the sitar, the *nadasvaram* in the south, and the *vina* in the form that it is seen today (with fretted strings) are indigenous to India, or if they were dramatically altered by Persian musicians.

Forms of music in northern India

The field of north Indian (Hindustani) music is a product of the synergism that came about from the encounter of Indian and Persian traditions. Amir Khusrow (1234–1325), poet, historian, and musicianm, was proficient in both the Indian and Persian systems of music and is considered to be one of the pioneers of the modern system of Hindustani music. He called himself a "Hindu [Indian] Turk" and was passionately involved with Indian music. He wrote: "Indian music, the fire that burns heart and soul, is superior to the music of any other country."[47] He is said to have learned music from Hindu musicians and "introduced

Persian and Arabic elements into Indian music thus giving to it an added grace and elegance."[48] In the fourteenth century, after Malik Kafur's conquest of south India, several musicians were apparently taken to the north and a considerable interchange is said to have ensued.

Amir Khusrow is credited with inventing new instruments, *ragas*, and forms of music such as the *qawwali*. *Ragas* such as *sarfada* (a combination of Sarang, Bilawal, and Raast) and *zilaph* (a combination of Khat and Shehnaz) are attributed to him, as are the more popular ones such as *yaman* (Hindol and Nairaze) and *sazgiri* (Purvi, Gara, and Gunkali).[49] The invention of the *sitar* is also attributed to him, although it seems probable that he modified the existing *veena*. The name *sitar* comes from the Persian *seh-tar* ("three strings"), but even if Khusrow was instrumental in this innovation, it seems probable that he did not name it. The name *sitar* apparently appears well after his time. However, during the reign of Allauuddin Khilji, Sultan of Delhi (1296–1316), a Hindu musician called Nayak Gopal translated the Sanskrit *Dhruvapadas* (verses sung in an austere manner) into the vernacular Braj-Bhasa, the language believed to have been spoken by the Hindu God Krishna. Nayak's choice of language is seen to have had religious sanction and the Sanskrit hold on music was apparently over. It became a convention in northern India to compose their religious and secular verses in Braj Bhasa. It is generally held that after Amir Khusrow's time, Hindustani (northern) and Karnatic (southern) forms of music became distinct.[50]

The integration between Indian and Persian styles of music continued during the time of Sikandar Lodi, Sultan of Delhi (1489–1517). Reginald and Jamila Massey write:

> At this point in history a Hindu–Muslim compact in the arts was being established. Sikandar Lodi . . . gave his blessing to the *Lahjat-e-Sikandar Shahi*, the first book on Indian music written in Persian and based upon Sanskrit sources. Ibrahim Adil Shah II, Sultan of Bijapur in the Deccan (1580–1626) and a famous poet-musician of his day, composed songs in praise of Hindu deities and published them in his *Kitab-e-Nauras*. Hindus learnt from Muslim *ustads* [teachers], masters, and Muslims from Hindu *gurus*. Hindu princes employed Muslim musicians and Muslim princes, Hindus.[51]

Music was also patronized by Mughal emperors such as Akbar, Jahangir, and Shah Jahan. Following Amir Khosrow, Muslim musicians took an active part in the performance and development of Indian music forms. Many of these songs had devotional lyrics which were minimized in later years to be mutually compatible with both religious traditions. During the time of emperor Akbar (1542–1605) legendary musicians like Tansen and Swami Haridas flourished. It would not be an exaggeration to say that the entire form of music in northern India as we know of it today comes through the synergism of Persian/Muslim and Indian/Hindu systems coming together. Amir Khusrow, Tansen, and Swami Haridas are some of the stars in this process. The integration of Muslim and Hindu musicians and music for over 700 years is a record that no other field can boast of. In this connection one may note that a genre of scintillating pure dance called *tillana* was introduced into south Indian classical dance form known as *dasi attam* (and in this century as *bharata natyam*). *Tillana* apparently is an adaptation of a Persian word. Instances of Muslim rulers fostering Hindu religious dance have also been recorded.[52]

Performers of classical South Indian "Karnatic" music adopted what were perceived to be "Muslim" melodies into the traditional *raga* structure of classical south Indian music. The ragas called Arabi, Husseini, and Paraz probably became popular around the seventeenth to eighteenth centuries, and some of the most famous kirtanas of Tyagaraja in praise of Rama are in these *ragas*. While Hindustani music is arguably neither Hindu nor Muslim, south Indian Karnatic music is definitely Hindu in nature. The striking feature of Karnatic music is the extensive attention paid to the lyrics. The composers were known as *vaggeyakarakas*, that is, musicians who composed both lyrics and the *ragas* to go with it. The lyrics are explicitly devotional and addressed to the various gods and goddesses. Even those who learn instrumental music in the Karnatic style have to learn the lyrics as they play the songs. However, Karnatic music has been influenced by other forms of music. Thanjavur had been a musical headquarters for south Indian music and experimental styles of music in the seventeenth through the nineteenth centuries. The local kings here had been patrons of classical Karnatic music and encouraged other forms of music as well, leading to a cosmopolitan fare. For instance, the royal accounts of King Sivaji II in 1856 speak of payments made to Englishmen and women for performance of western music, as well as to Said Hussain, a Muslim composer, and Krishna Ramaswami, a Hindu singer. The king was a patron of a Hindustani musician called Rahman and a woman percussion player called Kamakshi.[53] There is no doubt that here and even earlier, there was active experimentation in various styles of music.

Sheikh Chinna Moulana Saheb, son of Kasim Sahib, hails from Karavadi, Andhra Pradesh.[54] He learnt the instrument called *nagaswaram* or *nadaswaram* from Chilakaluripeta Adam Sahib, that is Adam Sahib who comes from a town called Chilakaluripeta. He moved to the state of Tamilnadu and became a disciple of Rajam and Dorarikkannu, Hindu *nadaswaram* players from Nacchiyar Koil who specialized in the "Than-javur" style of playing the instrument. One must note at the outset that the *nadaswaram* is not just any other musical instrument; it is one played on festive occasions like weddings and other rites of passage, and above all in Hindu temples. It is generally an outdoor instrument and connected closely with the *tavil*, a percussion instrument also played in temples.[55]

Sheikh Chinna Moulana started a school called Saradha Nagaswara Sangeetha Ashram in the temple town of Srirangam (this is the town where Lord Visnu or Ranganatha has a Muslim consort) for *nadaswaram* players. It is remarkable that the school is named after the Hindu patron goddess for music and the performing arts, Sarada or Sarasvati. The school is residential and is based on the older Indian system of *gurukula* where students lived with a male teacher and learned the art from him. Kasim and Babu, two of his grandchildren, accompany him in his concerts. He has received several civil awards from the government of India and has been honored by many performing arts groups around the country.[56] He was also given the title of "Saptagiri Vidwanmani" (the Gem among maestros of the Seven Hills) by the Tirupati Tyagaraja Festival Committee in 1984. This title is given by a group with explicit ties to a major Hindu temple. Tirupati is a major pilgrimage center for Hindus; in fact, the temple there is said to be the richest in India. This temple is reached after one crosses seven hills; and the whole area is considered to be sacred land by Hindus. The term Saptagiri (Seven Hills) is used as a synonym for the sacred land; thus the quarterly journal of the "branch" temple at Pittsburgh, Pennsylvania, is called *Saptagiri Vani* or the Voice of the Seven Hills. The title "Gem of maestros in the Seven Hills" thus has clear religious association.

While I have been arguing that Hindu participation in Muslim structures is largely on the level of ritual, and this is to be juxtaposed with Muslim scholarship of Tamil religious and secular literature, we must also note that these flows are not as unilateral as this chapter might suggest. There is some evidence that Tamil siddha works were influenced by Islamic literature and practice, but the appropriations seem somewhat limited and unclear. What is more striking are the few cases of Muslim participation in Hindu ritual structures; such of it that can be documented. I could not gauge the extent of Muslim participation in Hindu ritual in Tamilnadu; certainly we do not find them praying in

Hindu temples, but they did take part in the Sri Mushnam rituals when Visnu is brought to the samadhi/dargah of a Muslim ruler. But there seems to be more participation in the level of classical south Indian (Carnatic) music. Sheikh Chinna Moulana Saheb, his grandsons, and more recently, Sheikh Mahaboob Subhani and his wife Srimati Kalee-shabi Mahaboob,[57] play the *nadaswaram*, a wind instrument similar to the *shehnai* of northern India. As noted earlier, south Indian Karnatic music, unlike north Indian classical music, is strongly religious in flavor. Devotional lyrics dominate the exposition of Karnatic music; songs are identified by the words and the deity to whom they are addressed as much as the raga they are composed in. The musicians mentioned above, moreover, play the *nadaswaram*, an instrument used for domestic and temple celebrations. Temple liturgies frequently include nadaswaram music. Sheikh Mahaboob and his wife have played for the festivals at Tirupati and other temples; in fact, Smt. Kaleeshabi's first performance was for a Ganesha temple when she was 11 years old. They both played in Tirupati in 1978, and now live in Srirangam, another major temple town. They also participate at the annual devotional music festival to the composer saint Thyagaraja. The music is not just instrumental; in order to get the right *bhava* or emotional attitude when playing the songs, both Sheikh Mahaboob Subhani and his wife Kalee-shabi Mahaboob learned vocal singing for 4 years under Sri Chandra-mouli, the principal of the music college at Kurnool, Andhra Pradesh. During a conversation with me, to illustrate how important the lyrics were in the playing, Sri Mahaboob sang a (Hindu) devotional song in honor of Visnu at Srirangam. The song was in the raga Kambodhi; Sheikh Mahaboob first sang a technically correct musical version, and then one with the right devotional attitude of *bhakti* to show how the rendering of the song could be improved. The *sahitya* (lyrics) he said was the most important. Both he and his wife (they are cousins) claim to come from a family where their Muslim ancestors have played the *nadaswaram* for over seven generations. Both the players consider them-selves to be "proper" Muslims; whenever they can, they try to keep the "*vrata*" of the Ramzan fast. Such participation, not just in aesthetic musical forms, but in the spirit of the Hindu bhakti experience, cer-tainly mounts a melodious assault against dimorphic notions of Islam and Hinduism.

Scholarship, ritual, music: these are only some of the areas where we see communities coming together, and sharing ideas, concerns, melodies, hopes, and joys. One cannot talk of the communities with reified boundaries; what constitutes the identity of "Hindu" or

"Muslim" is fluid at most times, with harsher lines being demanded only recently in response to political pressures. While there was a reciprocally creative relationship at many times and in many places, political and economic considerations have now made some communalist elements highlight the antagonistic and suspicious attitudes that have also been part of Hindu–Muslim relations. It is important to note the shared spaces that have existed in the subcontinent along with the military conquests.

Responses to Hindu nationalism: the testimony of Tamil songs written by Muslims

In the wake of a new wave of Hindu nationalism in the last few years the identity of the Tamil Muslim is undergoing a crisis. The Tamil Muslims did not compare themselves with those from the north; they have been content with the antiquity of their origins. While they allied themselves with Arabic and Persian forms of literature and adapted them to Tamil genres, showed reverence to Muslim saints from other parts of India and the Middle East, the Tamil Muslims have on the whole maintained a distinctive linguistic and cultural identity without an intensive dialogic political or social relationship with Urdu-speaking Muslims in Hyderabad, or northern India, or the Bengali-speaking Muslims. When there was comparison, as with the Urdu-speaking Walajah court, the Tamil-speaking Muslims still maintained the antiquity of their Arabic origins and the linguistic importance of Tamil. This is particularly seen in the successful campaign mounted by the Tamil Muslims in the 1930s to ensure that Hindi would not be made a compulsory second language in the academic curriculum. While the Urdu-speaking Muslims from Tamilnadu supported this measure, the Tamil-speaking Muslims agitated against it along with the Tamil-speaking (non-Brahmin) Hindus. It was obvious that pride in linguistic identity proved stronger than aligning themselves with people who followed the same religion, but who spoke a different language.[58] The trauma of partition did not seem to affect the deep south and the Tamil Muslims were – as were all other south Indians – relatively insulated from the north. However, the aggressive stance of some Hindu nationalists in the 1980s and 1990s seems to have prompted a sense of insecurity among the Tamil Muslims. Their anger, sorrow, and bewilderment has now surfaced in public through Tamil songs sold in pre-recorded audio cassettes. Many of these are simply categorized as "Muslim Devotional (bhakti) songs" by the stores that carry them. However, packaged along with standard songs on the glory of Muhammad and Mecca are songs which are very patriotic and some filled with sorrow, and others filled with rage. These cassettes go under titles like "Makkanakar Manapi" (The Great Prophet of Mecca), "Makkavai Nokki" (Looking towards Mecca), or "Pallivacalil kutuvom" ("Let us gather at the gates of the mosque"). Let us look at some of these lyrics in translation:

Song from Makkanakar Manapi (The great Prophet of Mecca)

Refrain 1
India is our motherland
Islam is our way of life
Tamil is our language . . .
Who is it who said
who is it who said we are enemies?

Our forefathers worked and fought for freedom
Muslims fought to get rid of the nation's sorrow

Refrain 2
They have forgotten, they have forgotten gratitude
Is this betrayal? Are these the sins we have done?

The blood spilled by the Mappillas in Kerala is not yet dry
The wounds we got in Bengal are not yet healed

Mysore's lion Tipu's bravery will not change
Your heart cannot bear the grief of Bahadur Shah

Do you know we have ruled India for 800 years?
The Taj Mahal and the Kutb Minar are witnesses,
have you forgotten?
You cannot deny it, You cannot conceal truth.

Song from Makkanakar Manapi

Refrain
I swear on the earth
I swear on the heavens
I swear on the mother who bore me
I swear on God who created [all].

We will not lose our faith as long as we are alive
We will not weaken in resolve as long as we are alive
Leaving the Land of India,

forgetting it's glory
we will not flee in fear
we will not flee in fear of anyone.

This is the land where Muslim Kings ruled for 800 years
Say, does anyone have this pride [of rulership] other than us?
We have never betrayed this country
Muslims have served this land without end

Repeat refrain
Our crowd rose first to seek freedom
That is why blood began to flow in Kerala
Will my heart forget the sacrifice of the Mappilas?
We will do countless sacrifice again, for the country.

(*refrain*)
Think of the sacrifice of Bahadur Shah who ruled Delhi
when enemies gave him his son's head on a platter . . .
There is no one equal to us in devotion [*bhakti*] to the country
He was born as the brave son of Haidar, Mysore's king . . .
Tipu gave his life in war.
He tried hard to free his mother-country;
He bore endless grief in the British prisons
Maulana Muhammad Ali Saukat died pining for freedom.

Two strategies are immediately visible from these verses. The composers are now aligning themselves with Muslims from all over India, and not just the south, though the southern emphasis (Mappilas, Tipu) is evident. The second is the use of paradigms to remind the listeners of the sacrifices made by Muslims all over India during the independence movement. Since the simplistic war-cry of the aggressive Hindu is to tell the Muslim to go to Pakistan, the Tamil Muslim songs emphasize that India is their home. The patriotism is woven with songs on the Islamic faith.

The nationalistic Hinduism that we see today valorizes the perceived boundaries between Hindu and Muslim cultures, strengthening the ideas of difference in political and social ideologies, religious practices, and loyalties. The government has obviously not succeeded in keeping either the Hindus or Muslims happy. Both feel victimized, and it has been observed that the Hindu majority has for many years had a minority complex. At the root of the problems seems to be the concept of secularism espoused by India.

When India became a secular democracy, it was home to Hindus, Muslims, Christians, Parsis, Jains, and Jews. Its understanding of secularism is unique and has been the focus of more than a dozen books and hundreds of scholarly articles. Simplistically put, one may recognize at least three types of democracies in the world: one where there is a clear separation of church and state (such as the United States), one where religion is ignored and denied (as in the Former Soviet Union), and finally one where the state does not patronize a religion, but holds all religions to be equal, as in India. This translates to the state having four different sets of family laws: a reformed Hindu code, the Muslim Personal law, a family law for Christians and one for Parsis. Sikhs and Jains are clubbed under the Hindu code, and until the 1950s some Muslim communities such as Memmons and Bohras actually came under the Hindu code. Thus, because Hindu law was reformed and codified in the 1955, a Hindu man in India may have only one wife, even though historically Hindu laws have allowed a man to be polygamous. A Muslim man, on the other hand, may have up to four wives. Issues of divorce, child custody, inheritance, etc. are usually solved under these laws.

Two major issues seem to have precipitated the Hindu–Muslim crisis. The lack of a uniform civil code seems to be key concern for Hindus in the communal tensions today. The other is the caste issue. Although the constitution forbids discrimination on the basis of caste, the Mandal commission has made every citizen hyperaware of this issue. The caste system is prevalent among Hindus and Christians, and many Muslim communities are also included in the OBC. Reservations and quotas – the Indian version of an aggressive affirmative action – have given rise to demoralization and violence in many quarters. The Indian experiments in secularism and equality can only succeed if politicians stop manipulating religious fervor and instead provide economic and social opportunities which will override communal tensions.

In trying to understand the Tamil-speaking Muslim community, we can argue that language is an important factor in the construction of identity and acceptance of heritage. The intellectuals among the Tamil-speaking Muslims, those who present the "story" of the community, have stressed the importance of Tamil as their mother tongue. They are conscious of and emphasize the contributions of Muslims to Tamil literature; thus the titles of survey books on Tamil Islamic literature bear titles like "the service rendered by Islam to Tamil." Recent studies have suggested that it is only in the early twentieth century (1920s) against the background of British rule, Brahmin domination in government jobs, and anti-Brahmin feelings stirred up by E.V. Ramaswamy Naicker, that Tamil-speaking Muslims became "conscious of their Tamil identity."[59] P. Dawood Sha, the editor of *Dar ul Islam*, criticized some of the *moulvis* and *alims* for their inadequate knowledge of spoken and written Tamil.[60] The Self-Respect movement started by E.V. Ramaswami Naicker in 1925, criticized Hindu mythology, rituals, and the caste system, praised the religion of the Tamil Muslims for its rational basis and its belief in universal brotherhood, and urged the Untouchables of Hinduism to convert to Islam. The Self-Respect movement promoted its "Dravidian" roots and pride in the Tamil language, while pitting itself against the Bramanincal organization which was perceived to be "Aryan" and Sanskritized. In 1937, when the Congress party assumed power in the Madras Presidency, the Prime Minister, C. Rajagopalachari (a Tamil Brahmin), tried to introduce Hindustani as a compulsory subject into 125 secondary schools. It had been argued by Gandhi, Rajagoplachari, and Urdu-speaking Muslims that Hindustani was really the name for Urdu and Hindi, one language in two scripts. Urdu-speaking Muslims in the Madras presidency argued in favor of having Hindustani as a mandatory language; Basheer Ahmed Sayeed strongly defended this measure:

> There is no controversy over this. The language [Hindustani] is one, the scripts are two ... This government wants to propagate this spoken language [Hindustani] which is a Muslim language. It is up to the Musalmans to say "we welcome this movement."[61]

The Tamil-speaking Muslims did not buy this argument. Rather than aligning themselves with fellow Muslims, they backed the anti-Hindustani agitation of the Self-Respect movement. Caste and language issues dominated religious themes in the construction of a social and political identity for the Tamil Muslims.[62] In this episode, at least, language seems more important than religious affiliation in determining the parameters of the community.

The boundaries between Tamil-speaking Muslims and Hindus seem fluid in some areas and the common heritage of the language seems to transcend certain differences. The fluidity of this enterprise has to be emphasized; we are not dealing with a fixed or determinate sense of "mixing" of categories from two distinct, dimorphic cultures. Stewart and Shaw's description of the move from "melting-pot" to "multiculturalism" in the United States (a move which is not irreversible) seems to be applicable to the Indian milieu, where "syntheses, adaptations, assemblages, incorporations or appropriations are regotiated and sometimes denied and disassembled."[63]

By stating that the boundaries are permeable and that the gray areas are noticeable, I am not alleging that there are no boundaries. It is quite clear that Hindu communities and castes knew who they were and how different they were from the Muslims; the Hindu castes were quite clear about whom they married, whom they ate with, and whom they worshiped with in a temple. But these Hindu castes also adopted other rules, other customs, or exported their own customs into the worship of powerful beings such as the Muslim saints and some manifestations of the Virgin Mary, as in the Velankanni temple near Nagapattinam. The terms that one may use to describe these shared, negotiated spaces can be disputed. The term "syncretism" has been problematized in the last few years, and should be used with caution. Barbara Metcalf understands the concept of syncretism to be based on the fixed categories of "Hindu" and "Muslim." She adds:

> It encourages what one might call the "vertical fallacy," that it is possible to make lists, even contrasting lists, of what is "Hindu" in one column and "Muslim" in another. It also tends to call "Hindu" or "Muslim" elements in the culture that may be neither or both.[64]

Syncretism emerges when "bits of both in some sense mix." What Metcalf calls syncretism is called "bricolage" by anthropologists; Stewart and Shaw, in their efforts to rehabilitate the word "syncretism," offer many related words. They suggest that the term "syncretism" should be "limited to the domain of religious or ritual phenomena where elements of two different historical 'traditions' interact or combine."[65] This would distinguish syncretism from "bricolage, the formation of new cultural forms from bits and pieces of cultural practice of diverse origins."[66] Like Metcalf, Stewart and Shaw say that religions cannot be fixed; they go further and say that syncretism itself cannot be essentialized. They initially trace the history of the word "syncretism" from the time that Plutarch used it in an idiosyncratic sense to the positive tones given by Erasmus. Later in the sixteenth and seventeenth centuries the word had negative connotations when George Calixtus argued for the reconciliation of the various Protestant denominations. Opponents of the movement saw these efforts as a jumbled and confusing mixture of religions.[67] In the nineteenth century, the term "syncretism" is again used in a pejorative sense by scholars of comparative religion in their examinations of the religion of Rome and Greece, where it indicates disorder and confusion. It is also used to denote an imperialistic strategy by which all "the varieties of mankind would be called in and restamped at the Caesarian Mint."[68]

One may also add that "syncretism" is sometimes used in a derogatory fashion, to distinguish what scholars believe to be "hybrid" – and thus "lesser" – religions from what is "pure" and "authentic." It is because of the negative use of the term syncretism that scholars of religion shy away from it now. Anthropologists such as Charles Stewart and Rosalind Shaw are rehabilitating the word, but Tony Stewart and Carl Ernst urge caution in their analysis of the term.[69]

What then can we call the phenomena in the intersecting realms of Hindu and Muslim experiences in south India? Obviously it would not be sensible to argue that there are no boundaries between the Muslims and Hindus. There are strong boundaries within and between Hindu communities and castes, and all of them do distinguish themselves from the Muslims. What I am arguing for is a shaded area of "fuzzy" boundaries which is fairly large and permeable. If "syncretism" calls for harsh, discernible boundaries, with specific elements from both sides combining to form a third entity, the shared experience is evidently not that. What we find instead are common, intersecting areas of shared experience drawn from the matrix of language, myth, and ritual. One may argue based on these areas that colonial constructions of the labels "Hindu" and "Muslim" as discrete entities are problematic; softer, permeable membranes with bilateral osmosis have to be imagined. Michael Meister argues for the use of the "osmosis" metaphor[70] in his analysis of the styles of eleventh-century architecture in Rajasthan. This metaphor still uses the concept of boundaries, but at least makes them open to influences.

Until one can come up with a broadly acceptable term without the baggage that "syncretism" carries, it is tempting to consider using a variety of words commonly seen in social anthropology to describe the shared areas of culture between Hindu castes and Muslims in south Asia. Since there are diverse experiences, it would make sense to use different terms to describe them. If bricolage means the creation of a new culture with bits and pieces of others, one may point to the experience of the Meherats and the Maule-e-Salaam Garasiyas of Gujarat, who have elements from both religions in their lifestyle. The term "inculturation" can be used with qualifications (and with acknowledgment of limitations) in describing the lifestyle of the Muslims in Tamilnadu,[71] the modes of worship in dargahs, their intense scholarship of the Tamil

Ramayana, and incorporation of literary tropes from this epic in their *Cira Puranam.* Stewart and Shaw describe inculturation thus:

> In Catholic theologians' notions of inculturation . . . the Word of God, the message of the Gospel, is knowledge of a transcendental, timeless and transcultural Truth that is not tied to a particular human language of cultural form, but adaptable into local idioms and symbolic repertoires. Indeed the Church now contends that communities will apprehend the Christian message better if they do so in their own terms.[72]

One of the problems with this notion, of course, is that western notions of distinction between "culture" and "religion" may not always translate into other geographic regions. Moreover, in the phenomena we are considering, "inculturation" may be a misleading term at least in one way. Although it is not explicitly stated, inculturation may refer to a conscious adoption of local forms and styles of worship. In the case of the Tamil Muslims, there in no conscious adoption of something local; the Tamil literature and culture is perceived as their birthright and their inheritance. Inculturation also refers to the Muslim side of the phenomena in the worship at dargahs; it does not cover the Tamil Hindu's participation in such rituals.

One may also consider using the word "variation/variant" for some aspects of the shared culture in south India, but even if it can be used, this will again be applicable only for the Islamic side of the picture. This term has been used by anthropologists who studied indigenous churches in Africa. Peel (and in another study, Kiernan) have criticized the use of the word "syncretist" in earlier studies on African churches which practice faith healing. Rather than being a Yoruba or a Zulu practice, they argue that the use of faith healing in these churches have roots in the Western Christianity; Kiernan "affirms [like Peel] that Zulu Zionism is not syncretic but a thoroughly Christian variant."[73] The term "variant" can be used if a "native" of a religion shares a common ritual or concept that is or has been prevalent in another culture. Tamil Muslims who visit the dargah at Nagore frequently take their children there to have their heads shaven. This custom is common enough among Hindus in south Asia; a pilgrimage to a sacred site is undertaken when a child is 3 months or older. This is a Hindu samskara or sacrament; however, it is perceived to be a local Tamil (nonreligious) custom by Tamil Muslims who practice this ritual. While they did not show awareness of it, the tonsure of a child's head is, in fact, an Islamic custom. *Aqiqah* refers to the non-obligatory custom of tonsure on the seventh day after the birth of the child. However, the Muslims whom I interviewed in Nagore were not aware of this ritual as an Islamic one; their children whose heads were being shaved were older, and besides, this was just a "family" (read Tamil) custom. I would argue that for this custom to be properly called an Islamic "variant," at least some of the people in the dargah should relate the ritual to the prophet's life or to a textual source.

The term "bricolage," the replacement word for syncretism, can be used only for some restricted phenomena; the terms "inculturation" and "variant" miss the mark in conceptualizing the shared worlds of the Tamil-speaking Hindus and Muslims. One is left with four alternatives; we may go back to the osmosis metaphor of Meister, encourage the rehabilitation of "syncretism," nuance another term like "synergism" (which again presupposes distinct dimorphic entities), or come up with a neologism.

For lack of a word that is acceptable in the scholarly realm, I am tempted (at least for now) to lapse into the attitude suggested by a musician last summer. I was struggling to pinpoint whether some of the *ragas* like Todi and Arabi were originally from Persian music. While I was musing over the irony of using a raga like *Husseini* for a devotional song to Rama, and grappling with the geographic origins of the raga – which could not be fixed with certainty – the ethnomusicologist who gave me the different views on the subject advised: "If the aesthetic experience works, just enjoy the music which has come to you from the different sources." Muslim scholars of the Tamil *Ramayana* and Hindu pilgrims at Muslim dargahs would, I believe, agree.

Notes

1   The Sanskrit word *Ramayana* is written as *Ramayanam* in Tamil. In this paper, I will use *Ramayanam* to refer to the Tamil version by Kampan.
2   From Ahmed Khan, *Writings and Speeches* and *Akhari Madamin*. Quoted in *Sources of Indian Tradition*, ed. Stephen Hay, vol. 2, New York: Columbia University Press, 1988, 193.
3   A good visual account of Ayodhya's history can be seen in Anand Patwardhan's movie *Ram Ke Nam* ("In the Name of God"), 1991.
4   *India Today*, Oct. 31, 1984, 48.
5   Sreedhar Pillai, "Kerala: Brawl on the Beach." *India Today*, Feb. 29, 1984, 38–9.
6   "Thanjavur: Quiet Metamorphosis." *India Today*, May 31, 1988, 112.
7   Mumtaz Ali Khan, "Mass Conversions of Meenakshipuram." *Religion in South Asia*, ed. G.A. Oddie, Columbia: South Asia Books, 50.

8   "The Muslims: Anger and Hurt." *India Today*, March 15, 1986, 18–21.

9   For an account of the Mandal report and its repucussions, see Gerald Larson, "Mandal, Mandir, Masjid." *Religion and Law in Independent India*, ed. Robert Baird, Delhi: Manohar, 1993.

10 On the connection between the Shah Bano case and the Babri Mosque dispute, see Lloyd I. Rudolph and Susanne Hoeber Rudolph, *In Pursuit of Lakshmi: the Political Economy of the Indian State*, Chicago: University of Chicago Press, 1987, 44–5.

11 *India Today*, March 15, 1986, 19.

12 *India Today*, Aug. 31, 1989, 72.

13 "Communalism: Dangerous Dimensions." *India Today*, Oct. 31, 1989, 17.

14 *India Today*, March 31, 1993, 42.

15 Interview with Justice M.M. Ismail, July 1993. See also Mattison Mines, *The Warrior Merchants: Textiles, Trade, and Territory in South India*, Cambridge: Cambridge University Press, 1984, and Susan Bayly, *Saints, Goddesses and Kings*, Cambridge: Cambridge University Press, 1989.

16 Turnbull is quoted as saying, "The real Mahomedans are comparatively few [in Tirunelveli] in proportion to the Lubbays, amongst whom the vernacular language of the country prevails." Quoted in Bayly, *Saints, Goddesses, Kings*, 100n53.

17 See also "Andhra Pradesh: No Hindu Star rising" and "Kerala: Left Gains, Not Hindutva." *India Today*, March 31, 1993, 44–5.

18 *Dargah*, literally, "The king's court; a port, portal, gate, door . . . a mosque." The saint who is buried in a dargah is seen to be a door to the Lord, or someone who is a threshold between human beings and the divine.

19 Paula Richman discusses possible reasons for this neglect of Islamic Tamil literature in the appendix of "Veneration of the Prophet Muhammad in an Islamic *Pillaitamil*." *Journal of the American Oriental Society*, 113, no. 1 (1993), 57–74. The encounter between Hindus, Christians, and Muslims in Tamilnadu and Kerala has been discussed by Bayly in *Saints, Goddesses and Kings*. See also Shulman, "Muslim Popular Literature in Tamil: the Tamimancari Malai." *Islam in Asia*, 1, South Asia, ed. Yohanan Friedmann, Boulder, Colo.: Westview Press, 1984.

20 For detailed discussions, see the works of Carl Ernst.

21 Interview with Justice Ismail, July 1993. He voiced similar sentiments in an interview with a newspaper reporter the same month. See Rasheeda Bhagat, "M.M. Ismail: A Multi-faceted Personality." *The Indian Express*, July 11, 1993.

22 I have discussed Umaru Pulavar's life and the *Cira Puranam* in my paper "Religious Vocabulary and Regional Identity: a Study of the Tamil *Cirappuranam* ('Life of the Prophet')," (forthcoming).

23 To these five situations of love two more are added: *peruntinai* and *kaikkilai*, which have no corresponding landscape. *Peruntinai* indicates mismatched love and *kaikkilai* unrequited love. For discussions of the landscapes see A.K. Ramanujan, *The Interior Landscape*, Bloomington: Indiana University Press, 1967, 104–12, K. Zvelebil, *Tamil Literature*, Wiesbaden: Harrasowitz, 1974, 98–9; *Smile of Murugan*, Leiden: Brill, 1973, 85–110.

24 "Sankara, the teacher"; a title given to the abbots of five monastic institutions in India.

25   M.M. Ismail, *Oru marakka mutiyata anupavam* (An Unforgettable Experi-
      ence). Madras: Vanati Patippakam, 1992, 16. This is a reprint of an article
      by the same name originally published in the magazine called *Kalki*, dated
      Dec. 8, 1985. Justice Ismail called my attention to this episode and also nar-
      rated the incident to me in July 1993.
26   See Mangala Murugesan, *Sangam Age*, Madras: Thendral Pathipakkam, 1982,
      254. See also R. Champakalakshmi, *Vaisnava Iconography in the Tamil
      Country*, New Delhi: Oriental Longman, 1981, 44–5 and 117–18. She notes
      that in south India, the "inscriptional evidence . . . comes only from a record
      of about the seventh–eighth centuries AD and definite evolution of a Rama
      cult dates from the tenth century AD . . . the earliest sculptural representa-
      tions belong to about the first half of the tenth century AD. However, Rama
      occupies a place of great honour in the hymns of the . . . Alvars of the
      seventh–ninth centuries AD" (117). We may also note that Rama is men-
      tioned in Tamil literature between the second and fifth centuries CE.
27   Information on dargahs is derived from visits to Nagore, Kovalam and other
      places in Tamilnadu and Karnataka between 1995 and 1999.
28   See Bayly, *Saints, Goddesses and Kings*, 105.
29   For details of the Nagore dargah see J.M. Cali, *Nakur Nayakam varalaru* (The
      biography of the Chief of Nagore), Thanjavur: Kajiyar puk tipo (Kajiyar Book
      Depot), 3rd edn., 1989.
30   This paragraph is based on information given in "The Dargha v. The Clinic:
      An Examination of Treatment and Explanation of Mental Illness in
      Madurai," written by Jenefer Willem, an undergraduate student at Dickin-
      son College, as a term paper for the SITA program in November 1994. Ms.
      Willem did the fieldwork and also supplied me with photographs.
31   This information was initially given by Professor P.V. Arunachalam, Princi-
      pal, Sri Venkateswara University, Andhra Pradesh. Details were kindly sup-
      plied by S. Basha Mohiddin, journalist, *Navayugam* paper and written by
      Babar Ali Mohiddin (personal communication).
32   This festival is held in the Tamil month of Masi (Feb. 15 to March 14).
33   R. Srinivasaraghavachariar, *Srimushna Mahatmyam*. The author is the pub-
      lisher, and no other publishing details are given for this pamphlet. See pages
      17–18. There is no date of publication, but I got it in 1977.
34   This ritual has been written about and given prominence by Saba Naqvi
      Bhaumik in "In Good Faith: Mountain comes to Mohammed." *Indian
      Express Sunday Magazine*, July 4, 1993, 11.
35   For a brief discussion on the origins of this story, see my article, "*Arcavatara*:
      On Earth, as He is in Heaven," in *Gods of Flesh, Gods of Stone: the Embodi-
      ment of Divinity in India*, eds. Joanne Punzo Waghorne, Norman Cutler, and
      Vasudha Narayanan (Chambersburg, Penn.: Anima Books, 1984), 56–67.
36   See Saba Naqvi Bhaumik, "In Good Faith: They Cry for Hussain." Madras
      Indian Express Sunday Magazine, July 18, 1993, 11.
37   Quoted from Saba Naqvi Bhaumik's "In Good Faith: They Cry for Hussain,"
      11.
38   Quoted from ibid.
39   Syed Liyaqat Hussain Moini, "Rituals and Customary Practices at the Dargah
      at Ajmer." In *Muslim Shrines in India*, ed. Christian W. Troll (Delhi: Oxford
      University Press, 1992), 40, 61–3.

40 Saba Naqvi Bhaumik, "In Good Faith: Where a Cult Conquers Caste." Madras *Indian Express*, June 5, 1993.

41 "Rajasthan: Conversion Convulsions." *India Today*, June 30, 1986, 78–80.

42 Ibid., 79.

43 Uday Mahurkar, "A Mystic Blend." *India Today*, April 15, 1993, 53.

44 *India Today*, Feb. 15, 1986, 52–5.

45 *India Today*, Oct. 31, 1989, 18.

46 Ibid., 19.

47 Quoted in Reginald and Jamila Massey's *The Music of India*, New York: Crescendo Publishing, 1977, 43.

48 Ibid.

49 Sunil Bose, *Indian Classical Music: Essence and Emotions*, New Delhi: Vikas Publishing House, 1990, 50. See also Reginald and Jamila Massey *The Music of India*, 43.

50 Massey, *The Music of India*, 44.

51 Ibid., 46.

52 See Massey, *The Music of India*, 47, where they write about Abdul Hassan Tahnisha, the Nawab of Golconda, granting lands to Brahmin dancers in 1675 with the stipulation that these traditions should be carried on.

53 S. Seetha, *Tanjore as a Seat of Music*, Madras: University of Madras: 1981, 117–18.

54 Some of the information in this paragraph is derived from N. Rajagopalan, *A Garland (Biographical Dictionary of Carnatic Composers and Musicians)*, Bombay: Bharatiya Vidya Bhavan, 1990, 290.

55 There is considerable controversy on whether the *nadaswaram* itself is derived from or closely connected with the *shehnai*, a north Indian instrument clearly of Persian origin. The *nadaswaram* is referred to as the *nai* or *nayanam* by the players, making one assume that they see the strong historic connections between the two instruments. Sangita Kalanidhi (Professor) T. Viswanathan, professor of ethnomusicology at Wesleyan University, informed me that there were strong similarities, making one presume a common origin. However, Professor Skelton at Colgate University said the *nadaswaram* is independent, though bearing striking similarity to the *shehnai*. It would, of course, be dramatic if the instrument most used for temple music in south Indian Hinduism is of Islamic derivation, but there is no "hard" evidence on either side for this assumption and it is a matter of debate between scholars.

56 He was given the title of "kalaimamani" (the great gem of arts) in 1976 by the Tamil Nadu Eyal Isai Nataka Mandram (Tamilnadu Society for Prose, Music, and Drama), the well-recognized award of Padma Sri during the Republic Day honors (1977), and an Honorary Doctorate by the Andhra University in 1985.

57 I interviewed Sri Mahaboob Subhani and Smt. Kaeeshabi Subhani at length in December 1995 at Madras, India.

58 For a full account of this incident, see J.B.P. More, "Tamil Muslims and Non-Brahmin Atheists, 1925–1940." *Contributions to Indian Sociology (new series)*, 27, no. 1 (Jan.–June 1993), 83–104.

59 More, "Tamil Muslims and Non-Brahmin Atheists," 89.

60 Ibid.

61   Ibid., 98.
62   For a full account of this controversy, see More, pp. 95–101.
63   Charles Stewart and Rosalind Shaw, *Syncretism and Anti-syncretism: the Politics of Religious Synthesis*, London: Routledge, 1994, 6.
64   "Presidential Address: Too little and Too Much." *The Journal of Asian Studies*, 34, no. 4 (Nov. 1995), 959.
65   Stewart and Shaw, *Syncretism*, 10.
66   Ibid.
67   Ibid., 3–6.
68   Ibid., 4.
69   Tony Stewart and Carl Ernst, "Syncretism." *Encyclopedia of South Asian Folklore*, ed. Peter Claus, forthcoming.
70   Michael Meister, "The Membrane of Tolerance: Middle and Modern India." In *Art, the Integral Vision*, eds. B.N. Saraswati, S.C. Malik, and Madhu Kanna, New Delhi: D.K. Printworld, 1984.
71   J.B.P. More discusses the lifestyle of Tamil Muslims in his article "The Marakkayar Muslims of Karikal." *Journal of Islamic Studies* (Oxford), 2, no. 1: 25–44. He argues that while the Muslims believe in the basic tenets of Islam that most Muslims around the world believe in, they adopt local Tamilian practices for the celebration of weddings etc.
72   Stewart and Shaw, *Syncretism*, 11.
73   Ibid., 14–15; the quotation is from p. 15.

Index